WOMEN IN KHAKI
The American Enlisted Woman

Michael Rustad

Foreword by Helena Z. Lopata

PRAEGER SPECIAL STUDIES • PRAEGER SCIENTIFIC

FERNALD LIBRARY
COLBY-SAWYER COLLEGE
NEW LONDON, N.H. 03257

UB
418
.W65
R87
1982

Library of Congress Cataloging in Publication Data

Rustad, Michael.
  Women in khaki.

  Includes index.
  1. United States. Army—Women. I. Title.
UB418.W65R87 1982   355'.0088'042   82-9025
ISBN 0-03-060149-5   AACR2
ISBN 0-03-062193-3 (pbk.)

For Chryss and James

93715

Published in 1982 by Praeger Publishers
CBS Educational and Professional Publishing
a division of CBS Inc.
521 Fifth Avenue, New York, New York 10175 U.S.A.

© 1982 Praeger Publishers

All rights reserved

23456789 052 987654321
Printed in the United States of America

FOREWORD

Mike Rustad's *Women in Khaki* examines the life of women and of the men with whom they work at an American military base in West Germany. This book makes major contributions to four areas of sociological knowledge: military, occupational, gender relations, and social change.

Its contributions to the sociology of military life include an historical overview of the association of women to the military and to war. The study of token women in the voluntary army includes a portrayal of the community itself, which helps to fill the need for such knowledge pointed to by Roger Little in his "Friendship in the Military Community."[1] Little (1981:223) concluded his overview of early works on the military by comparing them to "studies in industrial sociology which concentrate on the work group while ignoring the larger organizational and societal context in which the worker lives." *Women in Khaki* locates the subjects in the community and shows how their situation is made difficult primarily because they are forcibly introduced by superiors into a male dominated base, but also because the base is located in a foreign country which lost the war with America and whose language most of the members of the American armed forces do not know (see also Wolf[2]). The servicewomen and men face hostility from the community outside of their Khaki Town (Rustad's name for the base) and restrict most of their lives to the base, making it not only a venal and greedy institution, but also a total one, as described by Coser and Goffman.[3]

That Rustad is describing the volunteer armed services is of itself significant. Janowitz, in his epilogue to *The Professional Soldier* (1960)[4], suggested several alternative ways the American military establishment could move in the future, including its conversion into a volunteer "professional" occupation in competition with civilian occupations. His comments were directed to the officer segment of the military, but he also envisioned a committed enlisted segment. Rustad shows how the women and men of the bases in which he taught and researched are very different from this ideal. The lack of "professional" or occupational identification with the military on the part of the majority of these young people is apparent. The women's lack of preparation for integration into the male dominated life and culture and the hostility with which they are received by the men makes identification with the military difficult. This is particularly true for women who are removed from the jobs for which they have trained and placed in traditional female jobs simply because certain jobs have been identified as male. Thus, the military has backtracked on what it has promised the women: an opportunity to learn and work in desexed jobs. The men, also alienated from the military for many situational and psychological reasons, respond by withdrawing into a variety of deviant life styles, often leaving without permission.

The questions posed and answered by Rustad—questions which rise immediately when we think of women in the military—are: Why would the military want women? and Why would women want to enlist? Rustad answers both of these questions consistently and logically, documenting his outline of the functions women perform for the armed services. By developing a typology of enlisted women in Khaki Town, he also shows the different roles the women adopt in order to cope with the hostility and frustrations of a life unlike the one they were promised at enlistment.

Women in Khaki likewise contributes to occupational sociology. It adds to the slowly growing but still slim literature on the occupations of women, especially of women in nontraditional jobs or settings. The sources of role strain, and of conflicts between the role of servicewoman and of other roles such as those of wife and mother, are clearly developed. The work complements Kanter's *Men and Women of the Corporation*, especially through the use of the concept of token women.[5] An interesting topic in occupational sociology is that of the job as a "greedy" institution and the contrast between jobs located in almost total institutions versus those separated from "private" or other roles in a person's role complex. One way in which the military maintains its life as a total institution, in addition to housing, leisure time control and so forth, is through the constant presence of rank which affects even friendship and off-base leisure (Little, 1981). Few other jobs in the United States insist that occupational rank influence life outside of work hours.

Recently blooming literature on so-called "sex roles" (but really on the pervasiveness of gender identity in role interactions) is definitely being added to by *Women in Khaki*. The hostility women face, the very concept of tokenism, the justification given by men for their hostility and behavior toward women (including their removal by superiors from the jobs for which they train simply because they are women), all reflect with strong emphasis the reports of other women in non-traditional, blue collar jobs. The hostility is accentuated by the male culture of the military, and by the fact that most of the enlisted men come from blue collar backgrounds and have limited schooling. These three characteristics would designate a tendency toward sexism, but in addition, the women toward whom they direct their hostility come with a higher, tested set of abilities and more schooling. Also, the majority of the women are white while a large proportion of the men are black. Rustad thus describes a situation in which many aspects mitigate against friendly relations between the sexes.

Finally, Rustad's *Women in Khaki* makes a contribution to our understanding of social change. Change was introduced by the top military hierarchy through its decision to allow women to enlist and train for non-traditional jobs, and its assignment of these women to various male-dominated units. Although there is available research on effective methods of introducing social change to people who must accept it, the military establishment has obviously not utilized the results of such studies. Rustad ends his *Women in Khaki* with several cogent recommendations to increase the number, "quality," and military effectiveness of women and men, and to integrate the armed forces in a positive manner. Both the newcomers and the established members of units must be anticipatorily socialized for such a major social change, and both male and female "coaches" or sponsors must be encouraged to help the token women adjust and integrate. The book shows the consequences of the lack of such socialization. By constract to the army, according to DeFleur who studied the integration of women into the Air Force Academy and mass media reports, various other academies have used numerous methods of introducing the change with relative success.[6]

Helena Znaniecki Lopata
Loyola University, Chicago

NOTES

1. Roger Little, "Friendship in the Military Community," in *Research in the Interweave of Social Roles: Friendship*, eds., Helena Z. Lopata and David Maines (Connecticut: JAI Press, 1981), v. 2, 221-235.

2. Charlotte Wolf, *Garrison Community: A Study of an Overseas Military Community* (Connecticut: Greenwood Press, 1969).

3. Lewis A. Coser, *Greedy Institutions: Patterns of Undivided Commitment* (New York: The Free Press, 1974) and Erving Goffman, *Asylums: Essays on the Social Situation of Mental Patients and Other Inmates* (New York: Anchor, 1961).

4. Morris Janowitz, *The Professional Soldier* (Illinois: The Free Press, 1960).

5. Rosabeth Moss Kanter, *Men and Women of the Corporation* (New York: Basic Books, 1977).

6. Lois B. DeFleur, conversation with author.

ACKNOWLEDGMENTS

Work on this book began in 1975 when I joined the faculty of the University of Maryland—European Division. As the first to discuss the role of military women with me, the faculty and students of the University of Maryland deserve, and have, my gratitude. I also appreciate the friendship and support that other members of the military community extended to me. Special thanks is due to the men and women of Khaki Town who confided in me and thereby made this work possible.

Since this book was initially written as a dissertation, I want to acknowledge the contributions made by my committee at the Sociology Department of Boston College. Joe Pleck's judicious editing helped to bind the diverse materials in this study into a coherent whole; my work with Joe over the past two years at the Wellesley College Center for Research on Women enriched the analysis. Ritchie Lowry's investment in this project as committee head was of critical importance. Ritchie was not only encouraging but also pointed out that military sociology and social policy do not have to be the red light districts of academic sociology. Paul Gray showed me how to make the field research experience more plentiful. Sy Leventman increased my understanding of the general problem of marginality.

Others whose comments on this manuscript helped to shape this work include Boston College professors John Donovan, David Karp, Michael Malec, Stephen Pfohl, Richard Quinney, Eve Spangler, and John Williamson; fellow graduate students, Dick Batten and Steve Dolliver; and my wife, Chryss Knowles.

I am indebted to the administrative staff of the Sociology Department at Boston College for preparing the manuscript. Lorraine Bone skillfully edited the final draft, while Alice Close, Shirley Urban, and Sara White typed it in record time.

I was frequently pointed in the right direction by librarians, Edward Bander and Harriet Nemiccola of Suffolk University Law Library and Boston College Social Work Library, respectively.

I was motivated to finish on schedule by the interest and enthusiasm of Lynda Sharp, my editor at Praeger, in the work-in-progress.

Janice Knowles provided me with work space at Joe's Pond, Vermont, and supported my research. Finally, my wife Chryss' familiarity with the overseas military community and sociological theory made for especially constructive discussions that helped me immeasurably. It is to her and our son James that this work is dedicated.

Grateful acknowledgment is hereby also made for permission to reprint material from the following sources:

Women as Force in History: A Study in Traditions and Realities by Mary R. Beard (New York: Macmillan, 1946; renewed 1974 by William Beard and Miriam B. Vagts)

The Soldier and Social Change by Jacques van Doorn (Beverly Hills and London: Sage Publications, 1974), pp. 16–17

The Marx-Engels Reader by Robert Tucker (New York: W. W. Norton, 1978)

Army Times and *Air Force Times*.

Michael Rustad
Boston College

CONTENTS

LIST OF TABLES AND FIGURES

TABLES

FIGURES

INTRODUCTION

This is a study of the emergence of the role of enlisted women in the U.S. Army. The first part of the book examines the female enlisted role from a social-historical perspective since it is necessary to study the social history of military women to understand the contradictions of their contemporary position. The second part describes the daily lives of contemporary female soldiers and the conflicts they face as token women in formerly male jobs in the U.S. Army in Europe.

Chapter One is a historical and cross-cultural review of women's past participation in armies. The evanescence of female participation in organized violence is demonstrated through an examination of four broad stages: (1) Stage One: Women in Pre-State Armies (antiquity to the Seventeenth Century); (2) Stage Two: Women in Early Industrial Armies (1600–1900); (3) Stage Three: External Crisis and Women as Military Reserves (1900–1945); and Stage Four: Peripheral Roles in Limited Wars and Peace (1945 to Present).

Looking first at the role of women in primitive warfare, it is concluded that the military has been, historically and cross culturally, a male dominated institution. However, in preindustrial European city-states and preindustrial cultures, individual female heroines served as crisis participants.

The hypothesis is advanced that bearing arms was associated with economic and political parity in Stage Two: Women in Early Industrial Armies (1600–1900). Much of the social history of the military woman is a history of nonparticipation. It is postulated that exclusion from the military retarded the extension of full citizenship rights to women.

Stage Three associates the inclusion of women in organized militaries with external crisis. In World War I and World War II, women were used as a reserve army of last resort. Women were mobilized only when the reserve pool of males was depleted. After each crisis, women soldiers and war workers were displaced without a permanent gain in status.

Stage Four describes how women have been relegated to the peripheral positions in armies in times of peace. With the sole exception of the United States, female military participation has been triggered only by total war.

Chapter Two examines the reasons why the U.S. military has expanded its uses of women during a period of peace. Contrary to the theory of external crisis, current female military participation does not seem to follow the cycle of crisis-mobilization-demobilization discussed in Chapter One. An internal crisis explanation for the recent increase in the number of women recruits is advanced, illustrated by the contrast of official Defense Department ideology and journalistic opinion with unpublished Defense Department data on the uses of military women.

Officially, the Defense Department and journalistic opinion promoted the theme that the military was a leading equal opportunity employer for contemporary women. This chapter compares popular myths about the military as an equal opportunity employer with the less acknowledged reasons for expanded female participation.

The discrepancy between official and unpublished sources reflects eight significant latent functions fulfilled in the peacetime military: (1) the Defense Department uses women to cultivate its image as a social welfare institution; (2) because high quality men will not enlist in the volunteer military, women serve as a reserve army of last resort; (3) female recruits have a higher educational level and score higher on military aptitude tests than do male enlistees; women smarten up the army; (4) an increase in female military participation contributes to a more socially representative force; (5) military women end up in the military justice apparatus less often than do men; since women soldiers are better behaved, they save the military management both time and money; (6) female military labor is cheaper to recruit, train, and retain than male labor; women help to stave off the military's fiscal crisis in manpower costs; (7) to the extent that women make the all-volunteer force work, they replenish the military's fund of legitimacy; and (8) at the enlisted level, women are a convenient pool of marriage partners for male soldiers.

Chapters Three through Seven present an ethnography of male-female relations in Khaki Town, a large community in southern Germany in which women were integrated into previously all male jobs in the Army.

Chapter Three compares responses of males and females to enlisted life. A question is raised that stimulates all that follows: "Was the Problem of Women in Khaki Town to Hell with Men or to Hell with the Green Machine?" The question is addressed by postulating two armies—two distinct interpretations of enlisted life. His Army is an occupation that already contained a number of social stresses, such as encroachments on time, family, and identity; but Her Army is all of His Army plus the stresses of being a token female in a male environment.

Chapter Four outlines the dimensions of female tokenism in Khaki Town. Lower-ranked females are in conflict with and are outnumbered by the men. In previous research on female tokenism in professional organizations, it was a clear-cut gain for women to weather the social injuries of being alone in a male environment, but in the case of low-status organizations such as the enlisted military, participation was both emancipatory and oppressive. Women found jobs in the military. However, the enlisted women were included not as a part of an affirmative action program but as temporary "dirty workers." Chapter Four describes the dimensions of tokenism that parallel the earlier work of Rosabeth Moss Kanter. Khaki Town women faced isolation from the work culture, sexual shakedowns, heightened visibility, and mistaken identity in the work place. As a response to those stresses, they developed two broad patterns that parallel what Spangler and her colleagues called "under-achievement" and "over-achievement" in their empirical study of token women in law schools. The "under-achieving" types of accommodation in which women resolved their status contradictions by discarding the soldier role were: (1) Daddy's Little Girl; (2) the Sex-Pot; and (3) Mama. In contrast, the "Super-Soldier" and "The Lone Ranger of Women's Liberation" were amplifications of the "over-achievement" pattern.

Chapter Five describes the responses of males to token women. The origin of negative male attitudes is traced both to antieffeminacy and to the "side bets" of higher command that women were doomed in khaki-collar jobs. Karl Marx studied male resistance to the first female coal miners in the 1860s. Like the men who worked in the mines, the Army male feels that nontraditional roles for Army women are "deplorable in the extreme."

Chapter Six examines the attributes of the *venal institution*. His Army is described as a task-oriented *total institution* with a contradictory compliance structure based on domination. The tension between femininity and militarism can be linked to the venal features of enlisted life. Participation for the enlisted soldier is compared to the status of the inmate in Goffman's *total institution* and the true believers of Coser's *greedy institution*. The *venal institution* is postulated as a new category of formal organization that further specifies Goffman's broad groupings of total institutions. The venal institution is a social hybrid encompassing features of both total and greedy institutions but having a contradictory character of its own. The venal institution is compared with Weber's concept of the pariah group, and a general portrait of life in the venal institution is drawn from unstructured interviews with the female and male soldiers of Khaki Town. This further describes the social context of female tokenism.

Chapters Six and Seven bring together earlier materials and recommend social policies that could improve life in the venal institution for soldiers of both sexes, with particular attention given to Her Army and the problems of tokenism. However, if women are to gain citizenship rights through military service, the structure of His Army must be completely transformed.

The Appendixes describe how I was able to study women and men of the U.S. Army for such an extended period. Beginning with my role as a lecturer for the University of Maryland's European Division, I describe the chronology of my research roles and the multiple methods used in this study.

Chapter One

WOMEN AND WAR

After the family and the school, the military is the most important socializing institution in American society. Since the end of World War II, 30 million people have experienced basic training. Currently, there are 5 million military and civilian workers on the military payroll, and nearly two and a quarter million people live on military reservations throughout the world. American soldiers shop in post exchanges, listen to Armed Forces network radio, live in military housing, and consult military doctors, lawyers, and dentists.

By all ordinary standards, the military is the focal institution of American society. Gallup reports that keeping out of war, winning war, and keeping peace have been America's major concerns during the past 45 years (1935 to 1980).[1] The Reagan administration proposes that over a trillion and a quarter dollars be spent by the Defense Department over the next five years.

However, despite the enormous power of the military institutions and its gargantuan dimensions, until recently it has remained nearly female free. From 1948 to 1972, women were employed in only about 1 percent of military jobs. When women did participate in the military, they were confined to low-status ancillary roles in medicine and administration.[2]

Within the past ten years, the role of women in the military has begun to change. Since 1972, the number of women soldiers in the U.S. military has quadrupled from 2 percent to 8 percent of the total enlisted employment. In 1972, there were only 40,000 women in all of the services. By 1981, the Army alone enlisted over 63,000 women, and there are currently over 200,000 women serving in the active forces. Furthermore, the latest expansion has taken place largely in traditionally male military jobs. Women have been integrated into previously all male domains such as air defense artillery, telecommunications, and mechanical maintenance. About 15 percent of all woman soldiers perform jobs equivalent to civilian blue-collar specialties, making the military the largest single employer of females in nontraditional work.

Despite the implications of female participation in the military, the subject has received little attention apart from Department of Defense-sponsored evaluation studies. There is a paucity of studies that have asked why women were historically excluded from the armed forces. Similarly, there has been little analysis of historical cases where women were included in martial roles.[3] Apart from military history performed under contract for the Defense Department, there is not a single study examining the history of women in organized armies. In sociology, the female experience in the military remains similarly unexplored. Most published studies have focused on military effectiveness questions without examining the structural antecedents of female participation. Researchers interested in the sociology of military life have been denied access to military-controlled data.[4]

THE DILEMMA OF MILITARISM AND FEMINISM

Another barrier to understanding the problem of female military labor has been the ambivalence with which scholars have approached the area of militarism and feminism. The question of expanded military service for women has given proponents the most difficulty. Feminists of both sexes ask whether participation in the military is really the vanguard of new sex roles or only the retrenchment of patriarchal society. Does participation in the military mean equity or does it mean that women will be disciplined by a total institution created, maintained, and controlled by males? Mrs. Elizabeth Jones, at the Women's Rights Convention of 1860, thought that feminists should oppose the militarization of women:

> I hope women will not copy the vices of men. I hope they will not go to war;
> I wish men would not. I hope they will not be contentious politicians; I am
> sorry that men are. I hope they will not regard their freedom as a license to
> do wrong! I am ashamed to acknowledge that men do.[5]

Early debate over whether or not women should receive the vote centered on such questions as whether women would use their citizenship rights to proscribe war. Would women be willing to declare war? Would they vote for supplies and equipment? More importantly, would women be willing to serve in the military? Emma Goldman thought that the

debate over whether or not women should take on martial roles expressed
the inconsistencies between traditional feminine socialization and full
citizenship rights. She argued that the social definition of maturity as
involving military participation was Janus-faced when applied to women.
On the one hand, the effect of freeing women from traditional constraints
was emancipatory. On the surface, military service for females was
a natural outgrowth of modernity. At the same time, however, arming
women was backward looking. Goldman characterized this bind—the
dilemma of feminism and militarism—as a linchpin of women's
emancipation:

> Woman is naturally perverse, I argued; from the very birth of her male child
> until he receives a ripe age, the mother leaves nothing undone to keep him
> tied to her. Yet she hates to see him weak and she craves the manly man. She
> idolizes in him the very traits that help to enslave her—his strength, his
> egotism, and his exaggerated vanity. The inconsistencies of my sex keep the
> poor male dangling between idol and the brute, the darling and the beast, the
> helpless child and the conqueror of worlds. It is really women's inhumanity
> to man that makes him what he is. When she has learned to be as self-
> centered and as determined as he, when she gains the courage to delve into
> life as he does and pay for it, she will achieve her liberation, and incidentally
> also help him become free. Whereupon my women would rise up against
> him and cry: "You're a man's woman and not one of us."[6]

The tension between militarism and feminism is apparent in the
current debate over whether or not women should be drafted. Compulsory
military service for women is the kind of issue that can easily fuel full-
scale ideological conflict. Jean–Bethke Elshtain characterized this debate as
the tension that haunts the women's movement:

> That my life is framed by one war and what seems to be the military and
> psychological build-up for another, despite Vietnam and the trauma of the
> '60s, is important for it indicates that the contemporary women's movement,
> just like its nineteenth century predecessor, has thus far, despite the efforts of
> many noble women, been unable to significantly influence public policy and
> the direction of political events away from war. Indeed, at this point, we are
> even told by some women that, in the name of feminism, they should be free
> to enter combat duty just like any man because, as one senior woman in the
> Pentagon, who calls herself a feminist put it, 'Women need a chance to prove
> themselves. You can't become a member of the Joint Chiefs of Staff unless
> you've earned your stripes in battle." Is this what we've come to? Well, it is
> part of what we've come to and it makes it all the more imperative to think
> through what feminism is, what it stands for—or ought to stand for—if the

new woman is not to be just a clone of the old man. Does, or ought, feminism represent some alternative to politics as usual, and war, and restless, rootless ambition and striving after material success, all the costly and damaging dimensions of a particular sort of upwardly mobile American male ethos?[7]

The National Organization for Women (NOW) has formulated a position paper on women in the military that simultaneously opposes the draft but favors female participation if there were to be a draft. The contradictory nature of this position obtrudes the issue of equal rights:

We are opposed to reinstatement of compulsory registration. As the first step toward reinstatement of the draft, registration is a return to the sexist and racist Selective Service System which gave us discrimination against the poor, minorities, and women while it lowered the quality of our military forces. Our longstanding position against violence combined with our determination to end discrimination makes us unable to support registration . . . As a matter of equity, no registration or draft which excluded women in 1980 could be deemed fair. If we cannot stop the return to registration and draft, we also cannot choose between our daughters and our sons. The choice robs women as well as men. In the long and short run, it injures us all.[8]

The issue of women's participation in the draft has been a source of ideological conflict within the women's movement as well as a source of conservative resistance to the Equal Rights Amendment. (ERA). Some feminists agree that equal rights are coterminous with equal responsibilities and that this dictum applies to military service. Another subgroup ducks this issue by not applying the "equal rights-equal responsibilities" argument to the military. Antidraft feminists see the issue of women's participation in the draft as a red herring which deflects attention away from issues of greater social import such as the radical restructuring of civilian employment. Compulsory military service is seen as a cynical twist to the overall citizenship rights for women. Representative of the perspective that military participation is actually antithetical to equal rights is the following account:

Feminists, both men and women, must resist the equal rights' arguments about the draft. We do not want an "equal right to commit murder, rape, and genocide." We do not want death jobs, for the women or men in our lives. We want the rights and responsibilities of life in a peaceful and non-authoritarian world that reinforces life, respect, and genuine equality among peoples.[9]

The tension between militarism and feminism is emblematic of a question that guides all that is to follow in the study of the enlisted woman soldier. Does the inclusion of women in martial roles mean greater opportunities or does it mean only that women will have the same rights as males to perform strenuous, dangerous, and obnoxious tasks? On the one hand, female participation in the focal institution of American society may symbolize the vanguard of new societal forms. Alternatively, female military participation may not be an unqualified gain. For instance, will the militarization of women mean a newly created right to the injuries of military service without a corresponding expansion of real citizenship rights? If women are privy to the military rites of passage, will other gender classifications be dismantled?

To begin to answer the question of the impact of military service on the status of women, it is necessary first to study the lineages of females in the military. The trajectory of accounts of women in armies is a broken history. Thus, it is necessary to draw together a brief social history of past involvement. This will provide a context for understanding the current role of enlisted women and also begin the rescue of the lost history of the female experience in armies.

A SOCIAL HISTORY OF WOMEN IN THE MILITARY

Any historical and cross-cultural survey of women in military organizations must begin with the proposition that the military has been an androcentric institution. The sexual division of labor traditionally excluded women from martial roles. Sex role proscriptions have been transformed only under the most exceptional circumstances. We will examine the historic range of cases where women were included in militaries and assess the consequences of military participation for social emancipation.

Much of the history and sociology of women in warfare has been irretrievably lost because military historians have centered and continue to focus nearly exclusively on the role of males. The insights that can be rescued from the past are derived from a content analysis of disparate sources—historical and anthropological references to women in the military. Myths, epics, poems, and sociological sources are also used to reconstruct accounts of women in martial roles. Together, these materials offer a springboard for the analysis of the legacy of the female soldier.

The history of female involvement in armies can be divided into four broad social-historical periods. Of course, any conceptual generalizations that encompass such large slices of history are replete with qualifications. The first period, which encompasses the role of women soldiers from antiquity to the seventeenth century is the most difficult to verify empirically. In the study of the pre-state women of war, it is difficult to separate mythmaking from social history. Ballads, poems, and the scattered historical accounts of the trajectory of female participation leads to the proposition that women were included in warfare only in time of crisis. Although, by way of exception, a few women served in limited permanent roles. On the whole, however, women were generally excluded from the military. This exclusion was ruptured most often during periods of siege.

The second period, which extends from the seventeenth century to the end of the nineteenth century, is characterized by the consequences of female exclusion from early professional armies.

The role of women in developed professional armies is the focus of the third period, from 1900 to 1945. A key feature of this study is an analysis of the temporary transformation of sex roles during periods of total war. However, women's participation was discontinuous as military organizations suspended stereotypes without changing the status of women.

The final period, from 1945 to the present, concludes the survey of female experiences in armies. A typology of female participation is constructed from the history of each period. This history sets the context for understanding the most recent expansion of female labor in the contemporary U.S. Army.

Stage One: Women in Pre-State Armies
(Antiquity to the Seventeenth Century)

Much of the history of female military participation in preindustrial armies is recorded in the epics, legends, and ballads of Western societies. The archetype of the woman warrior has been recorded by chroniclers as early as the *Iliad*. In Book Six of the *Iliad*, the Amazons are described as one of the epochal foes subdued by the Greek hero Bellerophon:

> First he bade him slay the raging Chimaera. She was of divine stock, not of men, in the fore part of a lion, in the hinder a serpent, and in the midst a goat breathing forth in terrible wise the might of blazing fire. Next fought he with the glorious Solymi, and this, said he, was the mightiest battle of warriors that ever he entered; and thirdly, he slew the Amazons, the women peers of men.[10]

In the earliest civilizations, it is not possible to disengage myth from history. Women's roles in primitive warfare are not known and cannot be known with any certitude. But the chronicler of female participation in warfare is expected to begin with the Amazons.

Of the Amazons, the historian Francis Gribble wrote in 1917 that the balance of opinion inclined to the view that the Amazons did actually exist: "But there was no foundation for the statement that they cut off their right breasts in order that they might better be able to draw the bow."[11]

In Mary Beard's 1946 social history of women, she wrote that, "evidence of armed women have been discovered in the European excavations of ancient ruins, reinforcing the Greek contention that fighting women, the Amazons, were real women, not creatures of imagery."[12]

Helen Diner, a German writer who used the pen name Sir Galahad, published a book in Munich in 1932 entitled *Mutter und Amazonen: Ein Umriss weiblicher Reiche* (Mothers and Amazons: Outline of Women's Kingdoms). Her thesis was that military females fulfilled a variety of martial roles.[13]

The earliest historical account of female military corps was promulgated by Herodotus, who portrayed Amazon warriors as a deadly species in his accounts of the battles between the Greeks and the women warrior castes: "I say that the Greeks, after gaining the battle of the Thermodon, put to sea, taking with them on board three of their vessels all the Amazons whom they had made prisoners; and that the women upon the voyage rose up against the crews and slaughtered them to a man."[14]

According to traditional accounts, Amazons were never subjugated militarily. Instead, their decline was attributed to the warriors voluntarily taking on wife and motherhood roles. The Scythians offered the Amazons all of their young males, provided that the Amazons would give up their arms and learn nurturance roles. "To draw the bow, to hurl the javelin, to bestride the horse, these are our arts—of womanly employment we know nothing," the Amazons responded.[15] The Amazons were said to have resided with the young Scythian men east of the Tanais River.

Goddesses on the Sidelines

The most prevalent image of women of war in classical literature was the goddess. Greek goddesses served the ancillary role of helpmate in battle. In Greek mythology, Pallas Athena was a goddess of both war and wisdom. In Book Five of the *Iliad*, a plea was made to Athena to assist males during a period of siege:

> Oh hear me daughter of Zeus
> who bears the stormcloud, tireless on Athena!
> If ever you stood near my father and helped him
> in a hot fight, befriend me as well![16]

In Norse mythology, Odin's special female auxiliary force, the Valkyries, also served as helpmates on the battlefront. The Valkyries remained immortal and invulnerable in the midst of combat only if they obeyed the orders of Odin and remained virgins. In Finn's Sage, the battle maidens transported war heroes to heaven. The term, *kiss of death*, is derived from the myth of the Valkyries; when dead male warriors received the Valkyries' kiss, they immediately ascended into heaven.[17]

Women were depicted in helpmate roles in warfare in other cultures as well. Mary Beard found women warriors in vicarious roles in the cultures of Egypt, Babylonia, and the Hittite Empires up to about 1000 B.C.: "Goddess functions ranged from guardianship of childbirth and all the arts of living to the partronage of kings and queens in empire building."[18]

An Interpretation of the Woman Warrior Myth

Women warriors have been an archetype in the folklore of every Western culture. The contemporary version of the female warrior is the Israeli woman depicted with an Uzi machine gun or the American woman of war with her M-16. Despite the fact that women have been traditionally excluded from warfare, the mystical woman warrior has enveloped thinking about women since antiquity.

A major theme in the female warrior myth is that armed women are an unnatural force. Only when female goddesses are subjugated is there a possibility of civilization. A nineteenth century historian, Keightley, believed that there was little historical basis for a female military corps. In fact, the invasion of Attica by female warriors recorded by the Athenians did not have the slightest foundation in classical mythology.[19] However, the function of the female warrior accounts, according to Keightley, was to justify female exclusion from warfare.[20] Male heroes such as Theseus or Heracles had to subjugate the women before civilization could flourish. More recently, Merck found that female warriors were variously depicted as subhuman, nonhuman, or superhuman. Merck contended that myths about women in war were contructed to legitimate male control over the means of organized violence. Since female warriors were atavistic and a threat to civilization, female military participation was inimical to the development of organized social life.[21]

If the Amazon myth was used to legitimate male control of the weapons of war, the myths of Athena and the Valkyries were part of the stock of traditional sex role ideology. Mary Beard found that the military goddess was used to legitimate a variety of ancillary roles, including support of male structures of domination: "The goddess became a war goddess whenever a ruler wished to have his sanction—a popular sanction—for his aggression against other peoples and rulers.[22]

It is difficult to know what role myths of women warriors have played in the construction of sex role ideologies in preprofessional armies. But, as we shall see, the image of Pallas Athena and the Valkyries paralleled the actual role of women as crisis participants. Only males were to wield arms routinely; only in the exigency of a state of siege were women to take up arms.

Pre-State Women of War

The earliest known historical references to women in organized combat appeared in the Anglo-Saxon chronicles of the Augustan Empire. In volume ten of the *Cambridge Ancient History* series, the role of women as crisis participants was documented. For example, when Paustagus died in 61 A.D., his widow, Boudicea, became a leader of the insurgents:

> The Iceni were made aware, that with every circumstance of indignity, that they had misunderstood their position. Instead of introducing the new regime with tact and moderation, the Roman officials left nothing undone to outrage the feelings of their new victims. The Iceni rose, Boudicea at their head. The Trinovantes were swept up into the revolt while the centres of Romanization went up in flames.[23]

Tacitus wrote the following account of the Roman's retaliatory attack on the female-led inhabitants of the island of Anglesea:

> On the shore was standing the battle line of the enemy, bristling with arms and men, while women were running back and forth, after the fashion of the Furies; in funereal garb with disheveled hair, they were bearing torches before them; and the Druids around, with hands raised to the sky pouring out their dreadful prayers struck our soldiers with consternation by the novelty of the sight, so that just as if paralyzed they offered their immovable bodies to wounds. Then at the exhortation of the leaders and encouraging themselves, not to tear this cowardly and fanatic array they charged, overthrowing their opponents, and enveloping them in their own attacks.[24]

Deo Cassius, the Roman historian, described the heroics of Boudicea in his monumental *Roman History of Britain*: "Boudicea rode in a chariot with her two daughters to the front and took charge of the fighting. When her forces were finally overwhelmed by the superior military skill of the Romans, Boudicca committed suicide thus sparing herself a worse fate at the hands of the Romans."[25]

Plutarch wrote about a number of battles that the Romans had with female defenders. At Aquea Sextiae, 102 B.C., Plutarch wrote: "The fight had been no less fierce with the women than with the men themselves . . . They charged with swords and axes and fell upon their opponents uttering a hideous outcry; . . . When summoned, they [women] killed their children, slaughtered one another, and hanged themselves from trees."[26]

Writing of the Germanic tribes beyond the borders of the Roman Empire, Tacitus commented on the presence of women throughout the garrisons. In *Germania*, he described women amidst the center of fighting: "They [women] are to every man the most sacred witnesses of his bravery . . . They are the most generous applauders. The soldier brings his wounds to his mother and wife."[27]

Mary Beard contended that there was not a type of war in which women did not participate: "They were among the primitive hordes which went on looting expeditions against their neighbors or stood fast on their own ground in defense of their lives, herds, and fields. Old Roman records testify to the savagery of women in the Cimbrian tribes that swept down from the north into Rome."[28]

The early social historical accounts of women in warfare are sparse. However, there is clear evidence that women participated in their own defense when invaders threatened to overrun their homes. Representative of the view that women were intermittent crisis participants were the numerous accounts of women heroines during this period.

The Vivandieres of Medieval Europe

Medieval women's most common role in warfare was as the spoils of war. In the fourteenth century, the indiscriminate slaughter of women and children was so common that one of the oaths taken by knights at the time of investiture was the protection of women and children. When the Crusaders under Richard I took Messina, they carried off and sold all of the women owned by the Sicilians. In 1194, Henry the Roman Emperor, took Salerno and auctioned to his troops the wives and children of the men whom he had slain.[29]

A second theme in the medieval period was the participation of women in warfare as individual defenders, according to the legends and epic poems of nearly every Western European city: "The city of Avila in Spain has a legend of the repulse of the Saracens by the women. We all know how nobly the maid of Sarragossa acquitted herself during the historic siege of that city; and we all ought to know how Kenau Hasserlaar and the three hundred women placed under her command helped to keep the Spaniards out of Haarlem."[30]

Medieval France had a long and continuous history of female leaders who emerged in times of crisis. Beginning with the women of Gaul, who took part in the fighting against Caesar in 61 B.C., heroines played a prominent role in French military history:

> Geneviève fought against Attila in A.D. 451 . . . In the case of Frédégonde, who fought against the Austro-Burgundians and reconstituted the kingdom of Neustria in 593, one is able to add just one interesting detail: Frédégonde rode at the head of her army, carrying her child Clotaire in her arms. There follow on our list Hermangarde, the great-granddaughter of Charlemagne, who defended the town of Vienne for two years against Boson Comte d'Autun, and Richilde, wife of Baudouin VI, Comte de Flandres, who allied

herself with Philip I of France, and went campaigning against her own husband.[31]

Medieval French history is replete with references of female military leaders and participants:

Those religious wars which rent France in the Sixteenth Century, and gave Paris to Henry IV at the price of a match, brought forth a crop of them. [faits d'armes] It was a time of sieges; and almost every siege produced its heroine or heroines. The historians speak especially of the heroines of Marseilles, Saint Riquier, Perronne, Meta, Montélimar, Poitiers, La Rochelle, Sanceree, Livron, Saint Lô, Aubigny, Cahors, Lille, Vitré, Autun, Montauban, Montpellier, Lamotte, Dôle, and Saint-Jean-de-Losne.[32]

"Women," wrote Jules Michelet in the *History of the French Revolution,* "are brave and make others so."[33] Female military participation in times of crisis was prominently proffered as a symbol of French unity by generations of historians: "Joan of Arc, of course, and Joan Laine, alias Joan Hachette [a reference to her lethal use of the axe] who galvanized the demoralized garrison of Beauvais and led the repulse of the besieging Bourguigons led by Charles Le Temeraire, are celebrated cases of female military leadership in the early stage of France's unification."[34]

Martin argued that the celebrated cases of female heroines and leadership were not isolated examples. Accounts of female crisis participants continued throughout the Renaissance:

Renaissance chronicles recount also the military virtues of Clorinde, a Bradamanne, the love for martial arts of a Louise Labe who fought under the officer accoutrement nicknamed Captain Loys by the Royal troops. Later with the Fronde, the King and his engineers, were confronted with both the conspiratorial proclivity and commanding skills of a few high born intrigantes: Anee-Genevieve de Longueville, Anne de Gonzague, and above all Anne-Marie-Louise de Montpensier, the grand mademoiselle, and her staff of female aides-de-camp.[35]

Much of the early trajectory of women's participation in preindustrial armies of Western Europe cannot be charted with any confidence. However, the accounts of Edwardian social anthropology and contemporary Anglo-American anthropology offer a more reliable source of data. Chronologically, of course, the studies of preindustrial cultures would be in Stage Three (1900–1945) and Stage Four (1945 to Present). Typologically, however, anthropological data illuminate the role of women in primitive warfare.

Anthropologists studied the female role in military organization as a portion of their overall studies of the division of labor. In general, anthropological research supports the proposition that preindustrial cultures define the military as men's work. Margaret Mead argued that most cultures have proscribed the arming of women in order to protect the means of reproduction. This proposition generally held true for hunting and gathering societies as well as in agricultural settings.

Edwardian social anthropologists supported Mead's general hypothesis in their early surveys of the female role in preindustrial cultures. However, Joyce and Thomas, in their report for the Royal Ánthropological Institute, proferred the hypothesis that female military participation was correlated with expanded political rights. Cultures that included women in warfare were also likely to include women in central decision-making roles.[36]

Samoa

In both Tonga and Samoa, women were included in both warfare and sacred rites, but the following incident culled from mariner records in the late nineteenth century shows a parallel to the role of women in pre-industrial Europe as crisis participants in warfare:

> Vavau who, when the people were discussing the proposal to throw off the yoke of Finow in revenge of his murder of their chief, rushed into the assembly demanding why they hesitated when honor pointed out that the only course to pursuse, "but if men are turned to women, the women shall turn to men, and revenge the death of their murdered chief; let then the men stand idly looking on, and when we women are sacrificed in glorious causes, our example may perhaps excite them to fight and die in the same spirited endeavor to support and defend their rights."[37]

African Women

In Niger and Chad women founded cities, led migrations, and conquered kingdoms in the fifteenth century. In Katsina, Queen Amina became important as a fifteenth-century military leader.

In Dahomey, a female warrior corps was an important line of defense. King Gezo recruited female warriors for the elite women's defense corps, and the female phalanx won a series of battles culminating with the attack on the Egba fortress town of Abeokuta. Sociocultural proscriptions were such that females in Dahomey occupied the more responsible positions such as hunting and gathering. Women were viewed as the more disciplined sex. Because female socialization was more disciplined, females were seen as the most able to withstand the adverse circumstances of combat. The decline of the female army was attributed to the sex role proscriptions of English colonials who excluded women from defense roles.[38]

Quincy Wright's encyclopedic *A Study of War* revealed that women participated in the militaries of relatively few preindustrial cultures. Women fought in the armies of Angola, the Canary Islands, the Valley of the Amazons, Patagonia, Central America, Hawaii, Tasmania, Arabia, Albania, and among the Ainu and Apache cultures.[39]

Wright's research supported the Edwardian anthropological view that female military participation was associated with greater political and economic status.

In summary, both historical and anthropological evidence from antiquity to the development of professional armies supports the general view that in Stage One, the military was considered the province of males. However, a second theme was also present: women played a significant role as crisis participants, as revealed in both myth and history. The transition to mass armies eviscerated the role of women as individual defenders. The primitive warfare technique of "pounce and retreat" was replaced by disciplined professional armies in the West. In Stage Two, we can trace how the impact of technical advances in the structure of warfare increasingly circumscribed the roles of women as military participants.

Stage Two: Women in Early Industrial Armies (1600–1900)

Bertolt Brecht's Mother Courage was a camp follower who provided succorance for the soldiers of the Germanic wars. Her role epitomized the disengagement of women from early mass armies. In the beginning, women, as portrayed by Mother Courage, served the men as laundresses and whores. They accompanied males into battle and nursed the wounded. They became the spoils of war. The army of 5,000 Spanish soldiers that marched from the Netherlands to Italy in 1577 had, for example, rations for 20,000 persons. There were three women and children for every soldier: "The army became the home of women and children. During the great war which raged in central Europe between 1618 and 1648, the Thirty Years War, each of the main armies as it moved about from one battle or siege to the next, became a vast moving city with its own community of life."[40]

But as the rational military apparatus became perfected, camp followers were gradually removed. It was more rational from an organizational point of view to segregate male soldiers from their families. It was easier to perfect military drill and discipline without women. Accounts of why women were excluded from early mass armies are nonexistent, and therefore it is not possible to know what role women played in the transition from the primitive to the professional army. Ostensibly, there were enough males to fill the enlisted ranks without the need to resort to recruiting women. It was Max Weber's thesis that the earliest mass armies lived on both the booties of war and the economic contributions of women.[41]

Because of the role that military participation played in the development of the capitalistic state, it is significant that women were excluded from the ranks of the first mass military organizations. Weber argued that military discipline gave birth to all discipline:

> The large-scale economic organization is the second great agency which trains men for discipline... No special proof is necessary to show that military discipline is the ideal model for the modern capitalist factory, as it was for the ancient plantation. However, organizational discipline in the factory has a completely rational basis. With the help of suitable methods of measurement, the optimum profitability of the individual worker is calculated like that of any material means of production.[42]

The exclusion of women from the early mass armies must have served as both a sword and a shield. On the one hand, females escaped being welded into the iron cage of industrial bureaucracy. On the other hand, women were denied the possible benefits of military service.

Women did not receive training for jobs in the industrial sphere. Worse yet, they were thought to be noncitizens. However, if Max Weber was correct in his belief that the military work place was fragmenting as well as frightening, women were saved from depersonalization:

> The psycho-physical apparatus of man is completely adjusted to the demands of the outer world, the tools, the machines—in short, it is functionalized and the individual is shorn of his natural rhythm as determined by his organism; in line with the demands of the work procedure, he is attuned to a new rhythm through the functional specialization of muscles and through the creation of an optimal economy of physical effort... Thus discipline inexorably takes over ever larger areas as the satisfaction of political and economic needs is increasingly rationalized. This universal phenomenon more and more restricts the importance of charisma, and of individually differentiated conduct.[43]

Van Doorn contended that the peasant was not useful to the mass army until he developed the necessary values of discipline and the mental acceptance of the decomposition of military work. There was a similarity between the soldier and the industrial laborer. Both were given precise training. Discipline, precision, order, and cleanliness replaced skill, craftsmanship, initiative, and heroism. While military discipline led industrial discipline, industrial development overtook it and remained ahead.[44] Van Doorn paralleled the founder of the mass military, Maurice of Orange, with the founder of the classical school of management, Frederick Winslow Taylor:

> But their similarity is also striking as far as their preoccupation with detail is concerned. The thing Taylor and his followers aimed at and effectuated, i.e., the decomposition of human labor into its components of movement in order to arrive, by its reconstruction, at the most efficient performance had been applied by Maurice three centuries earlier to the handling of weapons. In this fashion the handship of the musket was broken down into a prescribed series of 43 separate movements, and the use of the pike into 23, which had to be practiced one by one, individually at first and then in formation. The reorganization of army and industry went further, of course, than this. In agreement with the essence of organization, activities were mainly deployed in two directions: the hierarchical structure was made more rigid and performance was perfectionalized.[45]

From Military Amateurs to Military Professionals

From the sixteenth century to the end of the nineteenth century, the consolidation of the power institutions of the military, economy, and polity excluded women. Mass armies depended upon the machine production of weapons and men. This consolidation of power reduced any role women could play as "crisis participants." Since females were not socialized in the necessary values of discipline and decomposition, they could serve no useful role in times of war. Military service could never again be a part-time vocation. Abrahamsson contended that it was the rise of the nation-state, urbanization, bureaucratization, and full-blown industrialization that transformed the nature of military participation into an all-encompassing role: "Within a period of less than two centuries, military amateurs have developed into military professionals. In most countries, the military profession can command greater economic resources than any other single vocational group."[46]

For its lower-ranked participants, military service in the early mass armies was characterized by military servitude. The transformation of a group of poorly motivated peasants into laborers for the functional military apparatus must have involved much suffering. When the male proletariat refused to enlist, Van Doorn contended that early leaders used direct force:

> It is well-known that early capitalistic enterprises profited greatly from the population available in poorhouses and orphanages, and that the English navy was for a long time manned mainly via the activities of the press gang. In the eighteenth century, these forms of compulsion often coincided. Soldiers, expensively maintained in peace-time, were often made temporarily productive in workshops: "military barracks in Austria and Prussia were veritable spinning mills."[47]

The exclusion of females from the military service had clear short-run advantages but it also meant that they were denied the benefits of military service. Because they were not forced to sell their labor to the army, they avoided being transformed into fit specimens of the military machine, and yet they were also denied the skills and training useful in industrial roles. When men were mustered out, they could transfer skills to industry. While participation in mass armies must have involved boring, repetitive, and dangerous work, it also clearly involved training for industrial roles. As Van Doorn observed, peasants were transformed into trained men with an emphasis on discipline, self-sacrifice, and punctuality. While the decomposition of labor deskilled the craft tradition, it also created a new synthesis:

> In much the same way, new industry must have drawn on the skills of the tradesman, leaving the rest to experience acquired on the job. This could, indeed, be sometimes a very rational procedure. There were of old small units which aimed at the development of skills and which reflected in their hierarchical structure, differences in capacity and seniority.[48]

Military participation was, therefore, both oppressive and emancipatory for the male peasant. Because service in a rational bureaucracy allowed individuals to advance through the ranks, it placed a higher value upon individual competence than did the roles of the absolute state. By focusing on what a person could do in an army or factory, it allowed a person to be evaluated upon his abilities and skills. Of course, what a person could do in the mass military and later in the factory was always framed by the overall plan of labor decomposition.

For the male proletariat, then, military service operated as a dialectic. On the one hand, men were disembodied and thrust into roles of servitude. However, in other ways, men in this new organization benefited. The military per se was not the vanguard of the death of the *gemeinschaft* community. The male proletariat had already been uprooted from the farm and village during the transition from feudalism to capitalism. Females, of course, were also homeless. With the transformation in the economic substructure, military service provided technical education to males. In an ironic sense, military enslavement provided a new home for the landless and the dispossessed.

Because females were defined as being unfit to serve in the early mass militaries, they were relegated to noncitizenship. It is difficult to know the full implications of female exclusion and what it must have meant for women during this period. If military discipline was the precursor to industrial discipline, exclusion must have retarded the female's economic emancipation. Surely sex-role segregation retarded the recognition of the principle of equal treatment. Because women were never given recognition as coequals in the armed forces, they were never judged by performance norms in the society at large. Instead, they were judged by ascribed characteristics, with sexual attractiveness and fecundity serving as primitive measures of worth. If women had served as comrades-in-arms with men, the bourgeois concepts of chastity, ownership rights over women, and the sacredness of marriage itself may have been transformed. Unfortunately, a meaningful generalization as to whether the ultimate economic advantages of military service for women would have outweighed the disadvantages of military servitude cannot be easily formulated. Certainly exclusion impacted the subsequent patterns of sex segregation in the capitalist state. It takes no special evidence to demonstrate that exclusion from the military shaped the traditional sex-role ideologies. Because women were too weak to defend themselves, they were also too weak to work, vote, or think. Military parity seems to have closely correlated with economic and political parity. Exclusion from the military, if it did not create the sexually segregated division of labor, played and important role in reinforcing that structure of domination.

Female Grenadiers of the French Revolution

To women of the French Revolution, the line between military and political participation was not sharply drawn. Through military service, full citizenship rights were won. The French Revolution, itself, offered women training in self-defense. With the *levée en masse*, French women demanded to be included in the armed citizen's militia. Michel Martin's thesis was that the French Revolution was a historical period pregnant with anticipation of a militia of armed and trained females. Military participation was seen as the cutting edge of the rising class consciousness of women:

> The Revolution also offered a good training ground for women's familiarization with the interest in martial arts. Perhaps too much so for the taste of those revolutionaries scornful of these "female grenadiers" as Fabre d'Eglantine once put it. Soon after 1790, feminist clubs were established while pamphlets, petitions, and other memoranda demanding the integration of women in the armies circulated widely throughout the heated political circles of Paris.[49]

After the capitulation of Louis XVI, women played a prominent role in the popular agitation fermented by the revolutionary solution. The Paris agitators during the October days of 1789 included a significant proportion of women. Georges Lefebvre's *The Coming of the French Revolution* documented the role of women in the armed struggles, where they took on unorganized roles of militancy: "On Sunday the fourth (October 1789) a crowd swarmed at the Palais-Royal. Women were unusually numerous and declared their intention of marching to Versailles the next day; they were particularly vituperative against the queen. The National Guard broke up these assemblages, but listlessly and without conviction. That the morrow would be stormy was obvious."[50]

The revolutionary agitation for an expanded female role in the militia was cooled by the emergence of the Napoleonic state. As Abrahamsson put it, Napoleon perfected the French state machinery and knew how to use it for mobilizing and equipping huge armies:

> In the years between 1804 and 1813, a total of 2,400,000 men were called to arms. The human losses were enormous; already by 1806, some 1,600,000 men had died, part of them in battle, but the majority succumbing to various diseases and undernourishment . . . As a result of the greatly increased size of the armies, military strategy and tactics underwent profound changes. No longer was it possible for one commander to direct and lead a whole army; and, more important, no longer was it necessary to keep the whole army together in order to offer maximum protection during operations. Also, a half-million army allowed more complicated operations and movements designed to confuse rather than confront the enemy.[51]

Martin argued that the massive war machine of Napoleon did not immediately eviscerate the role of women. Women's role gradually became more tangential to military action with the maturity of the professional army. Even throughout the bourgeois century, individual women served in martial roles as crisis participants:

> Though after the Themidorian anticlimax, the "military bacchantes" and *tricoteuses* gave way to the more lady-like and fashion conscious *merveilleuses*, the Napoleonic saga was full of instances of feminine military bravery. Numerous women served as soldiers, even as officers in the uniforms of their regiment. Angelique Duchemin, an infantry lieutenant was the first woman ever to be awarded the much coveted Legion d'honneur, after seven campaigns and three wounds . . . Little by little, a camp follower tradition superseded the female warrior tradition. Yet the nineteenth century had also its contingents of female soldiers for whom 1848, the Franco-Prussian War and the Commune, for example, were occasions to manifest their martial pugnacity. The debate, during the Siege of Paris, over the constitution of a separate female military corps, although it was not authorized by General Trochu, is a proof of women's willingness to accept military responsibility. This responsibility carried over to the Commune barricades a year later and which won them various epithets—*petroleuses* being the best known one—evidencing both bourgeois retrospective fear as well as the audacity and the heroism of their protagonists.[52]

Ultimately, the professional armies of France became as balkanized as the mass armies of other Western European states. In the unrestrained

Napoleonic army, women's roles as intermittent crisis participants were restricted. Women's exclusion as armed *citoyennes* paralleled their exclusion from direct economic and political roles.

Females in the Early U.S. Military

Formal military organization in the United States was slow to develop. In contrast to the Prussian and British armies of the period, the Revolutionary army was primitive. In the guerilla warfare of the Revolutionary period, a few women participated in combat. But it was exceptional when women accompanied men onto the battlefront as direct participants. A few women participated, disguised as men, in the Revolutionary, Civil, and Spanish-American wars. Numerous accounts describe how women bound their breasts, donned mustaches, and cross-dressed in order to join their husbands or brothers at the front. The most prominent cross-dressed women soldiers were Deborah Sampson, in the American Revolution; Lucy Brewer, in the War of 1812; and Loretta Velasquez in the Civil War.[53]

However, in each war prior to the First World War, women primarily served as laundresses, cooks, and nurses without formal military status.

> Every day women went to the hospitals to care for the sick and wounded; they went to the battlefields to look for the wounded and dead; they buried friends and enemies. American prisoners waited for the women to bring them food. Women kept the farms going while the plowmen were on the battlefront—they raised grain, harvested it, and made bread to carry to their relatives in the armies or the prisons.[54]

During the settlement of the frontier, American women participated directly and in large numbers in a variety of hazardous roles as equal comrades with men. Women served on the Overland Trail, settled the Great Plains, and held a variety of roles with dangers tantamount to combat.[55]

As in Western Europe, the early U.S. armies excluded women except in frontier outposts where women often accompanied their husbands. Professional armies, however, wielded new weapons that inflicted injury and mutilation even more effectively than did the musket and pike. The exponential rise in war casualties created a need for women in the military, as trained nurses. A nineteenth century commentator described the expanded role of women in the embryonic field of military nursing during the Civil War:

> No pen can depict the sorrows that shadowed the lonely homes our soldiers left during those four years of bloodshed—four years of anxiety and watching

for news of the next battle and its results; four years of suffering on the part of our soldiers, tenting in swamps, marching through the mud of Southern soil, double-quick the carnage!

The fierce contest has begun—and they bare their defenseless bodies to the shot and shell of our Southern brothers, whose big guns sweep furrows through our ranks. The gaps are immediately closed, our boys falling dead or disabled. What more fitting place for women with holy motives and tenderest sympathy, than on those fields of blood and death, or in death, or in retreats prepared for our suffering heroes.[56]

The first formal ancillary role for women in industrial armies was in nursing, as the inefficiency of civilian nursing and volunteers in the American Civil War led to the development of a single unified nursing corps.[57]

The Legitimation of Military Nursing

Prior to Florence Nightingale, women who tended to the wounded and sick soldiers were stigmatized as prostitutes. But as high explosives created the need for trained medical personnel, the role of the war nurse replaced that of the camp follower.

In England during the Crimean War, there were difficulties finding enough civilian women volunteers to care for the wounded and sick on the Turkish front. This difficulty was due in part to the image of military nursing as a disreputable occupation. Gradually, a professional ideology arose that redefined military nursing as a legitimate and even patriotic role.

Florence Nightingale was the first to promulgate the professional ideology that trained nurses were respectable. Lord William Howard Russell's letter to the *London Times* during the Crimean War reflected the emergence of military nursing as a legitimate role for women in war: "Are there no devoted women among us, able and willing to go forth to minister to the sick and wounded soldiers of the East in the hospitals at Scutari? Are none of the daughters of England at this extreme hour of need ready for such a work of mercy?"[58]

War nurses worked under primitive and dangerous conditions. Much of the work involved tasks such as severing limbs and tending to endless lines of the sick and dying. Somewhat later, a nurse who served in the First World War described her work:

The nurses spoke of the restlessness which ate into them in the long months in which nothing had stability. Months in which the days were made up of meeting so many men, and seeing so many things they dared not think too deeply about . . . They listed the things that were everyday, but could never be everyday enough for fastidious women to stop minding. First of all the smells—so many, and so nasty. There was the smell of ether one never stopped tasting in the back of the throat, or the sweet, cloying smell of blood—one got that full on the tongue. Then there were the smells that made stomachs crawl, like the gangrenous ones, the smell of death, and the mixed smell of feces and chlorine in the latrines.[59]

The professionalization of military nursing was associated with the crowded and disease-ridden military encampments as well as with the greatly increased efficiency of military killing. Untrained civilian volunteers and civilian-followers were inadequate for the requirements of modern warfare. Thomas links the full development of the nursing corps in the case of England to the Boer War, in Canada to the 1885 rebellion, in Australia to the 1898 South African War, and in the United States to the Spanish-American War.[60]

In summary, the militaries of early capitalism envisioned no role for women except as prostitutes, laundresses, and canteenkeepers. After the seventeenth century, there were few references to individual female defenders as crisis participants. The role that heroines could play in the early mass armies was diminished by the organizing principle of the regiment, and there was a sufficient pool of impoverished males to field the early formalized armies of Western Europe. It has been argued that female segregation from early mass armies was double-edged. Exclusion from organized militaries was both oppressive and emancipatory. While it is difficult to know with certainty what long-range consequences military service might have had for females, it is clear that the segregated military retarded women's social emancipation. At the end of this period, the rise of military nursing legitimated female participation in a narrowly circumscribed sphere and forecast what was to come. The mature mass army found that it could use trained females in a variety of roles during the exigency of total war. The third stage (1900–1945) was a time of external crisis, with the inclusion of women as a reserve army. The large-scale mobilization of female labor in the military occurred as women were employed as an army of last resort during the total wars of the twentieth century.

Stage Three: External Crisis and Women as Military Reserves (1900–1945)

Civilian British Women and Total War (1916–1918)

In the latter part of the nineteenth century, the British military apparatus lagged behind that of the Prussian Army. War had grown to a complex and specialized social institution; yet the soldiers of the British army were poorly trained. Drawn from the poorest and least educated of the male proletariat, the British military participants were subject to absolute domination rather than to more complex training. In contrast, the French and Prussian armies had long since given their soldiers skills and toned down traditional military discipline:

> The increase in size of the armies since the turn of the eighteenth century, which in the long run has made the nobility and gentry an insufficient source, and the impact of military education, have contributed in diminishing the importance of ascriptive properties (such as noble origins and wealth) as criteria for military employment, so prevalent in the pre-revolutionary French and old Prussian armies.[61]

In the British Army, officers came exclusively from the upper class, while enlisted soldiers were from the déclassé. Raw domination was used to command the troops, in contrast with the education and training used in the Prussian and French armies: "The harsh and brutal conditions of [British] army life—long service and flogging—had made the army a kind of penal servitude. Men enlisted for twelve years—the most active years of their lives—and when they were eventually discharged, they were untrained and unfit for civilian employment."[62]

Cardwell's army reforms of the late 1870s corrected some of the most venal excesses such as the buying and selling of officer commissions, but by the beginning of the First World War the British Army had not been rationalized sufficiently to compete successfully with Germany's professional army. Jarman argued that the stalemate on the Western front necessitated the buildup of massive reservoirs of volunteers for the British Expeditionary Forces. During the first eighteen months of the war, two and a half million volunteers enlisted, but by 1916 the government increased the labor pool even further by introducing conscription, which was a marked break with the old tradition of relying on men untrained and unfit for civilian employment.[63]

By September of 1916, the War Office had exhausted its reserve army of males and began to call for the temporary mobilization of women. The mobilization propaganda of the War Office justified the employment of women in war work in order to release men for front-line duties.

The rapid growth in the number of British women workers and their entrance into hundreds of occupations as a supplementary labor source was one of the most striking industrial phenomena of the war:

> The decrease in women's employment which marked the beginning of the war disappeared month by month until the level of July, 1914, was passed in April, 1915. In the next month the *Labour Gazette* noted that the shortage of

male labor was now extended to female and boy labor in many lines. Now came Lord Kitchener's appeal for "men and still more men," and as the army grew the women had to fill the depleted ranks of industry. . . . In short, in four years of war more than a million and a third additional women entered work outside their homes.[64]

The temporary suspension of sex role proscriptions against women in heavy industry was justified in the War Office by the requirements of total war. In the report by the Adjutant-General to the forces, the rationale for replacing men with women in civilian war work was outlined:

In some measure the void can be filled by men not physically fit for Army work, but this source of supply is not enough for the country's needs. Since the outbreak of war, the women of Britain have shown themselves ready and anxious to undertake every form of work where their services could be accepted, and this book is intended not only to indicate women have shown themselves capable of successfully replacing the stronger sex in practically every calling, but is offered also as a tribute to their effective contribution to the Empire in its hour of need.[65]

While the total number of females substituted for male workers amounted to 1,392,000, including farm laborers, the total number of females substituted for male workers in selected occupations is even more dramatic. For example, the number of women workers in government was 9,120 times as great as the number of women so employed in July 1914. In banking and finance, the number of women was 555 times as great; in transport, 437 times; and in civil service, 152 times as great. By July of 1917, one working women out of three was replacing a man.[66]

During the war, Fabian socialists called for a wage and hiring policy that would put women and men on equal terms. The preliminary report of the Carnegie Endowment for International Peace on the effect of World War I on women's economic positions contained Beatrice Webb's Minority Report, which recommended:

1. The establishment of a national minimum wage.
2. The determination of a standard or occupational wage rate above the national minimum.
3. The adjustment of wages to the cost of living.
4. The requirement of efficiency qualifications rather than sex for applicants.[67]

Despite these attempts, the British government did not ensure equity in wages during the war, and at the coming of the Armistice, industry in Great Britain readjusted to the old structural constraints on female work. During the first weeks of March 1919, the number of women who were displaced and seeking employment reached half a million.[68]

British Women Soldiers (1916–1918)

Paralleling the role of British women in releasing men for the battlefront were the activities of numerous paramilitary auxiliaries. Because of the mutilation inflicted by modern munitions and the devastation wreaked by poisonous gas, trained nurses were in demand.

As Mauwick observed in his study of women in World War I: "Because the conditions of trench warfare were so horrific, with infantrymen pitted again and again against high explosives and machine gun fire, the rate of mutilation and serious injury was far higher than anyone had expected, leading very quickly to a dire shortage at the Front of trained nurses."[69]

Dalby's history of British women in World War I revealed that women in medical units performed competently under horrific conditions:

> No group so demonstrated the abilities of women to live the rough life demanded by war as the FANYS. In theory provided with barracks, they lived and ate in tents, even in the winter of 1917, the coldest on record to that date. . . . The drivers who waited to meet the ambulance trains or the canal barges loaded with wounded needed patience, endurance, flexibility, and strength, once setting the record of seventeen women carrying over 10,000 wounded in eight days and nights. . . . Of all women's units they had the greatest percentage of casualties and they won far and away the greatest number of decorations, mostly from the Belgians and French but including some highly coveted Mentioned in Dispatches.[70]

At the end of the war, the British women who served without formal status in the female auxiliaries received no veteran benefits. These women suffered the injuries of military service without even gaining the vote, as the House of Commons granted the right to vote to any woman aged 30 or over, effectively excluding most women who had served in the First World War.[71]

American Women in World War I

Whereas British forces encountered urgent manpower shortages, the United States had far greater manpower reserves in the First World War, due in part to the American Expeditionary Forces' (AEF) late entry into the war. With the exception of skilled clerical workers, there were relatively few shortages affecting the AEF. In particular, the AEF faced shortages of administrators, telephone operators, and persons with office skills. Of course, long before the military required these skills, the industrial sector had shifted to the almost exclusive employment of women as typists and telephone operators. In the latter campaigns of the war, skill shortages in administrative military occupations became critical. As early as October of

1917, General John J. Pershing, Commander of the Allied Expeditionary Forces, cabled a request to the War Department for 100 women telephone operators who were bilingual (French and English). After considerable discussion, the War Department informed Pershing that he would receive instead, 5,000 limited service males. As for woman's corps, the War Department was vehement in its stand that it was "not convinced of the desirability of such a radical departure in the conduct of military affairs."[72]

Ultimately, nearly 13,000 women served in the enlisted Army without formal status. The women who served in the Navy and Marines were granted formal status as Yeomanettes and Marinettes. In the official report issued by the War Department at the end of 1919, it was documented that a "continuance of the war would have required the United States in completing its program for the year 1919 to make a much more extended use of women."[73]

During the First World War, the War Department reluctantly employed women. Despite the military requirement for women in selected skills, women were not employed until all but the most unsuitable males had first been enlisted. When women were enlisted and even after they performed competently, male prejudice remained: "With careful supervision, female employees may be permitted in the camps without moral injury either to themselves or other soldiers."[74] With the exception of narrowly defined roles in nursing and administrative areas, the United States escaped the "manpower" pinch that Great Britain faced. As a result, sex-role definitions needed little adjustment.

American Women Between the Wars

Because the United States was not mobilized in World War I to its limits, only modest changes in women's industrial participation were required. The *New York Times* editorialized that the employment of women as subway toll keepers and streetcar conductors indicated that the United States would follow the example of Great Britain in using "woman-power." In an article entitled "Where Women Supplant Men Because of War," the *Times* stated that the reason for female employment in "male jobs" was not linked to present need but instead to the anticipation of increased shortages that would come with the prolongation of the war and a second draft.[75]

Women were both demobilized from the Army and forced out of their temporary war work at the cessation of hostilities. In both countries, when peace was restored, women soldiers and war workers were the first to be demobilized to the unemployment lines. In Great Britain, auxiliaries were demobilized the day after the signing of the Armistice. In the United States, women were dismissed from Marine and Navy units by the end of November 1918. In a curt one-page memorandum issued by the General

Staff of the War Department, women were stripped of any military status or benefits: "In view of the present situation it is believed no longer desirable that arrangements be made to form military organizations composed of women."[76]

In both the United States and Britain, women's expectations had been raised with respect to the potential benefits of military participation. In the early part of 1918, for example, former President Theodore Roosevelt introduced Harriet Stanton Blatch's book on the mobilization of "woman-power" for the war with the following declarations:

> Mrs. Blatch makes her appeal [for women's wartime service] primarily because of the war needs of the moment. But she has in view no less the great tasks of the future. I welcome her book as an answer to the cry that admission of women to an equal share in the right of self government will tend to soften the body politic . . . No man who is not blind can fail to see that we have entered a new day in the great epic march of the ages. For good or for evil the old days have passed; and it rests upon us, the men and women now alive, to decide whether in the new days the world is to be a better or worse place to live in, for our descendants. In this new world, women are to stand on an equal footing with men, in ways and to an extent never hitherto dreamed of. In this country they are on the eve of securing and in much of the country have already secured, their full political rights.[77]

However, the wartime appeals and promises were desiccated as the crisis passed.

Crisis Participation and Emancipation

World War I did not emancipate women, and the extreme depression that began toward the end of 1929 severely worsened their position. By 1930, 20 percent of women normally employed were permanently displaced,[78] as gender role proscriptions coalesced with economic depression to throw hundreds of thousands of women out of work.

British women's experience during the First World War and, to a lesser extent, the American women's experience demonstrated that they were adaptable to diverse roles within the mature mass army. In fact, the introduction of women into men's work was a frontal assault on the traditional practice of fixing wages on the basis of sex.

In the United States, immediately after women were enfranchised by the Nineteenth Amendment in 1920, the War Department began making plans to deploy females in the event of another total war. However, it was also evident that newly enfranchised females could wield considerable political power. The War Department feared that many female leaders were dangerously "susceptible to the charms of pacifism and other doctrines that advocated the abolition of the military":

To stem this tide of opinion the Army sought to teach women voters more about its own nature and purpose. To this end Secretary Baker in 1920 created a new position under the comprehensive title of Director of Women's Relations, United States Army ... The director was to maintain a liaison between the War Department and the women of the country and to secure their cooperation by explaining to them that the Army was "a progressive, socially minded human institution" and that women voters should not "fanatically demand the dissolution of a ruthless military machine."[79]

The Director of Women's Relations developed a questionnaire on the potential use of women in the military for the Army general staff. In the 1920s plans were discarded for a female corps.[80] While the Department was definitely interested in militarizing females, it was ambivalent about granting them formal military status:

Only six agencies favored giving them immediate military status. In view of later debate about the proper jobs for women in the Army, it was significant that at this time the concept of a menial type of corps of low-grade personnel loomed large in Army thinking. Not quite half of the requests were for clerks and stenographers; a few others were for small numbers of skilled workers such as draftsmen, dieticians, and telephone operators. The rest were chiefly for large numbers for unskilled work: approximately 5,800 laundry workers, 7,000 cooks, 1,300 charwomen and janitors, 5,000 chauffeurs, 2,000 messengers, 11,000 laborers, 8,000 seamstresses and so on.[81]

The military's refusal to give women military status was also strongly reinforced in Congressional hearings on women who had worked in France and were seeking compensation for the loss of their health. As Mattie Treadwell found in her exhaustive study of War Department policies toward women:

The War Department had already decided that such women were not entitled to veteran's gratuities, ruling in one case: "Female telephone operators have no military status whatever ... those serving with the American Expeditionary Forces (were) not even under civil service regulations ... It is not believed that Congress intended that a gratuity should be paid to any person not actually a member of the military establishment."[82]

Women in the U.S. Army in World War II

In May of 1941, the first bill to establish the Women's Army Auxiliary Corps for service with the U.S. Army was introduced in Congress by Representative Edith Nourse Rogers of Massachusetts. The first plans proposed that women not have full military status. Women were to be skilled temporary workers without the benefits of military service. As Treadwell documented:

Endless legal distinctions were also attempted. WAACs were to receive medical service from the Army, but no medical or other benefits after discharge except those provided by the Employees Compensation Commission. They were considered military personnel for benefits of the Soldiers and Sailors Relief Act but not for benefits of the act granting re-employment rights.[83]

By the fall of 1941, the WAAC bill was delayed by War Department staff officers who did not see an immediate need for large numbers of women in the Army. Only General George Marshall thought that the establishment of the Women's Army Auxiliary Corps (WAAC) was essential for the effective mobilization of the Army. Edith Nourse Rogers recalled conversations with General Marshall: "By the summer of 1941, General Marshall was intensely interested in the WAAC business. He foresaw a cycle of shortages; that of the moment was the supply shortage, in which the scarcity of supplies hindered mobilization, but he now became convinced that the bottleneck of the future would be that of manpower."[84]

From the date of Pearl Harbor, it became evident to others in the War Department that women had to be enlisted as soon as possible. But before mobilization was possible, public opinion had to be remolded. Although the crisis of total war worsened toward the end of 1941, public opinion continued to oppose War Department plans to militarize women. Negative attitudes toward the inclusion of women were manifest in the Congressional debate concerning the WAAC bill: "When the measure finally reached the House floor, the real opposition developed. Members argued that a soldier would go forward in battle even if his buddy was shot down beside him, but if his buddy was a woman he would stop and render first aid."[85]

In May of 1942, House Resolution 6293 created the Women's Army Auxiliary Corps with an authorized strength of 150,000. In July of that year, the first WAAC training center opened at Fort Des Moines, Iowa. By July of 1943, the first WAAC separate battalion consisting of 555 enlisted women officers arrived in England for duty with the Eighth Air Force.

The Women's Army Corps (1943–1945)

In September of 1943, the WAAC was dissolved and women received full military status in the Women's Army Corps (WAC). The law that established the Corps stated that women were to have full military status and benefits only for the duration of the war and for six months thereafter.[86] The public continued to view the Women's Army Corps with ambivalence despite the efforts of the War Department to carefully define and circumscribe female participation. At the first press conference given by the first director of the WAC, Oveta Culp Hobby, reporters' questions reflected the public view of the contradiction between traditional sex roles and military participation:

Q. *How about girdles?*
A. If you mean will they be issued, I can't tell yet. If they are required, they will be supplied ...
Q. *Will the women salute?*
A. Yes they will salute.
Q. *Will they march and carry arms?*
A. They will learn to march well enough to parade, but they will carry no guns.[87]

Newspaper headlines during the early period of the Women's Army Corps reflected resistance to the inclusion of women in the war effort even as temporary workers: "Petticoat Army Formed!", "Doughgirl Generalissimos!", "Fort Wackies!", and "Here Comes the Naked Amazons!"[88]

Fundamentalist religious leaders were the most vituperative in their opposition. An Arkansas radio evangelist gave a regional broadcast in which she alleged that women recruits were "lined up naked for the male officers to inspect":

Christ loves these girls and I know he does not like for them to have to line up naked and it is embarrassing for our girls every month. Please ask me to send you the book, *The Truth About the Mark of the Beast and Satan's Children.*[89]

During the first year of the Women's Corps, sex-role stereotypes retarded the mobilization of enlisted women. While the general public thought women who joined the Army were either whores or lesbians, enlisted males were another major barrier to the recruitment effort. According to military intelligence reports, enlisted male attitudes were the most important impediment to hesitant female prospects. The following accounts culled from the reports of military censors represented male stereotypes of female soldiers:

You join the WAVES or WAC and you are automatically a prostitute in my opinion.

I don't want you to have a thing to do with them. Because they are the biggest houres (whores).

I would rather we never seen each other for 20 years that to have you join the WACS for gosh sakes stay a good girl [civilian] and I'm not just kidding either.

Get the damn divorce. I don't want no damn WAC for a wife.

Honey don't you ever worry your poor head about joining the WACS for we went all over that once before. Ha! (Remember over my dead body Ha! Ha!) You are going to stay home.

Your letter shocked me and it was not appreciated by no means. If you join the WACS you and I are through for good, and I'll stop all allotments and everything.

The service is no place for a woman. A woman's place is in the home.[90]

Military intelligence reports also surveyed the attitudes of females in the Army and the views of female recruiters:

The trouble lies with U.S. men. The average serviceman absolutely forbids his wife, sweetheart, or sister to join a military organization and nearly all U.S. women are in one of these categories.

When a girl sees an Army officer refuse to return a WAC salute and even leave a restaurant because a group of WACs walk in, is that any inducement for her to enlist.

The catcalls, filthy remarks, and dirty stories floating among soldiers and sailors about service-women make a decent girl shudder.[91]

At the beginning, female military participation seemed to contradict traditional sex-role ideologies. The Women's Auxiliary units had been subject to the following rumors that carried over to the Women's Army Corps: (1) WAACs solicited men and engaged in sex acts in public places; (2) WAACs were issued prophylactics and required to carry them whenever they left the barracks; (3) WAACs were recruited to serve as sexual outlets for frustrated military males; (4) many of the WAACs had gonorrhea; immoral WAACs infected many of the men; (5) WAACs joined the service to meet other lesbians and to engage in homosexual orgies; (6) WAACs were drunks and brawled in bars; (7) WAACs who were not sexually active were rejected by Army physicians; (8) WAACs had to have large breasts and other anatomical specifications; (9) WAACs were immoral in conduct and appearance; (10) WAACs impeded the combat readiness of the Army.[92] Military intelligence investigated each of these rumors and traced them to the following sources:

1. *Army males:* Army officers and men who resented members of the WAAC ... who have obtained equal or higher rank than themselves. ... Male military personnel who are sometimes inclined to resent usurpation of their long established monopoly.

2. *Soldiers' wives*: Officers' wives over bridge tables. Women whose husbands are shipped overseas.
3. *Jealous civilian women*: Local girls and women who resent having the WAACs around. Younger to middle-aged women who deplore the extra competition. Women who ordinarily participate in community enterprise and who are losing publicity as a result of women in uniform.
4. *Gossips*: Thoughtless gossiping men and women. Men who like to tell off-color stories.
5. *Fanatics*: Those who cannot get used to women being any place except the home. Those whose rabid political convictions cause them erroneously to see in the WAAC another New Deal creation.
6. *WAACs*: Disgruntled and discharged WAACs.[93]

The Women's Army Corps was seen as an army of last resort. At the beginning of the war, the War Department preferred to utilize marginal males who were either sickly or unskilled rather than enlist women, however healthy or skilled. The view of the public was that marginal men should be enlisted before turning to women.

In 1941, a fourth-grade education was required for enlistment. By 1943, the War Department began dipping lower into the manpower reservoir. Toward the end of 1943, illiterates and parts of the prison population were conscripted. From June of 1943 to September of 1945, over 302,000 illiterate men received training for low-grade Army jobs,[94] yet the utilization of these limited men was not enough to stave off the manpower demands of total war. The exigencies of aggregate shortages and the prospect of future labor bottlenecks served as an impetus for a major recruitment plan to increase the number of Army women.

Rupp documented how public images were manipulated to help fulfill the desperate need for women in civilian war work. During the latter part of 1943, wartime propaganda had to somehow persuade women to take war jobs without challenging basic assumptions about women's role in society:

> The patriotic appeal had two aspects, the positive "do your part" approach and the negative "a soldier may die if you don't do your part" warning. The campaign slogan, "The More Women at Work—The Sooner We'll Win," promised women that their contributions could bring their men home sooner. The picture of a soldier and an empty machine, captioned "This soldier may die *unless* you man this machine," warned that if women did not take war jobs, their men might not come home at all. But in either case, the appeal to patriotism usually took on a personalized cast, urging women to work for their men rather than for their country.[95]

Coextensive with the propaganda campaign to legitimate women as civilian war workers, was the publicity campaign in 1943 by the War

Department to redefine the image of the female soldier. As manpower analysts estimated that over 50 percent of the military jobs could be filled by females, the publicity machinery of the War Department experimented with themes to marshal public support for the mobilization of women soldiers.

At the Conference on War and Post-War Demands for Trained Personnel, Representative James Wadsworth of New York drew the parallel between the utilization of women and the shortening of the war:

> We shall all have to give up something, men and women alike; and I think it is high time that we here in America mobilize every ounce of strength we have for if we don't do it and do it quickly, your son and mine will die ... Yes, we may muddle through, stumbling on the home front, and everybody knows it; we may win the finals but not without cost. I plead with women, conscious of their patriotism and conscious of their strength, to see this matter in the broader vision.[96]

From Whores to Patroits:
The Mobilization of Women Soldiers

One of the most important themes in the legitimation of women as soldiers was the "Release a Man" slogan. High school students in late 1943 received a book produced by military contractors entitled *Youth Goes to War*, which emphasized that women in support roles could be used to release men for direct combat:

> But this new war has seen women for the first time stepping into the places of men in the armed forces to release men for more strenuous duties elsewhere. The lead has been taken by our Russian allies, where there are now over thirty million women helping the Russian war effort, not only behind the lines, but in the fighting forces themselves ... Women in the United States are now being admitted to the armed forces, but only for noncombatant duty. The time may yet come when American women will have a chance to get in the fight, as in England, where women are already manning antiaircraft guns at defense posts throughout that island fortress. But American women for the time being are permitted only to perform detail work which will allow the men now in these positions to take over more active duty.[97]

A second theme in the recruitment campaign used guilt and fear to cajole reluctant females to enlist. The Director of the Women's Army Corps proposed a series of macabre advertisements and posters that would shock women into consulting their military recruiter:

> Her favorite advertisement was a "shocker" which showed a wounded

soldier dying on the battlefield while women played bridge, with the caption, MEN ARE DYING ON THE BATTLEFIELD—CAN YOU LIVE WITH YOURSELF ON THE SIDELINES?

Colonel Hobby next produced an advertisement showing soldiers' graves, with the caption, THEY CAN'T DO ANY MORE—BUT YOU CAN. She argued, "Something like this is needed to drive home a sense of shame to women not doing anything."[98]

Treadwell documented the ruinous expense and difficulties faced by the War Department's publicity machinery in attracting women. In January of 1944, the Army proposed yet another mobilization campaign labeled "Women in War." Its purpose was to urge women to accept some form of war work, either as soldiers or in industry:

The OWI (Office of War Information) leveled all its considerable forces against this apathy. Newspapers, motion pictures, magazines, radio, and all other civilian news media were fully at its command, and for several weeks all devoted their plugs to the theme of Women in War—urging women impartially to join one of the armed services or to take a job in industry. Fifty national radio shows a week and countless local shows used the OWI's Fact Sheet. Stars and producers of motion picture industry co-operated by making two-and-a-half minute bulletins to be attached to newsreels, and 16-millimeter films for showing in churches, schools, and war plants.[99]

Treadwell contended that all of the OWI activities had little perceptible effect on public apathy or on the armed forces recruitment of women. However, the All-States Campaign, the Station-Job Plan, and the Women-in-War drive had, to some extent, restored recruiting to a level that permitted the Corps' continued operation.[100]

By the end of 1944, recruitment of women began to expand. Feature articles on women in the military appeared in *Harpers, Life,* the *New York Times, The Saturday Evening Post,* and in local newspapers. A sampling of the headlines revealed the continuing effort to legitimate female military participation:

WAC ENLISTS AND MAKES FAMILY 100 PERCENT IN WAR EFFORT
FOUR WOUNDED SOLDIER HEROES HELP RECRUIT WACS
YANKS WELCOME WACS
GENERAL'S DAUGHTER, ARMY PRIVATE, AND WAC CREDITED WITH SAVING LIVES OF PLANE CREW[101]

The actual performance of women in the U.S. Army was exemplary, according to Treadwell's analysis of unpublished memoranda and letters from analysts at the War Department. General Eisenhower, for example wrote the War Department of the WAC's contribution: "During the time

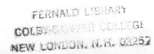
FERNALD LIBRARY
COLBY-SAWYER COLLEGE
NEW LONDON, N.H. 03257

that I have had WACs under my command, they have met every test and task assigned them. Their contribution in efficiency, skill, spirit, and determination are immeasurable."[102] Official military records substantiated this observation. The attrition rate for women was the same as for noncombat men (0.5 percent). Time lost to nonbattle hospitalization was lower for women than for men (2.2 percent as compared with 2.5 percent). Women developed psychological disorders less frequently than did males, and venereal disease was one-sixth that of the male rate. The pregnancy rate was negligible. WAC disciplinary rates were a tiny fraction of the rate for men.[103]

Other wartime services that included women were the Women's Reserve of the Navy (Women Accepted for Volunteer Emergency Service or WAVES), the Women's Reserve of the Coast Guard Reserve (SPARS), the Army Nursing Corps, the Navy Nursing Corps, the Cadet Nursing Corps, and the Women Air Force's Service Pilots (WASPS).[104] More than 350,000 women performed temporary duty in military roles. In comparison with the 18 million men that served, these numbers were small, but as in the case of British women in the First World War, women in the services were a valuable reservoir.

Within days of the end of the Second World War, the Women's Army Corps dismissed 98 percent of its members. In spite of the efforts of women's groups such as the American Association of University Women and the sponsorship of Eleanor Roosevelt, the women's services were disbanded. By January of 1947, the Women's Army Corps dwindled to 9,000 persons. Women once again found the cycle of proscription in peace after temporary suspension of sex roles for temporary "dirty work" in total war. Once again, women were relegated to their former roles without any appreciable increase in citizenship rights. Because women did not have the same reemployment rights as males after the war, they returned to the job market with a handicap. Representative of the remittable occupational roles was the plight of wartime women pilots who could find employment in the airline industry only as hostesses and typists.[105]

Women in War Industries

As Rupp has documented, women employed in war industries experienced the same cycle of remittance.[106] At the beginning of the war, government officials promised lasting changes in the wage structure. Harold Ickes, Secretary of the Interior, spoke at a conference to mobilize women for war and promised them permanent jobs as had Theodore Roosevelt in the mobilization campaign near the end of the First World War: "This participation of women in war and in industry, on such a colossal scale constitutes a major social and economic revolution. It will, in my opinion, have a fundamental effect upon society after the war. It will cause a change in the economic position of women everywhere."[107]

Ickes promised that women would be permanently accepted in male jobs and dismissed the fears of women who believed that no lasting gains would accrue from temporary war work:

> Some people, especially women, seem too worried about the future. They feel that when the war is over, they will lose their present jobs and with them, their economic independence. They are convinced the present need for labor cannot last. Some fret, while others try to make the most hay while the sun shines. Their actions remind me of the ditty that some disillusioned Thomas chalked on the wall of a railway station:
> Gather, ye rosebuds while ye may
>   For Time brings only sorrow.
> Girls you might have kissed today,
>   May wear gas masks tomorrow.[108]

Despite the excellent performance of women in "men's jobs" during the War, women were shifted back to women's industries—textiles, foods, processing, services, and household employment at the war's end. The popular mythology about the Second World War was that it expanded women's jobs. Rupp found that the wartime changes in female employment were only temporary:

> The OWI material on public opinion suggests that the public accepted the employment of women in war industry without revising traditional attitudes. Many men feared permanent changes, but the post-war situation assured them that little had changed. The proportion of employed women in the female population continued to increase after the immediate postwar layoffs, as it had throughout the twentieth century, but the war itself had no permanent impact on this trend . . . The seeming paradox of the intensely domestic 1950s following on the heels of a supposedly liberating war dissolves if one considers the form in which war participation was presented to the public.[109]

Temporary war work for some women resulted in losses of jobs in industries that had employed a large proportion of females prior to the war. The war actually reduced female employment in industries such as aluminum cooking utensils, silk-throwing mills, silk narrow fabric mills, broad fabric mills, hosiery, costume jewelry, cork, and asbestos jobs. After the production of luxury goods was restricted, many women were permanently displaced. In Washington hearings on national defense migration, Mary Anderson, Head of the Women's Bureau, expressed her concern about the displacement of women workers:

The ending of the silk throwing industry, in the anthracite area of Pennsylvania, has caused untold hardships to many families whose women worked in these mills. In Luzerne and Lackawanna Counties, in November of 1942, it was estimated that there were 10,000 unemployed women from silk mills and clothing factories... Out-migration of these women was suggested by the Employment Service. However, only one-eighth of a sample group interviewed were without dependents and these girls lived with their families and were not eager to move to new localities.[110]

Temporary war work involved may hidden injuries and conflicts for females. Males feared that women would be "scabs" who would drive down wages and hurt the collective bargaining position. In a survey assessing male industrial workers' attitudes toward the employment of women in war work, there was overwhelming evidence of sex-role strain between male and female workers; 50 percent of the married males were unwilling to let their wives work in defense plants under any condition. An intensive publicity campaign by the OWI was created to convince men that their wives should take jobs in the war economy to save the country.[111]

During the war, few executive positions were offered to women in order to release men for combat. Over 50 percent of the jobs offered to women were unskilled and semiskilled positions.[112] At the end of the war, defense plants disgorged women just as the armed forces had. Women's roles were redefined to encompass a narrow occupational span. The war, itself, produced few lasting gains.

Allied Women in World War II

The hypothesis that sex roles were dedifferentiated temporarily by the requirements of total war is supported by the female experience in other Allied armies during the war. The Axis powers, in contrast, did not militarize women as temporary participants.

Soviet Union. In the Soviet Union, because over 50 percent of all males born before 1939 were killed during the war, manpower reserves were not only threatened but exhausted as the war effort increased in 1943. Soviet women were then used in direct combat roles. The 46th Taman Guards light bomber regiment was composed of all female pilots. Women led air raids and filled armored task forces, infantry, and engineering corps jobs. Popova cited some of the following individual cases among the 100,000 women decorated for wartime bravery: "Guards Major E. Niklunia made six hundred night combat flights bombing enemy railway trains, bridges, and stores. The squadron commanded by Maria Smirnova made 3,260 combat flights, and Maria Smirnova herself, dropped 100,000 kilograms of bombs on enemy motorized units."[113]

Jackson believed that Soviet women played a key role in the destruction of the Sixth German Army at the Stalingrad Pocket:

> It was during the battle for Stalingrad that another women's air unit made its operational debut. This was the 586th Fighter Air Regiment; equipped with Yak-7 fighters it began to distinguish itself almost immediately. One of the 586th's pilots, Olga Yamschikova, became the first woman fighter pilot to destroy an enemy aircraft at night, shooting down a Junkers-88 over Stalingrad on 24 September 1942. During the remainder of the war the 586th remained a first-line unit, supporting the Soviet armies in their subsequent advance across Europe.[114]

Women units fought alongside male units in the defense of Leningrad, Odessa, Kiev, Sevastpool, Minsk, the Donbas, the Caucasus, and the Ukraine.[115] In the civilian sector, Soviet women replaced men in all areas of manufacturing, anti-air-raid defense, medical care, and fortress construction.

Great Britain. Great Britain faced severe labor bottlenecks in both the civilian and military spheres, as it had during World War I. As a result, women were temporarily employed in aircraft, small-arms ammunition, artillery ammunition, and other war industries. The Emergency Defense Powers Act gave the government the power to conscript female labor. In May of 1940, an agreement was reached with trade unions for the introduction of women in engineering, but the bulk of British women performed unskilled and semiskilled work. Working-class British women were required to migrate to remote army camps to perform cooking, cleaning, and domestic work. In addition, a large number of women found employment filling shells, producing ammunition, manufacturing airplane engines, and assembling armor.[116]

In 1938, the formation of the Home Auxiliary Territorial Service brought women into the military services. Nolan noted that the difference between the ATS and the regular army was due to the restrictions on organized combat by the former. The auxiliary women's forces totalled over 200,000 by 1943: "During the last week of August, 1940, 19,000 women received their call up papers and by June 1941, over 40,000 women were serving. These women worked alongside the men in many of the trades open to them by 1943 but, in most cases, training for their employments was carried out on a single sex basis."[117]

In 1941, the Auxiliary Territorial Service was retitled as an official branch of the military. According to Thomas, as such, they became subject to military law. During the three years of conscription, 125,000 women were drafted, and 430,000 volunteered for service.[118]

The United Kingdom was only one of four countries that developed a policy to conscript women during wartime, according to Binkin and Bach (the others were Germany, the Soviet Union, and later Israel):

> Women in the Auxiliary Territorial Service (ATS), the Women's Royal Navy Service, and the Women's Auxiliary Air Force first served as drivers, cooks, orderlies, and telephone operators. Later, as the manpower shortage became greater, they worked in ordnance maintenance and repair, and as brick-layers, electrical engineers, and range finders and fire controllers in anti-aircraft batteries. Some women volunteers serving in integrated anti-aircraft artillery batteries saw action both at home and overseas, suffered casualties, or became prisoners of war. However, despite their close proximity to actual combat, women were never considered to be in a direct combat role.[119]

In Britain as in the United States, women were restricted at first to a narrow band of military occupations, but as the total war gained momentum, women assumed a wider range of duties. Of the women who served in the armed forces in the United Kingdom, approximately 1,500 became casualties (624 killed in action; 98 missing in action; 744 wounded in action; and 20 prisoners of war).[120]

France. In July of 1938, the passage of the Paul Boncour Law required women to enlist in times of wartime crisis. As Martin observed, it was planned that women were authorized to enlist in a variety of occupations in addition to medical roles. The Vichy regime sought, however, to limit, if not to actually put to an end, the employment of women in the military. However, women served with the liberation armies in the North African, Italian, French, and German campaigns: "The Resistance movement constituted a powerful impetus for women's involvement in military actions. Numerous were those who served beyond the expected yet peripheral roles of nurses and liaison agents in military operations... Many, for that matter, did pay in the hands of the occupants, in French jails or German camps, a high price for this role."[121]

Women Partisani

Despite severe manpower shortages, the Axis powers failed to use women effectively during the war. The sex-role ideology promulgated by the Third Reich was antithetical to the use of women even as crisis participants.

Officially Holland, Belgium, Norway, France, and other European countries had New Orders during the war. Women played an important role in the subterranean armies of the resistance. In Yugoslavia, 25,000 women guerillas were killed in action. Women in Belgium served as couriers, radio operators, and printers of underground newspapers. Notable women who were killed in the resistance include Germaine Devalet, for harboring fugitives; Marguerite Bervoets for espionage; and Louise Henine, who was beheaded for subversion.[122] The role of the *partisani* was similar to that of the crisis participants in preindustrial Europe, who defended their homes during states of siege.

In summary, throughout the modern epoch women became temporary dirty workers for the military in times of extreme external crisis. While military participation was originally defined as a male-only activity in the early mass army, women were needed for the armies in periods of total war. With the growth of the fully rational military, women became a surplus army to be mobilized in times of crisis and demobilized during peace. The result was that women were clamped back into their traditional positions when they were no longer needed.

Stage Four: Peripheral Roles in Limited Wars and Peace (1945 to the Present)

Since the end of World War II, women have played an insignificant role in both NATO and Warsaw Pact armies, constituting less than 1 percent of total enlisted positions.[123]

Women in the U.S. Military Since 1945

By far the most important developments since the war have occurred in the United States. In 1948, women were granted military status as a small permanent unit restricted by law to a strength of 17,500 enlisted soldiers and 1,000 officers. These numbers were small when compared with the nearly 200,000 women who served in WAC and WAVE units during 1944.[124]

In 1950, George Gallup found that over 40 percent of his nationwide sample felt that the United States would find itself in another major war within the next five years.[125] Military leaders, too, felt that women should be mobilized just in case, and in November of 1951, when it became apparent that the Korean War would be protracted, an attempt was made to increase the number of American women soldiers. However, the Korean War did not constitute the type of total war effort that required the Army to dip into the female labor pool, and the 1951 mobilization campaign remained primarily a contingency plan developed in the event that the Korean hostilities resulted in total war. The campaign motto was, "Share Service for Freedom." The publicity machinery of the Defense Department used extensive radio, magazine, and newspaper advertisements to induce women to join the war effort. A representative of President Truman again cajoled civilian women to do their part: "Today the very existence of our democratic way of life is threatened and we must call upon all our strength. Every one of us must understand that our young women, no less than our young men, must come forward to accept the challenge with which our country is faced."[126]

However, in the months after the publicity campaign, the number leaving the Women's Corps exceeded the number of new enlistments. As the Korean War lost further legitimacy and mass support in 1953, the Army was ordered to reduce its female strength and to slow down the influx of new female personnel. As Binkin and Bach put it, "The general lack of interest and the war's unpopularity doomed the effort [recruitment of women] to early failure."[127]

The case of the Korean War supports the hypothesis that women are not included in industrial armies until male labor reservoirs have been depleted or exhausted.

Vietnam

The Vietnam War, too, was a limited war that did not require the United States to resort to an army of last choice—women. The Vietnam War mobilization effort supports the general hypothesis that external crisis must be urgent to legitimize the large-scale, temporary participation of women. During the war, only 10,000 women out of a total of 2 million soldiers served in Southeast Asia, and these women were confined to the nursing corps.[128] In general, the larger the depletion of the male reservoir, the more diversified are the roles in which women are able to participate. Both the Korean and Vietnam limited wars did not require women because of an adequate pool of males.

Israel and the Woman Warrior

No review of female military participation is complete without a discussion of women in the Israeli Defense Force. Nowhere in the history of military women since the Second World War is there a more enduring popular myth than the combat role of Israeli women. As Hazleton correctly observed, Israeli women in war, representing the duality and simultaneity of life and death, continue to capture public attention: "And they are the stars in the firmament of the myth of Israeli women's liberation, beckoning to legions of hopeful admirers including such eminent feminists as Betty Friedan and Simone de Beauvoir. But the stars are evanescent, fading on close inspection to a reality in direct confrontation with the image."[129]

While Israeli women are conscripted for two years of military service and training, not one Israeli woman has performed a combat role since 1948.[130] Instead, the Israeli government views women as a source of routine administrative and semiskilled labor. The CHEN, or Women's Corps, serves the following functions: (1) secretarial work, (2) communications, (3) medical support, (4) entertainment roles, (5) graphics work, (6) psychological services, and (7) miscellaneous administrative and support functions. Women are the folders of parachutes rather than the combatants of paratrooper units. In 1978, while 52.2 percent of eligible women were inducted, they filled purely support functions.[131]

The popular conception of the Israeli woman, weapon in hand, is based on myth rather than reality. The myth has its roots in the early 1930s when women were used extensively to transport arms for the Haganah, the preprofessional Jewish army formed prior to the establishment of Israel. Later during Israel's War of Liberation, women *did* perform offensive and defensive roles in combat. However since 1948, the role of women in the Israeli Defense Force has been peripheral and distinct from the all-male combat units. This pattern is familiar. Women were included in diversified combat roles only because the expanded guerilla war between the Arabs and the Jews exhausted male reservoirs, but since the War of Liberation, the absence of total war has circumscribed female participation.

Women in the Warsaw Pact Armies

Soviet Union. As was previously noted, women played a vital role in the defense of the Soviet Union during the German invasion of World War II. While women were used in combat assignments, their most prominent role was to release men from the rear units for participation at the front. But today, Soviet Army women number less than 10,000, and women soldiers' assignments are largely in the paramedical, administrative, and tactical communications specialties.[132]

East Germany. Women serve in the East German Army in accordance with the Defense Obligation Law of 1962. Under this directive, women between the ages of 18 and 50 are subject to conscription in the event of total mobilization. In peacetime, women may volunteer for service in two areas: they may join as short-term soldiers (*Soldaten auf Zeit*) or as career soldiers (*Beruf Soldaten*).[133] The military occupational specialties open to women include administration, communications, and medical services, as is the case in the Soviet Union.[134]

Women in Other Warsaw Pact Armies. In Rumania, a 1972 law stipulated that it was the "holy duty" of every male and female to defend the motherland. The contemporary Rumanian army conscripts females for nine months' service. Because women soldiers are trained in combat arms, they are viewed as a valuable reserve force in the event of a national emergency.[135]

The Czechoslovakian Army assigns volunteer women to sexually integrated units. After three years of duty, women may continue to have formal military status either as professional soldiers or as reservists. There is, however, no available information as to whether women would play a direct combat role in a confrontation with the West.[136]

Hungarian women are required to register in peacetime. In addition to volunteer service for women, national defense instruction in military schools is compulsory for all females. In times of crisis, women would be conscripted for combat roles.[137]

In general, Warsaw Pact countries have a pattern similar to NATO countries. Women constitute less than 1 percent of total personnel in the armies, but compared with the NATO countries, these countries have more extensive military instruction in peacetime. Consistent with the hypothesis that women are a reserve army to be mobilized in times of crisis, women have low status in the peacetime forces.

Women in NATO Armies

Two generalizations are clear with respect to women in NATO armed forces. First, the United States has relied most heavily and gone much further than the other NATO allies in the expansion of the female military role. Secondly, women are not used in an active combat capacity, nor do there appear to be any NATO-wide plans for such a role.[138]

In 1976, nine of the NATO countries included a small percentage of women in their armed forces—Canada, Denmark, France, the Netherlands, Norway, Belgium, Turkey, the United Kingdom, and the United States. The Federal Republic of Germany, Greece, Iceland, Luxembourg, and Portugal did not have any female military participation.[139]

There has been protracted debate as to whether the number of women in uniform in the United States should be expanded. Recently, the question of women in arms was debated in West Germany. German demographic projections indicate that there will be a manpower shortage in the armed forces beginning in the late 1980s, creating the first labor bottlenecks in the Bundeswehr. As in the United States, German feminists, socialists, and pacifists view expanded military participation with much ambivalence. While socialist and women's groups consider the inclusion of women an advance toward remilitarization, others have advocated female military service in the hope of expanded citizenship rights.[140]

In Britain, women have been assigned more hazardous roles than in the other NATO militaries. For example, women have been assigned to the

Ulster Defense Regiment in Northern Ireland. In this capacity, they have been exposed to the dangers inherent in guerilla activity. In general, however, the bulk of British women serve in support roles.[141]

In Canada, women are subject to the same disciplinary code as males and have attained the same benefits and status as that of males. The 1971 Royal Commission on the Status of Women ordered the complete integration of the services in all military occupations except direct combat.[142]

Institution of the all-volunteer force in 1973 has transformed the role of women in the U.S. military. Over 90 percent of the military specialties are now open to women, and women constitute 9 percent of the total strength. Unlike the other cases discussed in this chapter, women's expanded participation in the United States came in a period of peace. In Chapter Two, we shall examine the uses of women in the peacetime U.S. military.

SUMMARY

Women, War, and the Role of Crises

Female military participation since World War II reflects the pattern of peripheral roles in limited wars and in peacetime. While there have been variations in the utilization of women during periods of stability, women have continued to serve as the reserve army of last resort. External crisis is the most important determinant of female participation. While women have had limited permanent roles as nurses and as aides-de-camp in peace, participation has been associated largely with violent politico-military events. The periodization of participation has been propelled by the conduct of external war. When international armed conflict ends, women are forced to relinquish any benefits they have received as temporary laborers for the military apparatus, and sex-role stereotypes that define the military as the province of males are recalcified.

The evanescence of female participation has been demonstrated through an examination of four broad stages: Stage One: Women in Pre-State Armies (antiquity to the seventeenth century); Stage Two: Women in Early Industrial Armies (1600–1900); Stage Three: External Crisis and Women as Military Reserves (1900–1945); and Stage Four: Peripheral Roles in Limited Wars and Peace (1945 to the present).

Looking first at the role of women in primitive warfare, it was concluded that men had nearly exclusive dominance of the army. In preindustrial European city-states and preindustrial cultures, individual female heroines were limited to the role of crisis participants. The patriarchal hegemony of military organization had been observed much earlier by Max Weber:

> The men's house, which has been studied by Schurtz with so much sympathetic care, and which, in various forms, recurs in all parts of the world, is one of those structures resulting from such a consociation of warriors, or in Schurtz's terminology, a men's league... Only those are members who have demonstrated prowess in the use of arms and have been taken into the warriors' brotherhood after a novitiate, while he who has not passed the test remains outside as a "woman," among the women and children, who are also joined by those no longer capable of bearing arms.[143]

In Stage Two: Women in Early Industrial Armies (1600–1900), the hypothesis was advanced that bearing arms was associated with political and economic rights. Much of the social history of this stage was a history of the nonparticipation of women. The militaries of early capitalism had no role for women. Although the role of women in the transition from primitive warfare to professional warfare remains an obscure area, it seems clear that exclusion from the military must have worked to maintain women's low political and legal status.

In Stage Three (1900–1945), women did not gain anything significant by being in the military as temporary dirty workers. Military participation did not lead to new functional roles for women in the industrial and political spheres. Because these women had a transitory status, they did not even find career opportunities in the military itself. Since the Second World War, military women have again been relegated to the peripheral positions characteristic of past patterns. With the sole exception of recent developments in the U.S. volunteer military, female military participation has been impacted only by external crisis. We have seen that, historically and cross-culturally, the greater the depletion of male reserves, the higher the military participation ratio for women.

Types of Female Participation in the Military

Table 1.1 depicts six types of female military participation extracted from the four stages that have been considered.

Numbers I and IV represent women's most common role, historically and cross-culturally—military nonparticipation. In preindustrial armies women were routinely excluded from warfare as they were in the industrial army.

Number II represents women who served as camp followers and the first military nurses. In primitive warfare, women accompanied their husbands to the battlefront and served as informal nurses, laundresses, and

TABLE 1.1. A Typology of Female Participation in Military Labor

	Exclusion	Civilian-Military Support	Military Roles
Primitive armies	I Men's consociation	II Camp followers	III Crisis participants
Industrial armies	IV Limited functional roles	V Temporary dirty workers	VI Combat support & *partisani*

Source: Compiled by the author.

cooks. By the end of the nineteenth century, the industrial armies began to functionalize these roles.

Number V represents the role of women as temporary participants in civilian war work. In both World Wars I and II, females replaced males in order to release them for direct combat.

For both II and V, female participation was similar to the role of Pallas Athena in Greek mythology and that of the Valkyries in Norse mythology. Women were mobilized by patriotic images. They provided vicarious support rather than direct combat support. Of course, there is no quick and easy division between the vicarious roles of II and IV. Women who worked in the munitions industry participated more directly than did those who knitted stockings for the boys overseas.

Number VI represents the historical examples of women who performed combat-support roles in total war. In both World War I and World War II, allied countries included large numbers of women in the military. In the case of the *partisani*, the division between combat and support roles was not sharply drawn. Number III, which characterizes the role of individual heroines in preindustrial armies during states of siege, is similar to the role of women resistance fighters in the industrialized armies. When warfare threatened home and motherland, individual women always played some role in their own defense.

The theory of external crisis is useful for explaining the role of women as temporary military participants. In peacetime, women are routinely proscribed from performing martial roles (Numbers I and IV). This exclusion has negative consequences on women's economic, political, and legal parity. Whether military participation creates full citizenship rights or simply follows them is debatable, but participation is clearly a correlate of traditional rights and autonomies.[144] However, privileges and rights gained by temporary participation in the army do not give rise to permanent citizenship guarantees. Women have often paid the price of military participation as temporaries without corresponding gains in privileges.

External crisis theory cannot, however, explain the recent expansion of women in the U.S. military, since this latest expansion has occurred during a period of relative stability. The cycle of crisis-mobilization-demobilization is not evident. Does increased female military participation mean that the volunteer military is in disarray? Or is the American military at the cutting edge of female emancipation? The remainder of this study will examine the social forces responsible for the seemingly divergent trajectory of female involvement in the contemporary U.S. Army.

In Chapter Two, I will develop an internal crisis explanation for the recent expansion of women in the U.S. military. It will be argued that females serve latent functions and are providing the margin of success for the volunteer military. The contention that the U.S. military has included women to stave off a continuing legitimation and fiscal crisis will be examined through an analysis of Defense Department studies and unpublished data on the utilization of women.

The remainder of the book focuses on a case study of U.S. Army women who were assigned to nontraditional military jobs in the Signal Corps. Chapter Three describes the community of Khaki Town and the social setting for the study. The backgrounds of male and female soldiers are compared, using both field data and questionnaires. When responses to male and female enlisted life are compared, two distinct interpretations of enlisted life are detected—His Army and Her Army. His Army is a status of politico-legal coercion, but Her Army combines the stresses of His Army with the marginality of being a token female in a male-dominated occupation. Chapter Four looks more closely at the characteristics of Her Army. In Chapter Five, the responses of males to token women in Khaki Town are considered. Chapter Six examines further the quasi-occupational nature of enlisted life in His Army. His Army is described as a *venal institution* with a contradictory compliance structure, based upon domination. The tension between femininity and militarism is traced to the venal aspects of the military. In Chapter Seven, the earlier findings are brought together and recommendations are made for reforming the more backward aspects of the military as an occupation. Policy suggestions for transforming Her Army are also advanced. The premise of this work is that no plumb line can be drawn between the structures of His Army and Her Army. The tension between militarism and feminism can only be resolved through the transformation of enlisted life for soldiers of both sexes. Appendix A is a description of how I was able to study Khaki Town and gain successful access, including the chronology of my research roles. My use of multiple methods and the peculiar problems I faced gaining access may be instructive to others driven to study marginal groups.

NOTES

1. George H. Gallup, *The Gallup Opinion Index: Report No. 175* (February 1980), p. 9.

2. Department of Defense, *All-Volunteer Data Base* (AVF), unpublished statistics compiled by the Office of the Assistant Secretary of Defense (OASD (MRA & L) RRA/R & D), (March 1980).

3. Leila Rupp's analysis of the World War II campaign by the American and German governments to mobilize women for war work does not study the role of women soldiers, per se. However, her examination of wartime propaganda is illuminative of the parallel campaign to legitimate women for military service. See Leila J. Rupp, *Mobilizing Women for War: German and American Propaganda, 1939–1945* (Princeton: Princeton University Press, 1979).

4. The extant research on military women has been largely supported by the Department of Defense, the U.S. Army Research Institute, the Naval Personnel Research and Development Center, and by contracted research for the Defense Department. For a review of military sponsored studies, see the December 1978 issue of *Youth and Society* or the August 1978 issue of *Armed Forces and Society*.

Relatively few sociologists have conducted research of any kind outside the aegis of military sponsorship and control. Only 15 of the more than 5,000 sociologists listed in the 1980 American Sociological Association's *Guide to Graduate Departments of Sociology* indicated competence in military sociology. During the period from 1972 to 1982, two to five times as many sociologists studied U.S. rural communities as studied the military. Thus, one of the reasons why the study of women in the military has been undeveloped is due to the overall poverty of military sociology. An important obstacle to critical research on the military has been the access and sponsorship barriers. Hutchinson observed that some general sociologists researched issues in the military, but this group was small when compared to the group studying military effectiveness: "Sociologists who do not work directly with the military departments in a supporting role are likely to avoid interaction with the military because it functions as a fairly closed system with effective insulation from civilian investigators." Researchers unwilling to cooperate with military management find themselves closed off from research settings. See Charles E. Hutchinson, "The Meaning of Military Sociology," *Sociology and Social Research* 41 (1957): 417–422. For a more recent and critical study of the restrictions placed on military sociology, see Ritchie P. Lowry, "Toward a Sociology of Secrecy and Security Systems," *Social Problems*, vol. 19, no. 3 (Spring 1972): 437–50.

5. Elizabeth Jones, "Speech to The Women's Right Convention," held at the Cooper Institute, New York City, May 10-11, 1860. (Proceedings published by Yerrington and Garrison, Boston, 1881).

6. Emma Goldman, *Living My Life* (New York: Alfred A. Knopf, 1931), reprinted in *The Essential Works of Anarchism* (New York: Quadrangle, 1972), p. 334

7. Jean Bethke-Elshtain, "A Feminist's Journey," *Commonweal*, vol. 109, no. 11 (June 5, 1981): 331.

8. Eleanor Smeal, "NOW Opposes Draft; Supports Women's Regirstration," *NOW Times* 14:3 (March 1980): 1.

9. Wendy Kohli, "Militarism and Feminism: A Future of Death or a Future of Life?," *Peace Newsletter*, vol. 1, no. 1 (March 1980): 10.

10. Homer, *The Iliad*, quoted in Mandy Merck, "The Patriotic Amazonomachy and Ancient Athens," in *Tearing Down the Veil*, Susan Lipshitz (London: Routledge, Kegan, and Paul, 1978), p. 97.

11. Francis Gribble, *Women in War* (New York: E. P. Dutton, 1917), p. 1.

12. Mary S. Beard, *Women as Force in History: A Study in Traditions and Realities* (New York: Macmillan, 1946), p. 278.

13. Ibid.
14. Herodotus, *The History of Herodotus*, trans. George Rawlinson, ed. Manuel Komroff (New York: Tudor, 1928), pp. 237–39.
15. Ibid.
16. Homer, *The Iliad*, trans. Robert Fitzgerald (New York: Anchor Press, 1974), p. 113.
17. Helene Adeline Guerber, *Myths of Northern Lands* (New York: American, 1895), pp. 162–65.
18. Beard, *Women as Force in History*, p. 278.
19. Thomas Keightley, *The Mythology of Ancient Greece and Italy* (New York: Appleton, 1866), pp. 489–99.
20. Ibid., p. 499.
21. Mandy Merck, "The City's Achievements," in *Tearing Down the Veil: Essays in Femininity*, ed. Susan Lipshitz (London: Routledge, Kegan and Paul, 1978), p. 106–13.
22. Beard, *Women as Force in History*, p. 279.
23. S. A. Cook, F. E. Adcock, M. P. Charlesworth, *The Cambridge Ancient History* vol. 10, *The Augustan Empire 44 B.C.–A.D. 70*. (New York: Macmillan, 1934), p. 802.
24. Tacitus, in *Readings in English History Drawn from Original Sources* (New York: Ginn, 1908), p. 22.
25. Beard, *Women as Force in Hstory*, pp. 280–82.
26. Ibid.
27. Tacitus, *Readings in English History*, p. 22.
28. Beard, *Women as Force in History*, p. 279.
29. James Anson Farrer, *Military Manners and Customs* (New York: Henry Holt, 1885), pp. 38–39.
30. Gribble, *Women in War*, pp. 2–3.
31. Ibid., p. 69.
32. Ibid., p. 128.
33. Quoted by Michel L. Martin, "The Military and Women in France," in *The Role of Women in European Armed Forces*, ed. Gwyn Harries-Jenkins (Hull, England: University of Hull, Adult Education Department, for the U.S. Army Research Institute for the Behavioral and Social Sciences, Final Technical Report, DAERO–77–G–092, July 1980) no pagination.
34. Ibid.
35. Ibid; see also Michel L. Martin, "From Periphery to Center: Women in the French Military," *Armed Forces and Society*, vol. 8, no. 2 (Winter 1982): 306.
"Actually, they (early forms of female military participation in France) seem rather the residues of an early, imperfect historical differentiation within the society's organizational division of labor." According to Martin, the first institutionalized encounter between women and the military occurred in the health services area. As nurses, French women served in the 1870 Franco-Prussian War, in China (1900), in Morocco (1970), but more especially in World War I as nurses and ambulance drivers.
36. T. Athol Joyce and N. W. Thomas, *Women of All Nations: A Report of Their Characteristics, Habits, Customs, and Influence*, Royal Anthropological Institute (London: Casell, 1909), p. 43.
37. Ibid.
38. John Laffin, *Women in Battle* (London: Abelard-Schuman, 1967), pp. 16, 48; see also Joyce and Thomas, *Women of All Nations*, p. 43.
39. Quincy Wright, *A Study of War* (Chicago: University of Chicago Press, 1942), p. 84.
40. Geoffrey and Angela Parker, *European Soldiers: 1550–1650* (Cambridge: Cambridge University Press, 1972), pp. 4–6.
41. Guenther Roth and Claus Wittlich, *Max Weber's Economy and Society: An Outline of Interpretative Sociology* (New York: Bedminister, 1968), vol. 3, chap. 14, pp. 1153–54.
42. Ibid., p. 1156
43. Ibid.

44. Jacques Van Doorn, *The Soldier and Social Change* (Beverly Hills: Sage Publications, 1974), pp. 16–17.

45. Ibid., pp. 11–12.

46. Bengt Abrahamsson, *Military Professionalism and Political Power* (Beverly Hills: Sage Publications, 1972), pp. 22–23.

47. Van Doorn, *The Soldier and Social Change*, p. 15.

48. Ibid., p. 9.

49. Martin, "Military and Women in France."

50. Georges Lefebvre, *The Coming of the French Revolution* (New York: Vintage, 1947), p. 169.

51. Abrahamsson, *Military Professionalism*, pp. 24–25.

52. Martin, "Military and Women in France."

53. For historical studies of women who took up arms on the battlefield in the early U.S. militias, see John Laffin, *Women in Battle*; J. L. Arthur, "Women of the Revolution," *New York State Historical Association Preceedings* 5 (1905): 153–61; James R. Power, *Brave Women and Their Wartime Decorations: A Study* (New York: Vantage Press, 1959); and Frank Moore, *Women of the War: Their Heroism and Self-Sacrifice* (Hartford, Conn.: n.p., 1866).

54. Paul Engle, *Women in the American Revolution* (Chicago: Follett, 1974), pp. 14–15.

55. See J. Clement, *Noble Deeds of American Women with Biographical Sketches* (New York: Auburn, 1855). This early study contains a variety of references to women in martial roles. There is also an early biographical sketch of Deborah Sampson, who joined the Massachusetts Regiment of the Revolutionary Army disguised as a man.

There are a growing number of excellent studies of women's role in the settlement of the West; see Winnipeg Manitoba Women's Club, *Recollections of Women Surviving From the Red River Era* (Winnipeg, Manitoba: W. J. Healey, 1923). For a contemporary analysis of women's role in the nation's settlement, see Beverly J. Stoeltjie, "A Helpmate for Man Indeed: The Image of the Frontier Woman," *Journal of American Folklore* 88 (1975): 25–41, and Christine Stansell, "Women on the Great Plains, 1865–1890" *Women's Studies* vol. 4, no. 1 (London: Gordon and Breach, 1976) pp. 87–98.

56. Mary A. Gardner Holland, *Our Army Nurses: Interesting Sketches, Addresses, and Photographs of the Noble Women Who Served in Hospitals and Battlefields During Our Civil War* (Boston: B. Wilkins, 1895), pp. 16–17.

57. Patricia Thomas, *The Role of Women in the Military: Australia, Canada, the United Kingdom, and the United States* (San Diego: U.S. Naval Personnel Research and Development Center, 1978), p. 3.

58. Gribble, *Women in War*, p. 31.

59. Iris Carpenter, *No Woman's Work* (Boston: Houghton Mifflin, 1946), p. 55.

60. Thomas, *Role of Women in the Military*, p. 3.

61. Abrahamsson, *Military Professionalism*, p. 40.

62. T. L. Jarman, *A Short History of 20th Century England* (New York: Mentor Books, 1963), p. 21.

63. Ibid., pp. 136–37.

64. Irene Osgood-Andrews, "Economic Effects of the World War Upon Women and Children in Great Britain," in David Kinely, *Preliminary Economic Studies of the War* (New York: Carnegie Endowment Fund for International Peace, Division of Economics and History, April 1919), p. 40.

65. Report by the Adjutant-General to the Forces, "Women's War Work" (London: Home War Office, Whitehall, S. W., August 1, 1916), p. 7.

66. Great Britain, "Report of the War Cabinet Committee on Women in Industry" (April 1919), pp. 80–81; see also Osgood-Andrews, "Economic Effects of the World War," p. 40.

67. Osgood-Andrews, "Economic Effects of the World War," p. 10.

68. Ibid., p. 8.

69. Arthur Mauwick, *Women at War: 1914–1918*. (Glasgow: Fontana, 1977), p. 83.

70. Louise Eliot Dalby, "The Great War and Women's Liberation" (Paper read at Skidmore College, May 1970, Faculty Lecture).

71. Ibid.

72. Mattie E. Treadwell, *The Women's Army Corps: United States Army in World War II, Special Studies* (Washington D.C.: Office of the Chief of Military History, Department of the Army, 1954), p. 6.

73. Ibid., p. 8.

74. Ibid., pp. 7–8.

75. Editors, "Where Women Supplant Men Because of War," *New York Times*, February 2, 1917, p. 1.

76. Treadwell, *Women's Army Corps*, p. 8.

77. Theodore Roosevelt, Introduction to Harriet Stanton Blatch, *Mobilizing Woman-Power* (New York: The Woman's Press, 1918), pp. 6–7.

78. Osgood-Andrews, "Economic Effects of the World War," p. 8; see also Mary Elizabeth Pidgeon, *Women in the Economy of the United States of America: A Summary Report* (Washington D.C.: Government Printing Office, 1937), p. 6.

79. Treadwell, *Women's Army Corps*, p. 11.

80. Ibid.

81. Ibid., pp. 11–12.

82. Ibid., p. 21.

83. Ibid.

84. Ibid., p. 23.

85. Ibid., p. 25.

86. "WAACS Now in Army; Name Becomes WACS," *New York Times*, July 3, 1943.

87. Treadwell, *The Women's Army Corp*, p. 48.

88. Ibid., p. 49.

89. Ibid., p. 197.

90. Ibid., pp. 212–13.

91. Ibid., p. 689.

92. Ibid., pp. 206–7.

93. Ibid., chap. 11, p. 206.

94. Ibid., chap. 2.

95. Leila J. Rupp, "Woman's Place Is in the War: Propaganda and Public Opinion in the United States and Germany, 1939–1945," in Carol Ruth Berkin and Mary Beth Norton, *Women of America: A History* (Boston: Houghton Mifflin, 1979), p. 357.

96. James Wadsworth, U.S. Representative, speech given to the Proceedings of the Conference on War and Post-War Demands for Trained Personnel, Mayflower Hotel, Washington D.C., April 9, 1943 (Proceedings published by Connecticut College, Institute of Women's Professional Relations 1943).

97. Science Research Associates, *Youth Goes to War* (published under contract by Science Research Associates, Washington D.C.: Department of the Army, 1943), chap. 8.

98. Treadwell, *Women's Army Corps*, p. 232.

99. Ibid., p. 254.

100. Ibid., p. 255.

101. Ibid., pp. 699–707.

102. Ibid., chap. 2.

103. Ibid., pp. 615–20.

104. Ibid., Appendix A.

105. Dorothy Schaffter, *What Comes of Training Women for War?* (Washington D.C.: American Council on Education, 1947).

106. Rupp, "Woman's Place Is in the War," p. 357.

107. Harold Ickes, Secretary of the Interior, speech given to Proceedings of the Conference on War and Post-War Demands for Trained Personnel, Mayflower Hotel, Washington, D.C., April 9, 1943, pp. 1–2.

108. Ibid., pp. 2–3.

109. Rupp, "Woman's Place Is in the War," p. 357.

110. Mary Anderson, testimony before the Select Committee Investigating National Defense Migration, U.S. House of Representatives, pursuant to House Resolution 113 (Washington D.C.: U.S. Government Printing Office, 1942).

111. Chester W. Gregory, *Women in Defense Work During World War II: An Analysis of the Labor Problem and Women's Rights* (New York: Exposition, 1974), pp. 10–11.

112. Ibid., p. 30.

113. Nina Popova, *Women in the Land of Socialism* (Moscow: Foreign Language Publishing House, 1949), pp. 164–65.

114. Robert Jackson, *Heroines of World War II* (London: Arthur Barlow, 1976), p. 29.

115. Popova, *Women in Land of Socialism*, pp. 164–65.

116. See Treadwell, *Women's Army Corps*, pp. 780–81 and Martin Binkin and Shirley J. Bach, *Women and the Military* (Washington, D.C.: Studies in Defense Policy, The Brookings Institute, 1977), pp. 121–22.

117. Mary Anderson, "Women's Status in Industry in World War II," in *Yearbook of American Labor*, vol 1, ed. Colston Warne (New York: Philosophical Library, 1945); see also Eileen Nolan, "Woman Management," in *The Role of Women in European Armed Forces*, ed. Gwynn Harries-Jenkins (Hull, England: University of Hull, 1980); and Department of the Army, *Women in the Army Study*, sec. 7, "British Women in WW II" (Washington D.C.: Department of the Army, prepared as the Final Report of the 1976 Women in the Army Study Group, ODCSPER, Washington, D.C. 20310), p. 2–F–1.

118. Thomas, *Role of Women in the Military*, pp. 5–6.

119. Binkin and Bach, *Women in the Military*, pp. 121–22.

120. Department of the Army, *Women in the Army Study*, p. 2–F–5.

121. Martin, *Military and Women in France*.

122. Joan and Kenneth Macksey, *The Book of Women's Achievements* (New York: Stein and Day, 1976), pp. 61–78.

123. Binkin and Bach, *Women in the Military*, pp. 113–31; Department of the Army *Women in the Army Study*, Appendix.

124. "Women Get A Special Place in the U.S. Services," *New York Times*, June 13, 1948, p. 1.

125. George C. Gallup, *The Gallup Opinion Index: Survey #453–K, vol 1* (March 1950), p. 899.

126. Armed Forces Radio Talk No. 425, Armed Forces Network (October 1, 1952), reported in Department of the Army, *Women in the Military*, Chief of Military History (1961).

127. Binkin and Bach, *Women in the Military*, pp. 11–12.

128. Grover Heiman Jr. and Virginia Heiman Myers, *Careers for Women in Uniform* (Philadelphia: J.B. Lippincott, 1971), chap. 7, p. 260.

129. Leslie Hazleton, *Israeli Women: The Reality Behind the Myths* (New York: Simon and Schuster, 1977), p. 137.

130. "In Israel, Women Drafted But Not to Fight," *Boston Globe*, April 5, 1980, p. 1; Tom Bowden, *Army in the Service of the State* (Tel Aviv: University Publishing Project, 1976), p. 106.

131. Bowden, *Army in the Service of the State*, p. 106.

132. Department of the Army, *Women in the Army Study*, p. 2–R–1.

133. Ibid., p. 2–S–1.

134. Ibid.; Binkin and Bach, *Women in the Military*, pp. 126–27.

135. Binkin and Bach, *Women in the Military*, p. 127.

136. Ibid., p. 125.

137. Ibid., p. 127; Department of the Army, *Women in the Army Study*, p. 2–U–1.

138. Ibid., pp. 2–E–1 – 2–T–1.

139. Ibid.

140. Editors, "German Women as Soldiers," *Social Report*, Sozial-Report, SR 12–79 (E) (Bonn: Bundesrepublik Deutschland, 1979).

141. Department of the Army, *Women in the Army Study*, pp. 2–G–1 and 2–H–1.

142. Ibid., p. 2–I–1.

143. Roth and Wittlich, *Max Weber's Economy and Society*, vol. 2, chap. 9, pp. 906–7.

144. For a recent argument that the right to bear arms is an integral aspect of the normative definition of citizenship, David R. Segal et. al., "The Concept of Citizenship and Attitudes Toward Women in Combat," *Sex Roles*, vol 3, no. 5 (1977): 469–80.

Michel Martin argues similarly that the integration of women into the French armed forces reflects a process by which heretofore peripherized social clusters are pulled into the "central institutional and value systems of the society."

See Michel Martin, "From Periphery to Center: Women in the French Military," *Armed Forces and Society*, vol. 8, no. 2 (Winter 1982): 303–33.

Chapter Two

THE USES OF WOMEN IN THE MILITARY

We are attempting to create an environment in which men and women regardless of their racial, ethnic, or religious background—can fulfill their personal and career objectives.

> —Department of Defense, *Equal Opportunity Current News*, January 15, 1978

We have programmed decreases in first-term attrition for each of the four military services. There will be an increased utilization of women with superior skills and abilities.

> —John P. White, Assistant Secretary of Defense, 1979

A strong argument could be made that it has been the female entrants, virtually all of whom possess a high school diploma, that are the margin of success in the All-Volunteer Force.

> —Charles C. Moskos, 1978

The booklet, *Women Serve Proudly*, developed for Defense Department recruiters, contains the theme that the military is the leading equal opportunity employer for contemporary women:

> During this time, significant changes began to get underway regarding equal opportunity for women in the military services ... Today's military women sharing increased participation in the defense mission often hear the exclamatory, "You've come a long way, lady!"[1]

There is no question that, in terms of numbers, women have come a long way during the years of the all-volunteer force when compared with the draft years.

FIGURE 2.1. Trends in Female Enlistment (Enlisted Women as a Percentage of the Total Active Duty Enlisted Strength)

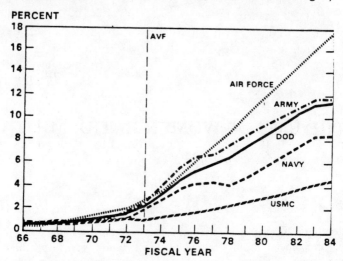

Notes: The broken vertical line indicates the break between the Draft Years (1964–1972) and the All Volunteer Force Years (AVF)(1973–1980). The figures for 1981–1984 are projections.

Source: Assistant Secretary of Defense for Manpower, Reserve Affairs, and Logistics, *Use of Women in the Military,* 1978; according to unpublished tabulations from the All-Volunteer Force Data Base, the total number of enlistees increased from 8,730 in 1964 to 47,600 in 1979—from 7/10ths to 1 percent to 9 percent (March 1980, unpublished tabulations, Assistant Secretary of Defense, Manpower, Reserve Affairs, and Logistics).

For the volunteer military years, 1973 to 1979, an average of 35,000 women joined the military as compared with an annual average of 12,000 a year during the draft years. During the draft years, women constituted less than 1 percent of total strength, while they presently account for nearly 9 percent of enlisted persons. By the end of fiscal year 1984, the Defense Department expects that women will constitute 11 percent of the strength for all the services. In the Air Force women will constitute nearly 18 percent of total strength. As Figure 2.1 indicates, there will be a slower growth in the utilization of women in the Marines and Navy than in the Air Force and Army.

While the number of women officers increased less dramatically during the transition to the volunteer forces, Figure 2.2 reveals substantial gains. In 1979, there were 19,000 women officers, as compared with 11,000 in 1964.

The recent expansion of women in the U.S. military is contrary to the general proposition that women are used as a reserve army in the face of external crisis. In this chapter I will argue that the recent expansion of women in the military can be attributed to internal crisis. The popular myths about the military as an equal opportunity employer for women will be contrasted with the less acknowledged imperatives for increased female participation. To accomplish this, it is necessary to penetrate official ideology.

In order to understand what is really happening with the transformation of the role of women in the U.S. military, it is necessary to look beyond the official statements and press releases of the Defense Department. To put the matter a little differently, it is necessary to "debunk" what passes for knowledge about the uses that women fulfill in the military.[2]

FIGURE 2.2. Active Duty Women Officers: Trends from 1964 to 1984

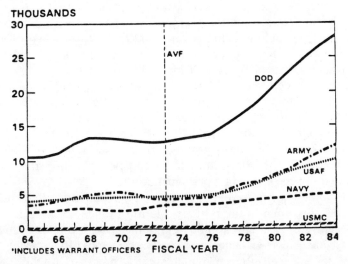

Notes: The broken vertical line indicates the break between the Draft Years (1964–1972) and the All Volunteer Force Years (AVF) (1973–1980). Figures include warrant officers. The figures for 1981–1984 are projections.

Source: Assistant Secretary of Defense for Manpower, Reserve Affairs, and Logistics, *Use of Women in the Military*, 1978; according to tabulations from the All-Volunteer Data Base, the total number of women officers increased from 11,293 to 19,000 in 1979; by fiscal year 1984, the number of women officers will be 28,900 (March 1980, unpublished tabulations, Assistant Secretary of Defense, Manpower, Reserve Affairs, and Logistics).

Erving Goffman provides a conceptual framework for understanding how the military "launders" its policies toward military women. Goffman's frontstage-backstage distinction illuminates the discrepancy between the Defense Department's public relations and cost-accounting voices. On the one hand, the military is portrayed as the leading edge of the war on sexism: "We don't ask for experience, we give it." But in its cost accounting voice, the military knows that "a high quality female can be recruited at the same price as a low quality male."

Goffman considers two kinds of bounded regions in organizations. The frontstage is the place of the public performance. Here, behavior is filtered to create an impression of a favorable product or image. In contrast, backstage regions are where the suppressed facts and less acknowledged realities make their appearance; the backstage is hidden from the public. Backstage strategies are available only to knowledgeable insiders.[3]

In order to fully understand how the military says different things to different audiences about women, it is necessary to study the backstage behavior of Defense Department planners. Obviously, the backstage area of the Defense Department is buffered and controlled so that an observational study is not possible. An interesting way to study the difference between the frontstage—public relations voice and the backstage—cost-accounting voice of the Defense Department is through the perspective of *critical functionalism*. Critical functionalism had its roots in the work of Robert Merton, who defined functions as "those observed consequences which make for adaptation or adjustment of a given system." Merton later extended the theory to encompass "manifest" and "latent" functions. Manifest functions are objective consequences that are recognized by participants. They are the official reasons for a social process, including the outward appearance. In contrast, latent functions are those that are neither intended nor recognized by participants.[4]

Manifest functions, in the sense used here, are the official reasons for the uses of women in the military. Manifest functions are constructed by the Defense Department and are represented by press releases to those on the outside. However, beneath the smoke screen of official ideology (front stage) are the real interests, which socially produced myths serve (back stage).

Herbert Gans was the first to demonstrate the radical potential of using functionalism to illuminate socially constructed myths. With great acuity, Gans used functionalism to explain the ubiquity of poverty. While on the surface poverty appears to be an insidious social problem, it really benefits powerful interests. Without poverty, politicians, slum landlords, loan sharks, antipoverty workers, and federal bureaucrats would lose business. Gans described how poverty and the poor satisfied a number of positive functions for many privileged groups in American society. Although there is a general impression, sedulously cultivated by official opinion, that poverty must be eliminated, it stubbornly persists. Poverty resists all apparent efforts to eliminate itself because too many powerful interests are dependent upon it for their own well-being.[5]

Following the lead of Herbert Gans, the manifest functions of military women can be compared with the latent functions. In order to study this, "frontstage" press releases of the Defense Department are compared with "backstage" unpublished Defense Department data on the uses of women.[6] It should be noted that manifest functions can be detected by participants and observers, whereas latent functions can be seen most clearly by outside analysts. It is difficult to know to what degree Defense Department planners are aware of some of the elements that I describe as "latent." Top officials are perfectly well aware of some of the "latent" functions, such as the higher intelligence and lower administrative costs of female recruits. Clearly, the presentation of the image of military women to the public uses a different imagery than that reflected in their own data. While the Defense Department may be aware of the "latent" functions of women, the public and women soldiers themselves may not recognize these patterns. What I am really demonstrating is that top officials of the Defense Department construct a frontstage image of women that becomes and shapes what the public perceives as manifest functions of women soldiers. The latent functions are understood in the backstage regions of the Defense Department and by critical observers outside the military. There are at least eight significant latent functions that women fulfill in the peacetime military:

1. The Defense Department uses women to cultivate its image as an equal opportunity employer.
2. Women serve as a reserve army of last resort.
3. Women smarten up the army; they have a higher educational attainment level and higher scores on military aptitude tests than do men who volunteer.
4. An increase in female military participation contributes to a more socially representative volunteer force.
5. Military women end up in the military justice apparatus much less often than do men; the employment of women saves valuable management resources.
6. Female military labor is cheaper than male labor; women help to stave off the fiscal crisis in defense manpower costs.
7. To the extent that women have helped to make the volunteer military work, they have replenished the military's *fund of legitimacy*.
8. Women serve as a convenient reservoir of marriage partners for enlisted males.

THE "FRONTSTAGE" IMAGE OF MILITARY WOMEN: MANIFEST FUNCTIONS

In January of 1978, the Director of the Women's Army Corps reported that "the opportunities for women in the Army have never been greater." She went on to describe how women, in the same fashion as blacks, had found equity in the military that could not be found in the industrial sector:

> As we take advantage of these opportunities, we must fully accept the challenges of service to the nation, giving positive recognition to these women who set the high standards, fought the hard fight, and have made our today a reality and our tomorrow possible.[7]

From the beginning of the volunteer military, official Defense Department statements affirmed the military's willingness to lead the war on sexism. General Bernard Rogers, Army Chief of Staff, stated that women would find that the Army would give them a chance for equal pay for equal work: "The purpose of this message is to emphasize the Army's commitment to the integration of women and to provide fundamental guidance to ensure that this integration is completed smoothly and rapidly."[8]

Both official and unofficial military periodicals reported that women were cracking the barriers of sexism in the military. A sampling of articles from 1980 headlined the military as a leading avenue of upward mobility:

From *Sergeants* magazine:
She Operates a Gas Station at 20,000 Feet

From *Air Force Magazine*:
They Are the First

From *Air Force Times*:
35 Proposals Eyed (by Air Force Uniform Board):
   Skirts to Come Down!
Women Get More Specialties
Women to Get Centrifuge Tests at SAM
DACOWITS [Defense Advisory Committee on Women
   in the Services] Gaining New Clout
DACOWITS—No Sexism in Recruiting Literature
What Happens When the Boss Is a Woman
Women Denied Husband [Health] Care Get Break
Women Graduates of the Academies

From *Parameters* (U.S. Army):
   Women and the Combat Exemption

From *U.S. Aviation Digest*:
   Army's [2d Lt. Marcella A.] Hayes, First Black Woman
   Aviator in U.S. Forces

From *Defense Management Journal*:
   The Changing Face of Army Basic Training:
   More Flexibile and Coeducational

From *Soldiers* (U.S. Army):
   Working Together: The Army's Assault on Sexism

From *Marine Corps Gazette*:
   Women Marines in FMF [Fleet Marine Force] units[9]

   The services' unofficial newspaper, *The Stars and Stripes*, characterized the military as a vanguard of women's liberation: "A Myth is dying. Women in uniform are shooting it full of holes. With more occupations open to American military women than ever before, women in uniform are literally everywhere: driving trucks, flying airplanes, repairing engines, climbing telephone poles, and even handing out traffic tickets."[10]

   Paralleling official military accounts of military women were reports in the civilian media that reinforced the image of liberated women in combat boots. The *New York Times* published 82 articles on the topic of military women from June of 1972 to July of 1980. Pentagon reporters during the period of female expansion do not appear to have challenged Defense Department ideology. The *Times'* lack of general critical reporting on the military prompted Murray Kempton to write of the *New York Times'* Pentagon correspondent:

> The *Times* has always been a curiously uninquisitive servitor of whatever plate the defense establishment sends from the kitchen. William Beecher, its Pentagon correspondent, so faithfully passed on whatever vagaries the Joint Chiefs happened to light upon as their received wisdom that there were those of us who came to suspect that Beecher did not exist and was only a name that the *Times'* copy desk put at the top of Pentagon press releases before printing them unaltered.[11]

   Much of the *New York Times* reporting on military women appeared to be a conduit for Defense Department press releases. Reporters were not able to penetrate the "frontstage" presentations of the public relations office, or their interest was piqued only by the image of the military as an equal opportunity employer. A representative article during this period supported the Defense Department "definition of the situation":

> Women will soon be permitted to fly naval aircraft as part of the services' program to equalize opportunity.[12]

An August 11, 1972 article on the appointment of the first women generals contained a similar theme:

> The military is also making moves to appeal to the liberated woman. Last June, the Army named Elizabeth P. Hoisington of the Women's Army Corps and Anna Hays of the U.S. Army Nurses' Corps as the first woman generals in its 196-year history. And last month, the Air Force named Jeanne Holm, director of the Women in the Air Force (WAF) as its first woman general.[13]

While *New York Times'* reporters were correct in noting expansions in numbers of women, there was little reporting on the structural constraints impeding women in newly integrated settings. The congruence between Defense Department press releases and journalistic opinion is partially the result of the press's general difficulty in gaining access to military reservations. Even when correspondents are allowed access to military settings, they are not allowed backstage. As a result, reporters reinforce the images created by public relations officers of the Defense Department. Most reports from 1972–80 described the numerous "firsts" for women in military occupational fields. As a consequence, the military was depicted as an equitable and accessible employer for women.

Headlines during 1972 highlighted the following achievements of women:

> WAFs Permitted to Fill Most Jobs Not Combat-Linked
> Navy Seeks Eight Women to Volunteer as Pilots
> Air Force Anticipates Up to 80 Women Cadets
> Woman Heads Mixed Air Force Unit
> Woman's Army Corps to Grow with More Jobs and
> New Styles
> WAVES Will Serve On Warships Once Equal Rights Amendment
> Is Law[14]

During the first years of the volunteer force, articles focused on women as leaders in sex-integrated settings:

> WAVE General on the Way Up
> Marines Pick Mary E. Bane as Commander of Mixed Unit
> Woman Becomes Lieutenant in Military Police

Integrated West Point Prepares for First Women Cadets
Army Will Train Women on Rifles[15]

In the same period, paralleling the reports in the *New York Times*, features in the *Boston Globe* and *Washington Post* reflected official military accounts on the gains of military women. The following headlines are representative of the *Boston Globe*'s reporting on military women during the period from 1972 to 1980:

Women Soldiers Pull Their Own Weight
Army Plans to Double Number of Women
Lady General with a Conscience
More Women in Uniform
Women's Push for Equality Gets Help from High Courts
Army Eases Rules of Motherhood
Marines Pick Woman to Direct 2,000 Men[16]

When compared with the coverage of women soldiers in Defense Department publications and the *New York Times* and *Boston Globe*, the *Washington Post* was more likely to report the conflicts faced by women. In particular, the *Post* conducted independent research on the litigation that was initiated by military women to trigger institutional changes in promotion, benefits, and job opportunities.[17]

LATENT FUNCTIONS OF MILITARY WOMEN IN THE BACKSTAGE REGION

How can the expanded female soldier population be explained in the 1970s and 1980s? Is the expansion of female labor a reflection of changing sex roles? Is the military the vanguard of new definitions of female work? Is the military attacking the bastions of sex segregation? Alternatively, is the present status of women in the military due to internal problems? Are women a source of cheap labor? To begin to answer these questions, it is necessary to explore the latent functions of women.

The Military as a Social Welfare Institution

During the most recent expansion of military women, the Defense Department has been legitimized as a social welfare agency for women. As Defense Department press releases and media accounts indicate, the military has used women to cultivate its image as an equal opportunity employer. As a large-scale training and rehabilitation program for females unable to find equity in the industrial sphere, the military pays women at the same rate as men. Bernard Beck has noted that both the military and welfare institutions function as kinds of responses to persons residual to the civilian economy:

> Among the criteria which the military fulfill are: public subsidy of a social need which is not and cannot be treated in the private sector; provision of subsistence to persons who are not economically productive in a direct way; suspension of the ordinary rules of earning a share in the allocation of rewards, justified by an appeal to a higher social good. This higher social good is characteristically phrased in terms of the well-being of the total society and of all the members. The conceptual result is not that the military is really some form of welfare, but rather that is has such a divergent public reputation while being so similar structurally.[18]

That public opinion had been molded to view the military as a training and rehabilitation center for women was evident in media accounts between 1972 and 1980. A manifest function of including women in larger numbers was the public view that the military was giving a residual population, working class women, an opportunity denied to them in civilian society. A latent function of the public view was that even if women had only an imperceptible impact on the success of the volunteer force itself, their inclusion improved the military's image.

Military Women as a Reserve Army

The ghost of Marx's "reserve army" hypothesis is emerging in the U.S. military. Since the volunteer era began, the military has been faced with the problem of attracting 2.5 million persons to enlist. Each year, the military has experienced difficulty in attracting its quota of 400,000 to 450,000 persons between the ages of 17 and 21 years to sign up for a term of service. To attain these numbers without conscription, three out of every ten eligible males would have to be inducted.[19]

As in the Industrial Revolution, the current period reveals many paradoxes. Faced with both a declining reservoir of male youth in general and acute shortages of "high quality males" willing to volunteer, the military has turned to women.[20] The increase in female military labor constitutes a major test of the classical reserve army theory.

In *The Eighteenth Brumaire of Louis Bonaparte*, Marx explained how capitalism produced an unemployed surplus population. The army, in Marx's view, was the first structure to transform paupers, vagabonds, and criminals into a new class. Of the state's use of the peasant population, Marx wrote:

> Finally, it [economic development] produces an unemployed surplus popu-

lation for which there is no place either on the land or in the town, and which accordingly reaches out for state offices as a sort of respectable alms, and provokes the creation of state posts . . . Finally, the culmination of the *"idées napoléonieenes"* is the preponderance of the *army*. The army was the *point d'honneur* of the peasants, it was they themselves transformed into heroes, defending their new possessions against the outer world, glorifying their recently won nationality, plundering and revolutionising the world.[21]

Marx, like Weber, viewed military organization as the precursor of the emergence of bourgeoise industrial organization. Both saw military domination as a process that was reproduced in the industrial sphere.

If the army seeded the original relations of production and forecast the use of peasants as a surplus population, it was the industrial sphere that perfected the system to "cheapen human labor in every way." The influx of women in today's U.S. military resembles the situation described in Engels' *Condition of the Working Class in England in 1844*: cheap female laborers were preferred by factory owners to more expensive male labor. Engels argued that inclusion of women in this way degraded both men and women; when women replaced men in traditionally male jobs, it "unsexed" the man and took all dignity away from women.[22]

However, E. P. Thompson argues that the inclusion of women as an industrial reserve army was Janus-faced:

> On the one hand, the claim that the Industrial Revolution raised the status of women would seem to have little meaning when set beside the record of excessive hours of labour, cramped housing, excessive child-bearing, and terrifying rates of child mortality. On the other hand, the abundant opportunities for female employment in the textile districts gave to women the status of independent wage-earners.[23]

Ultimately, the character of female wage labor was segmented into men's work and women's work. When jobs were segregated in this way, women could not as easily serve as an industrial reserve army. Industry could not easily release women from the marketplace if all typists or textile workers were women. As Hartman found, the reserve army hypothesis was not affirmed as the industrial revolution progressed:

> As industrialization progressed and conditions stabilized somewhat, male unions gained in strength and were often able to preserve or extend male areas.
>
> Thus, in periods of economic change, capitalists' actions may be more instrumental in instituting or changing a sex-segregated labor force—while workers fight a defensive battle. In other periods, male workers may be more important in maintaining sex-segregated jobs; they may be able to prevent

the encroachment of, or even to drive out, cheaper female labor, thus increasing the benefits to their sex.[24]

It is therefore debatable whether women served as an *industrial* reserve army, but it is evident that women served as a literal reserve army. As we learned in Chapter One, women were a literal reserve army in both civilian war work and in the military itself during periods of total war. The pattern of employment in war and demobilization in times of peace has been emblematic of women's past military participation. To the military, women were redundant when the supply of males was ample. If, during times of war, women enjoyed expanded rights as citizen-soldiers and war workers, they were also an elastic part of the military labor force who could be driven out during periods of peace.

The present status of women in the military is the direct result of an acute shortage of males willing to volunteer. As we have seen, it is highly unusual for the participation of women to be expanded during a period of peace. How are women being used in today's military?

There is no question that the U.S. military has faced a serious labor problem during each year of the volunteer force. Significantly, the Defense Department has lowered its labor requirements each year since the end of the draft, as Table 2.1 indicates. Even if the quality of enlisted accession is disregarded, the military has still never been able to meet its authorized strengths.

The shortfall in strength reported in Table 2.1 appears, on face value, to be inconsequential, but the inability of the armed forces to meet its

TABLE 2.1. Authorized and Actual Enlisted Trends (1972–1979) All Services

Fiscal Year	Authorized Department of Defense Strength	Actual Department of Defense Strength
1972 (Draft)	2,322,000	2,553,000
1973 (Volunteer)	2,329,000	2,252,000
1974	2,190,000	2,161,000
1975	2,149,000	2,127,000
1976	2,091,000	2,081,000
1977	2,093,000	2,074,000
1978	2,085,000	2,049,000
1979	2,051,000	2,014,000

Source: Assistant Secretary of Defense for Manpower, Reserve Affairs, and Logistics (March 1980, unpublished tabulations, All-Volunteer Data Base).

requirements, coupled with the enormous amount of money spent on recruitment, demonstrates a crisis in labor supply. However, the real crisis in military labor is to come. In the decade of the 1980s, the labor force is expected to constrict by nearly 20 percent. This includes a 17 percent decrease in the pool of available 17 to 21-year-old males.[25]

During the period of the all-volunteer forces, women have already helped to stave off the "manpower" crisis. At the same time that popular press accounts were sustaining Defense Department ideology of the military as a social welfare institution, manpower analysts were planning the further expansion of women in all of the services. The background study entitled "Use of Women in the Military," prepared by the Assistant Secretary of Defense for Manpower, Reserve Affairs, and Logistics argued that recruiting high quality women in lieu of available low quality men was the solution to demographic constraints:

> The marginal recruiting cost is expected to rise sharply, as the supply of qualified 18 to 20 year old males shrinks in the 1980s. A decrease in youth unemployment would make the market even tighter. The success of the all-volunteer force may well depend on reducing the number of young male high school graduates the Department needs to recruit each year. This is potentially the major benefit of using more women, but it is not without costs.[26]

During the period in which the proportion of women in the military increased from less than 1 percent to 9 percent, the military began experiencing recruitment shortfalls. In the 12-month period that ended September 30, 1979, the Army fell nearly 16,380 recruits short of its goal of 158,700. Despite increased enlistment bonuses and lowered standards for enlistment, the Army missed its objectives in every category.[27]

Therefore, as a cheap reservoir to replace "high quality" males, women fulfill a second latent function, as a literal reserve army. As the male pool constricts further, manpower analysts will turn increasingly to women. According to the Department of Defense planning report, the annual number of female accessions is expected to double by 1990.

Smartening Up the Military

Manpower analysts have also turned to women increasingly to improve the quality of the enlisted force. In 1977 the Navy conducted studies of the literacy of its recruits and found that some of their high school graduates could not comprehend fourth-grade-level materials; 37 percent of its recruits were unable to understand materials written at the tenth-grade level. While the Army did not conduct such extensive tests as did the Navy, it estimates that their average recruit reads at the ninth-grade level.[28]

Because male entrants read poorly, they had problems learning their military jobs through training manuals. Although training manuals were rewritten from the ninth-grade level to the sixth-grade level, in comic book style, male soldiers were still having difficulties in learning their military jobs. Table 2.2 is excerpted from the fiscal year 1980 Department of Defense results on Army Skill Qualifications Tests, which are special performance tests given to soldiers in their specialized military jobs.

In 1979, 10 percent of Army specialists passed the skills qualification test for radar crewman; less than 2 percent of soldiers tested passed target accuracy tests. Not a single soldier passed the following skills tests: (1) tank turret repair, (2) flight operations, (3) quartermaster equipment repair, and (4) dental auxiliary. Less than a quarter of the soldiers tested had minimum competence in the following areas: (1) fire direction specialist,

TABLE 2.2. 1979 Army Skill Qualifications Test Results

Military Occupation	Number Tested	Percent Passed
11B Infantryman	25,259	83.5
11C Indirect fire crewman	5,701	75.4
13B Cannon crewman	3,920	41.7
13E Fire direction specialist	725	16.0
15D Lance missile crewman	325	48.4
15J Lance/Honest John	61	93.5
17B FA radar crewman	88	10.3
17C FA target acquisition	119	1.7
82C FA surveyor	439	15.8
16B Hercules missile crewman	57	33.4
55B Ammunitions specialist	302	37.5
44B Metal worker	82	2.5
44E Machinist	42	40.5
45K Tank turret repair	8	0
63B Wheel vehicle repair	496	21.2
63C Track vehicle mechanic	775	9.2
63J Quartermaster equipment repair	49	0
74B Card and tape writer	398	8.1
74D Computer/machine operator	2,639	21.4
42D Dental laboratory specialist	30	0
71G Patient administration	65	6.2

Source: Hearings before U.S. Senate, Department of Defense Authorization for Training, FY 1980, U.S. Congress, p. 1,836.

(2) surveyor, (3) wheel vehicle mechanic (4) track wheel mechanic, (5) metal worker, (6) card and tape writer, and (7) computer/machine operator.

Partly as a response to the difficulties of attracting a sufficient number of trainable recruits for skilled and semiskilled jobs, the Army adopted a new recruiting slogan: "It Takes Brains to Join the Army." Bulk mail advertisements were sent to high schools seniors in June 1979. "Don't laugh", the ads read, "If you're a recent high school graduate, joining today's Army might be the smartest move you could make ... We also give you your choice of over 300 valuable technical jobs, and many job-training school courses. Excellent courses with some of the best equipment available anywhere, with professional instructors to train you in a skill you can turn into a career. In the Army or later in civilian life." The message was reinforced using television and billboard advertising.

The women recruited during the campaign to "smarten up the Army" were less likely to require training manuals to be rewritten as comic books. The military has found that educational level, rather than physical strength, is the best predictor of whether a recruit can learn a military job. The possession of a high school diploma is also the best predictor of a person's potential for adapting to military life. For the Department of Defense, nearly one-third of its recruits from 1974 to 1979 were high school dropouts.

A third latent function of women recruits is that they improve the quality of the forces. Table 2.3 reveals that the proportion of male high school dropouts was four to six times higher than that for females during the years of the volunteer military. Across all services, women recruits were more likely to hold a high school diploma, when compared with their male counterparts. Until 1980, females who did not formally complete high school were required to pass the high school equivalency test and to score at least 90 percent on an occupational area of the Armed Forces Qualification Test. Male dropouts, during the same period, were not required to pass the high school equivalency test and could enlist even if they scored as low as the sixteenth percentile on the Armed Forces Qualification Test.

For all services during the draft years, males were slightly more likely than females to have completed some college. During the years 1964 to 1973, an average of 14 percent of the males had some college training as compared with only 11 percent of the female population. However, during the volunteer years, these trends reversed. Females were twice as likely as males to have attended some college prior to enlistment (9.4 percent versus 4.5 percent).[29]

There were interservice variations in how much difference females could make in quality. During the volunteer years between 1973 and 1979,

TABLE 2.3. Percentage of Non-High School Graduates for Males and Females (1964–1979) (Enlistees)

All DOD Services

Fiscal Year	Males (%)	Females (%)	Total (%)
Draft years			
1964	31.1	5.0	30.6
1965	31.7	5.2	31.1
1966	22.4	5.0	22.2
1967	24.0	5.0	23.7
1968	26.7	4.9	26.4
1969	27.3	5.7	27.0
1970	28.7	6.6	28.2
1971	32.3	7.0	31.7
1972	34.3	6.8	33.5
1973	35.2	7.2	33.9
Average	28.3	6.1	27.9
1974	41.5	10.8	39.0
1975	36.3	8.3	33.8
1976	33.1	8.9	31.2
1977	32.5	9.6	30.6
1978	24.8	9.0	22.9
1979	30.0	8.7	27.2
Average	33.4	9.2	31.1

Notes: GED (high school equivalency holders) were considered to be non-high school graduates.

For volunteers during the draft years, an average of 31% did not possess the high school diploma versus 22.8% of the draftees.

Source: Assistant Secretary of Defense for Manpower, Reserve Affairs, and Logistics (March 1980, unpublished tabulations, All-Volunteer Data Base).

only 4.8 percent of Air Force males lacked the high school diploma as compared with 3 percent of females. In the Navy, no female high school dropouts were allowed to enlist. In the Marine Corps, an average of 38 percent of the males lacked the high school diploma during the volunteer years, as compared with only 5 percent of the females. Of all of the services, the Army has had the greatest difficulty attracting both sufficient numbers and quality. In the Army, 44 percent of the males recruited did not hold a high school diploma versus only 10 percent of the females. Females smartened up the Army and Marine Corps more than the Navy and Air Force, where the sex differences in educational attainment were not so pronounced.

When compared with males, female recruits excelled in military aptitude tests. Despite the fact that military vocational test batteries test mechanical aptitudes, which are incongruent with traditional female socialization, females easily outdistanced males. Military aptitude is measured by scores received on the Armed Forces Vocational Aptitude Battery Tests (ASVAB). From the ASVAB, a standardized test score called the Armed Forces Qualification Test (AFQT) is computed. Based on percentile scores on the AFQT, enlistees are classified into one of five mental categories, with category I the highest level. The average score is 50, which divides category III. In a standardized test population, the top 8 percent will score in mental category I. The next 27 percent will score from 65 to 92, in category II. Mental category III contains the middle third of the population, scoring from 31 to 64, and mental category IV contains those scoring from 10 to 30. Finally, those scoring in category V (0 to 10) are disqualified from consideration.

Figure 2.3 presents a graph of the AFQT scores for the Army,

FIGURE 2.3. Average Armed Forces Qualifying Test Scores (AFQT) by Sex and Race for Army Recruits (1971–1980)

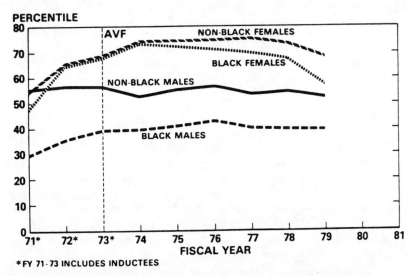

*FY 71-73 INCLUDES INDUCTEES

Notes: The broken vertical line indicates the break between the Draft Years (1964–1972) and the All Volunteer Force Years (AVF) (1973–1980). The figures for 1981–1984 are projections.

Source: Department of Defense, Assistant Secretary of Defense for Manpower, Reserve Affairs, and Logistics (March 1980, unpublished tabulations, All-Volunteer Data Base).

presenting breakdowns by race and sex. Females scored considerably higher than males, regardless of race. While white females have consistently scored the highest on the AFQT, black females have also scored higher than either white or black males.

There is a caveat in the interpretation of AFQT data. In the 1980 U.S. Senate Armed Services Commitee Hearings, Defense Department analysts admitted that the problem of quality in the volunteer military was much more serious than previously admitted because they had systematically overrepresented category III and underrepresented category IV. Traditionally, comparisons have been made on the basis of five categories. However, from 1976 to 1980, the Defense Department transformed the distribution by subdividing category III into IIIA and IIIB. Five senators of the Armed Services Committee charged in June of 1980 that the Army was conducting a "campaign of deception in covering up deficiencies of the all-volunteer force." Senator Sam Nunn (D, Ga.) said in a June 25 news conference that Army leaders should come forward and tell the truth about the condition of the Army: "Our Army is not an armed WPA (Works Progress Administration) and we must not permit it to become a Job Corps equipped with tanks and nuclear missiles."[30]

Nunn also contended that the Army covered up mental test scores of many new recruits. As the *Army Times* reported in July of 1980:

> He said that 43 percent of artillerymen failed to pass qualifications tests last year as did 49 percent of combat engineers tested, 51 percent of military intelligence people, and 69 percent of communications operators . . . He said figures supplied to the Senate Armed Services Committee by Assistant Secretary of Defense for Manpower Robert R. Pirie indicated that up to 45 percent of recent recruits were in the Category IV group: "The cause of this unacceptable situation is apparently the failure to properly score the aptitude tests that were introduced in 1976. This is a most serious revelation and one that took real courage by Pirie to admit. Yet," Nun said, "the Army continues to issue press releases with optimistic numbers on the quality of new recruits." [31]

In Senate Armed Service Committee Hearings, it was documented that 25 to 50 percent of the recruits classified in mental category III should have been placed in category IV. In 1978, before the figures were changed, the services recruited more than 90,000 persons in category IIIB. As many as 45,000 of these recruits should have been classified in category IV. The Defense Department has consistently argued that its relatively low number of category IV recruits (fewer than 17,000 in 1978) was an indication of the quality of the volunteer force.[32]

While it is unclear how many recruits were in the lowest military aptitude categories, the percentage in the top categories of achievement are

TABLE 2.4. Male and Female Percentages for Top Two Categories of Mental Quality as Measured by the Armed Forces Qualifying Test (AFQT) (1964–1985)

Years	Males (%) Army	All DOD	Females (%) Army	All DOD
Average draft years (1964–1973)	33.3	37.3	54.7	49.1
Average volunteer years (1974–1979)	23.9	33.0	76.0	61.2
Projected (1980–1985)	19.8	29.9	65.5	54.7

Source : Abridged from Tables 66 and 562, Department of Defense, Assistant Secretary of Defense for Manpower, Reserve Affairs, and Logistics (March 1980, unpublished tabulations, All-Volunteer Data Base).

unchallenged. Table 2.4 presents data from the highest categories for both the Army and the Defense Department as a whole.

When only the top categories of military aptitude are compared by sex, the sex difference is even greater than indicated in Figure 2.3. For the Defense Department as a whole, females were almost twice as likely as males to be in the top two categories during the volunteer years (61.2 percent versus 33 percent). During the draft years, females were also more likely to score in the highest categories of military aptitude (49.1 percent versus 37.3 percent).

Sex differences in military aptitude were most pronounced in the Army, as Table 2.4 indicates. In the Army, females were more than three times as likely to score in top categories as were males (76 percent versus 24 percent). The Army expects to find only 20 percent of its male recruits in the top categories for the period 1980 to 1985, as analysts concede that it will become increasingly difficult to find highly qualified men. This is doubtless an important reason why projected plans for 1980 to 1985 include expanding further the number of female soldiers. In the Army, 66 percent of new female recruits are expected to score in the top categories versus less than 20 percent of the males. For the Defense Department as a whole, 55 percent of the females should score in the top categories versus only 30 percent of the males.

Comparisons on both educational level and aptitude indicate that females help to solve the quality problem in the volunteer military. It is not that females are inherently better suited for military jobs. The decision to enlist in the military is a function of relative rates of pay, prior employment histories, and perceived advantages of military service.[33] Unfortunately, the disaggregation of studies of enlistment by sex is unavailable; however, it is clear that the military can attract high quality females more easily than high quality males. It is also true that the higher the level of education and military aptitude, the easier it is for the Defense Department to train a recruit. With these realizations in mind, the Defense Department has continued a major expansion in the number of females.

A Socially Representative Force

By 1974, observers were commenting that the volunteer military was becoming an army of the poor. Morris Janowitz and Charles Moskos, for example, thought that the military was becoming both racially and economically more unrepresentative of the general population than the draft military had been.[34]

Public confidence in the volunteer forces was shaken with reports such as the ABC News program entitled, "The American Army: A Shocking State of Readiness." The program, aired on prime time, pointed to the collective poverty and alienation of American soldiers stationed in overseas garrisons.[35]

By the middle of the 1970s, many noncommissioned officers were withdrawing public support for the all-volunteer concept. One sergeant first class, quoted by the *Army Times*, expressed a representative view of first-line supervisors of volunteers: "Those generals in the Pentagon, sipping coffee and checking enlistment charts, can say what they want. But we're down here at the grass-roots level, partner, and I'm telling you the all volunteer army is a loss."[36] A drill sergeant contrasted today's volunteer recruits with the draftees of the Vietnam period:

> Most of them [draftees] were mature, many of them were bright. Now we're getting immature kids, mama's boys. Cry babies . . . they cry the minute you snap at them. We're getting a lot of sick people too. We had to medically discharge one guy who was missing the big toe on his left foot. Could hardly walk. How these guys get through the entrance examination station, I don't know.[37]

Since the inception of the volunteer force, it has been easier to recruit a more socially representative female than even a marginal male. Females not only fill slots in the military, but they are also a more socially representative group than are the male recruits. Although the Defense Department will not release measures of social class background of their recruits, it is possible to surmise sex differences in representativeness through oblique measures. Two such measures, educational level and military aptitude, have already been discussed. Both measures can be compared with national populations. In a national population, the high school dropout rate is between 20 and 25 percent of an 18- to 21-year-old cohort. For the Defense Department, over a third of its recruits for the years 1974 to 1979 were high school dropouts. To the extent that women improve the educational level of the forces, they also contribute to a military population convergent with civilian society. As was documented earlier, females tended to score higher on military aptitude than the general youth population, whereas male recruits scored lower than their civilian counterparts. Since the average woman recruit is brighter and more likely to hold a high school diploma, the presence of women improves representativeness.

A final more subtle measure of social representativeness identified by Moskos is the marital composition of the volunteer military:

> From 1965 to 1976, the proportion of married enlisted men increased from 36.4% to 56.9%. The average number of dependents increased from 1.02 to 2.47. These significant changes have occurred since the end of the draft in 1973. The changes in marital composition of the enlisted ranks runs counter to national trends where the median age of males at first marriage has increased. It is apparent that the all-volunteer Army has been overrecruiting from the group of young married men.[38]

Female recruits are less likely to be married and have dependent children than their male counterparts. For example, in December of 1975, the ratio of dependents to women soldiers was only one to five. In contrast, each male soldier averaged one dependent each.[39] Males had far more family responsibilities than did females, which escalated personnel costs. Prior to 1971, women who became pregnant during their term were automatically discharged. Revised policies now allow women to choose whether they wish to remain in the service after a pregnancy. In May 1973, the U.S. Supreme Court decided the case of *Frontiero* v. *Richardson*, 411 U.S. 677, which invalidated a military regulation that discriminated against women soldiers in the area of dependent allowances. The military regulation presumed that wives of male soldiers required military support, while husbands of female soldiers had the burden of proving that they were dependent upon their spouses. However, since *Frontiero*, women have continued to have fewer dependents than their male counterparts and saved the military considerable expense in the area of family allowances, medical fees, travel costs, and relocation expenses.

Because the average woman recruit is brighter, more likely to have a

TABLE 2.5. Total Disciplinary Incidents: Department of Defense
(1968–1979)

(Rates per 1,000 soldiers)

Year	Court Martials	Desertions	Nonjudicial Punishments	Totals
1968	29	18	141	188
1969	36	24	151	211
1970	31	31	168	230
1971	29	40	168	237
1972	25	32	169	226
1973	23	29	185	237
1974	24	29	211	264
1975	21	26	202	249
1976	16	20	191	227
1977	12	18	176	206
1978	11	17	178	206
1979	13	17	171	201

Source: Department of Defense, unpublished tabulations, DOD Report System, 1979.

high school diploma, and less likely to be involved in an early marriage, female recruits are important to the Army in maintaining at least some convergence with a civilian population of young adults.

Women and Social Control in the Military

One of the indirect costs of enlisting high school dropouts in large numbers in the military is the increased problem of social control. Young male dropouts between the ages of 18 and 21 are a particularly high-risk group for criminal activity in any population. Table 2.5 presents official Defense Department disciplinary rates. These figures indicate that at least one in five soldiers had some contact with the military justice system during each year. While nonjudicial punishments may involve relatively minor infractions, they do involve considerable administrative and management time and money.

One of the advantages that was proffered for the volunteer military was that it would result in fewer social control problems because recruits were in the Army of their own volition. However, Table 2.5 shows that the average of disciplinary incidents has decreased only slightly during the volunteer years. In fact, the average number of incidents has exceeded the number reported during the peak of the Vietnam protest years of 1968–69.

In addition, during the first four years of the volunteer force, 608,000 soldiers were absent without leave for a period greater than 30 days. In only 42 percent of the more serious cases studied were individuals given administrative discharges rather than formal court maritals. In fiscal year 1979, the Army alone issued nearly 11,426 general discharges. Each case of official Absent Without Leave (AWOL), desertion, and first-term attrition resulted in major training, administrative, and management costs.[40] Whether individuals were administratively discharged or imprisoned, the result was the same. As General Bernard W. Rogers of the U.S. Army recently put it, "In the units, we captains and first sergeants spent 90% of our time with 10% of our soldiers."[41]

Finally, during the years of the volunteer military, both alcohol and drug abuse were major concerns to military management. Nearly 25 percent of all enlisted men surveyed used drugs or alcohol during work hours at least once per year; one out of four soldiers missed at least one day of work due to alcohol abuse. According to the Defense Department, an additional 10 percent of the sample were impaired at work at least once during the past 12 months because of drug use. Arthur D. Little's self-report study of drug use in the services conducted in 1975 found that 38 percent of the respondents were regularly using marijuana. In addition, 14 percent were using hallucinogens. Another 11 percent regularly used cocaine, uppers, barbiturates, downers, and Darvon.[42] Whether or not military drug abuse is higher than in a group of young civilian males is debatable. However, General William C. Louisell, Deputy Assistant Defense Secretary for Drug and Alcohol Abuse Prevention, correctly states, "The military could take no great comfort that it shares with the civilian world a drinking and drug problem: We're in a high-risk business and the tools of our trade are lethal weapons, so we have to be better and think clearer."[43]

One of the traditional canards for excluding women from the military is that they would lose too much time due to pregnancy. However, when lost time for enlisted men and women in the Navy was compared, females lost only half as much time as men. Women were much less likely to lose time due to alcohol abuse. They were six times less likely to lose work time due to drug use. The female AWOL (unauthorized absence) rate was 20 percent of the male rate, and women were ten times less likely to desert. For women, pregnancy was the major cause of lost time.[44] However, pregnancy taxed administrative time at a fraction of what it took to process males through a court martial hearing. Much of the male's lost time was due to desertion, alcoholism, and drug abuse. In contrast, female lost time was disproportionately due to nondisciplinary factors such as pregnancy. Because the female soldier is less likely to end up in the military justice system, she is less likely to tax administrators' time, and because she is a more reliable worker, she also costs less.

Female Military Labor and the Fiscal Crisis

James O'Connor, in the *Fiscal Crisis of the State* argues that economic theorists have ignored the role of government expenditures in the current peril of advanced societies. O'Connor contends that the accumulation of social expenses creates tendencies toward economic, social, and political crises. Two lines of analysis were explored by O'Connor. First, he argued that the state has socialized more and more capital costs. The socialization of capital costs and private appropriation of profits creates a fiscal crisis, or "structural gaps between state expenditures and state revenues." The result is a "tendency for state expenditures to increase much more rapidly than the means of financing them." Secondly, O'Connor found that the fiscal crisis was exacerbated by the private appropriation of public funds. A host of "special interests"—corporations, industries, regional and other business interests—make claims on the public budget for various types of social interest.[45]

There is no greater social expense than defense. Military expenditures constitute a larger and larger share of state expenditures. Whereas President Carter had proposed a 1 trillion dollar defense budget for fiscal years 1981 to 1985, President Reagan has upped the ante to 1 trillion, 600 billion. Emma Rothschild found that U.S. military expenditures began to rise dramatically in the mid-1970s:

> Military contracts for goods and services—what the Defense Department comptroller calls "procurement," which includes spending for maintenance goods and for foreign military sales—increased from $45.8 billion in 1976 to $55.6 billion in 1977 and $69.0 billion in 1979. . . . If one considers the history of the American economy in the twentieth century, it seems possible that military industries have functioned as a "leading sector"—in the economist Joseph Schumpeter's sense of a dominant industry—during the long expansion of the 1940s to the 1970s.[46]

Much of the increase in defense spending occurred in the weapons industry: "The greatest increase in any major category within the 1981 budget is for 'research, development, test and evaluation, or RDTE.' Spending on strategic and other nuclear weapons increases particularly fast, as does futuristic research at the 'leading edge' of military technology."[47]

James Fallow, in his book on defense spending, warns about the new culture of procurement:

> [Procurement] draws the military toward new weapons *because* of their great cost, not in spite of it . . . United Technologies, which makes

helicopters and jet engines, among other things, received $2,553,600,000 [in Pentagon business during one year, 1978] . . . the president of United Technologies was Alexander Haig—former four-star general, former Supreme Allied Commander of NATO forces, Reagan's Secretary of State, and perhaps the most dramatic example of the traffic between defense contractors and the Government.[48]

Even a 1 trillion, 600 billion dollar budget cannot buy everything. Increasingly in the 1970s, defense manpower costs competed with weapons procurement for the defense dollar. During the decade of the volunteer force, defense manpower costs increased exponentially. Total defense manpower costs expanded from 24 billion dollars in fiscal year 1964 to 64 billion by fiscal year 1979.

Since 1974 the percentage of the Defense budget allocated to manpower has ranged between 56 percent and 60 percent, up from 47 percent in 1964 and 46 percent in 1968. While increased personnel costs reflect inflation, the increased proportion of the budget devoted to labor is, in large part, due to the greater overall cost of the all-volunteer force. The enormous outlays for defense manpower have caused Congressional concern about whether the country can afford the volunteer force. Despite the dramatic increase in total defense spending, would the increased

TABLE 2.6. Trends in Defense Manpower Costs (1964–1979)
(in billions of dollars)

	Actual					Budget
	FY 1964	FY 1968	FY 1974	FY 1977	FY 1978	FY 1979
Total manpower costs	24	35.8	46.7	56.3	60.1	64.0
Total minus retirement	22.8	33.7	41.6	48.1	50.9	53.9
GNP deflator	49.7	64.7	57	54.6	54.3	53.9
Defense manpower costs as a proportion of the Defense budget (%)	47	46	60	59	57	56

Source: U.S. Senate, Armed Services Committee, Department of Defense Authorizations for Appropriations, Fiscal Year 1980.

manpower costs contribute to a fiscal crisis that would threaten the federal budget priority of weapons procurement? To the extent that manpower costs can be cut by enlisting more women, more funds are left for weapons.

That manpower costs are considered a problem is evident from Congressional hearings on the volunteer costs. In hearings before the Committee on Armed Services of the U.S. Senate, Senator Nunn asked Admiral Baldwin of the Navy what kind of money it would take to ensure the success of the all-volunteer force in the 1980s. The following exchange was recorded during Senate hearings on defense appropriations:

> Senator Nunn: Do you have any idea what we are talking about in terms of expense if we want to use financial resources to try to insure the success of the All-Volunteer Forces in the 1980s? Have you ever quantified that?
> Admiral Baldwin: Several people have made those kinds of projections, I believe.
> Senator Nunn: CBO (Congressional Budget Office) says $6 billion to $8 billion a year additional funds would be required. Is that in the ball park?
> Admiral Baldwin: I would think so sir, yes.[49]

When compared with a 1.6 trillion dollar budget, a 6 to 8 billion dollar increase in personnel costs seems insignificant. However, when that figure is compared with cutbacks in state expenditures for social welfare, as indicated in Table 2.7, the enormous price of the volunteer force is underscored. Since the late 1970s, militarism has eclipsed social welfare as the major federal budgetary priority. However, this does not mean that Congress has not expressed increasing concern about the impact of manpower costs on the budget.

Prior to the late 1960s, Congress "rubber-stamped" Defense Department authorizations, but since then, Congress has become more critical. Handberg and Bledsoe found, in their analysis of the Congressional impact upon the defense budget, that the attitude of Congressional committees has changed from positive support to criticism or skepticism:

> In the 1950s and 1960s, the American Congress' basic posture was that of a ratifier of executive budgetary decisions. Congressional involvement came only in those instances where the American defense establishment was severely split along service and/or doctrinal lines. In the "Vietnam era" of the 1960s, there were more frequent splits within the American defense establishment (especially its civilian component) over the war itself and, more recently, the strategic arms race with the Soviet Union.[50]

By the mid-1970s, defense manpower costs began to be scrutinized by the Congress and by the Defense Department itself. Increasingly, cost cuts

TABLE 2.7. A Comparison of Increased Manpower Costs in Defense to Proposed Federal Budget Cuts for Fiscal Year 1982 (in millions of dollars)

Area	Fiscal Year 1981	Reagan Budget (Proposal)	Difference
Health and social			
Medicaid	18,016	17,089	927
National Science			
Foundation	1,088	1,049	39
Aid to families with			
dependent children	8,588	7,480	1,100
Child nutrition	5,482	3,461	2,021
Legal Services			
Corporation	338	26	312
Head Start	886	0	886
Guaranteed student			
loan programs	3,006	2,623	383
Total FY 1982 cuts in selected programs			5,668
Increased manpower costs each year for the all-volunteer force			6,000–8,000

Sources: Congressional Budget Office, "Federal Budget Scorecard—Selected Programs," as reported in New York Times, June 21, 1981, p. 4E; Senate Subcommittee Hearings on the Cost of the All-Volunteer Force, 1978, U.S. Senate, Subcommittee on Manpower and Personnel of the Committee on Armed Services, Ninety-Fifth Congress, February 6, 1978.

began to be proposed in the areas of military housing, education, and medicine. Defense manpower analysts began to look for ways to cut costs and simultaneously to maintain minimum recruitment standards.

In 1978 hearings before the U.S. Senate, Senator Nunn expressed doubts about whether the military could continue to afford increased manpower costs without cutting back in the area of weapons procurements: "To summarize, despite favorable economic and demographic conditions, the AVF (All Volunteer Force) is now operating on the ragged edge of viability, with mushrooming recruiting costs, unacceptable rates of attrition, severe shortages of critical skills, shortages in qualified recruits, and dangerously undermanned, lower-quality reserves."[51]

The armed forces spent over $18 billion in additional expenses to reach authorized strengths in the first years of the volunteer forces. Increasingly, both Congressional members and Defense manpower analysts publicly asked how much money it would take to keep the volunteer forces at a steady state.

For example, General Louis H. Wilson, Commandant of the Marine Corps, believed that fiscal year 1978 represented the optimum amount of money that could be spent, "There is a point beyond which we cannot spend for additional talent."[52] Similarly, Army General Bernard W. Rogers concluded that current trends were not encouraging, "Despite the Army's best efforts, the quality of accessions has fallen below requirements. The volunteer Army and its continuing success require increased support.[53] Finally, Admiral James L. Holloway, Chief of Naval Operations, testified before the Senate Subcommittee on Manpower and Personnel, "Services that are having problems today will have problems in the future. There is a price for everything, but I think it would be so exorbitant that it is unreasonable to think about it . . . We have no give. We are at the limit of our resiliency."[54]

One of the ways in which costs have been lowered has been to increase the number of women soldiers. Defense Department analysts believed that women could be used to partially alleviate the crisis in defense personnel costs. As the Assistant Secretary of Defense for Manpower stated, women soldiers were a cheaper reservoir of labor than their male counterparts:

> To put the question bluntly: Is recruiting a male dropout in preference to a smaller, weaker, but high quality female erring on the side of national security, in terms of the kinds of jobs which must be done in today's military?
>
> The tradeoff in today's recruiting market is between a high quality female and a low quality male.[55]

Binkin and Bach of the Brookings Institute first alerted military planners to the economic advantages of sex integration. While there were one-time costs associated with modifying facilities to accommodate women, the inclusion of women could result in substantial savings. The Binkin and Bach study identified the following ways that women could alleviate the crisis in manpower costs:

1. Women were cheaper to recruit than males. Because of sex discrimination in the civilian economy, it was comparatively more advantageous for high quality females to enlist.
2. Women had fewer dependents, which resulted in lower costs for housing, medical care, travel, and allowances.

TABLE 2.8. Sex Differences in Recruitment Costs*
(in dollars)

	Army	Navy	Marines	Air Force
High quality male	3,700	1,950	2,050	870
High quality female	150	150	150	150
Low quality male	150	150	150	150

*Active force recruiting costs for enlisted personnel were $422 million in FY-1977. The proposed costs for FY-1979 were $515 million.

Source: Assistant Secretary of Defense for Manpower, Reserve Affairs, and Logistics, Use of Women in the Military (1978).

3. Women had a higher first term completion rate, which resulted in lower training costs.
4. Women had fewer disciplinary problems, such as drug abuse, alcoholism, absenteeism, desertion, and unauthorized leave.
5. While women live longer than men, they are less likely to remain in the service to collect military retirement compensation.[56]

As personnel expenditures began to constitute a larger share of defense spending, the inclusion of women partially compensated for some of these costs. While Binkin and Bach were cautious about their estimates of savings through the increased utilization of women, their report confirms women's role in alleviating the military's fiscal crisis:

Far and away the most important financial consequence of increasing the proportion of women in the military services—and one that is likely to attract more attention—is the prospect of being able to maintain desired quality standards among volunteers without incurring large increases in the military payroll, using up resources that might otherwise be put to better use elsewhere in the defense establishment or in nondefense activities. Indeed, whether this nation can sustain its armed forces solely by voluntary means could well depend on how effectively the female labor resource is employed.[57]

Women Soldiers and the Military's Fund of Legitimacy

While the manifest reason for the inclusion of women, according to Defense Department press releases, was to create job opportunities for women, in reality, a more powerful argument has emerged. Women have been the all-volunteer military's margin of success. They have helped to alleviate the problems of numbers, quality, social representativeness, and social control. High quality women have been recruited at the same cost as low quality males. While equal opportunity may have been a genuine Defense Department concern, the role of women in staving off the endemic problems of the volunteer forces must also be considered.

In this section, I shall argue that women have helped to restore public confidence in the military as a social institution. However, before this latent function is examined, it is necessary to understand the economic, political, and military problems that led to the loss of public confidence in the U.S. military. Further, it is necessary to understand why the military needs legitimacy.

Max Weber first used the term *legitimacy* in defining four justifications for a social institution: tradition, affect, rational belief, and law. According to Weber, every institution must find some way to dominate persons legitimately:

> Domination was defined above as the probability that specific commands [or all commands] will be obeyed by a given group of persons. It thus does not include every mode of exercising "power" or "influence" over other persons. Domination ["authority"] in this sense may be based on the most diverse motives of compliance: all the way from simple habituation to the most purely rational calculation of advantage. Hence every genuine form of domination implies a minimum of voluntary compliance, that is, an *interest* [based on ulterior motives or genuine acceptance] in obedience.[58]

The most effective way in which mass support could be marshalled for the military was based on rational belief. The public has to be convinced that military domination is consistent with their economic and political interests. Once this voluntary compliance is secured, military power can be accepted as natural and inevitable.

The work of Jürgen Habermas provides the impetus for examining the problem of legitimacy as process and as a persistent problem rather than as a static phenomenon. Habermas views disturbances in the flow of legitimacy as a ubiquitous problem of the state:

> Legitimacy means that there are good arguments for a political order's worthiness to be recognized. This definition highlights the fact that legitimacy is a contestable validity claim; the stability of the order of domination [also] depends on its [at least] de facto recognition. Thus, historically as well as analytically, the concept is used above all in selection in which the legitimacy of an order is disputed, in which as we say, legitimation problems arise. One side denies, the other asserts legitimacy. This is a process—Talleyrand endeavored to legitimize the House of Bourbon. Processes of this kind were rendered less dramatic in the *modern* con-

stitutional state [with the institutionalization of an opposition]; That is, they were defused and normalized. For this reason it is realistic to speak today of legitimation as a permanent problem.[59]

Jacques Van Doorn, writing from a different perspective, also views the military legitimation crisis as an endemic problem of contemporary civil-military relations. Van Doorn defined the present crisis of military legitimacy in this way:

> This term [military legitimacy] implies a comprehensive complex of developments such as the diminishing acceptance of military force, the increasing public criticism of the military, the popularity of compulsory military service, the decivilianization of the military and the concomitant loss of institutional identity . . . The crisis of legitimacy is not so much characteristic of the political order as of the military establishment.[60]

The Legitimacy Fund

Legitimacy for military organizations is sustained by the belief that the armed forces reflect sacred social values and shore up economic and military power as well. The problem of legitimacy in the military has a "boom and bust" quality. The concept of a *legitimacy fund* captures the public's roller-coaster views of the military; as such, the legitimacy fund serves as a gauge of public loyalty. The legitimacy fund, as measured by public opinion, can plummet or rise sharply in the same fashion as a monetary fund. For example, during the early years of the Korean War and the Vietnam War, the military borrowed on its past accomplishments in order to stave off a crisis in public confidence. However, when public disaffection became too great, the legitimacy fund experienced a crisis comparable to a "run on a bank" during a monetary crisis. When public confidence plummets too much, the exercise of military power can be vitiated. Because the exercise of military domination is dependent upon the voluntary compliance of the public, there will be a crisis in military legitimacy when there is too much deficit spending from the fund. Because legitimacy circulates between institutions, a crisis in military legitimacy will create steering problems in other areas, such as the economy and polity. Habermas argues that when a legitimizing system does not succeed in maintaining the requisite level of mass loyalty, crisis tendencies occur both in the administrative (political) and economic systems.[61]

The legitimation problem of the military is to keep public confidence at least at the minimal level, where it won't create contradictory steering problems in the economy and polity. The Vietnam War was a case in which the military came perilously close to endangering its fund of legitimacy. During the middle 1960s, there was a long period of deficit spending from the legitimacy fund. An understanding of the latent functions of military women is not possible without considering how they have helped to restore military legitimacy.

Vietnam as a Run on the Legitimacy Fund

During the Vietnam conflict, arguments about the detrimental effect of the war shifted to a critique of military domination itself. At one point, the fund of legitimacy was so depleted that fundamental questions were raised as to the necessity for large military spending and a permanent war economy. By the end of the 1960s, the withdrawal of mass loyalty from the military's fund of legitimacy had also created difficulties for the political and economic systems. By 1969, public confidence in the military had fallen to a 40-year low. George Gallup reported that in 1969 only 8 percent of the public felt that defense spending was too low, while 52 percent felt that too much was being allocated to defense.[62]

The military's legitimacy crisis was also indicated by the following critical incidents and developments documented by David Cortright:

1. During the five peak years of Vietnam involvement, the Army desertion rate increased nearly 400 percent.
2. Growing antimilitarism led to trouble in the Reserve Officers' Training Corps (ROTC) program. Total college enrollment dropped from 218,000 in the 1968 academic year to 72,500 in 1972–73. From 1969 to 1972, 38 ROTC units were expelled from college campuses.
3. For the Vietnam War period, 206,000 persons were reported delinquent to the Justice Department by the Selective Service.
4. Massive antiwar demonstrations were launched from 1968 to 1972.
5. Dissent and disorder within the Army reached its peak during the spring of 1971. The growing antimilitary insurgency within the nation, evident in the massive upsurge in civilian peace action and the national emergence of "Vietnam Veterans Against the War" kindled an intense outpouring of soldier resistance within the military.[63]

Morris Janowitz wrote in *Foreign Affairs* in 1972 that the military was in the midst of a legitimation crisis: "The military establishment, and especially its ground forces, are experiencing a profound crisis in legitimacy due to the impact of Vietnam, internal racial tension, corruption, extensive drug abuse, leadership imbalance, a high UA (unauthorized absence) rate, lack of motivation . . . in an unpopular war."[64]

Charles Moskos observed that, in World War II, the military establishment had unprecedented public support. In contrast, support for the military during the latter stages of the Vietnam War was at an all-time low:

Although there was a brief spate of glory attached to the Green Berets, opposition to the war soon led to negative portrayals of the armed forces. Indeed, as the antiwar movement gained momentum it began to generalize into a frontal attack on the military system itself—particularly within elite cultural and intellectual circles. The 1967 March on the Pentagon crossed a symbolic threshold. Not only was the war in Vietnam opposed, but for a growing number the basic legitimacy of military service was brought into open question.[65]

Much of the opposition to the Vietnam War was fanned by the draft. Eventually the threat to the political and economic institutions posed by these developments was considered so severe that there was a movement in Congress to end conscription. In 1971, members of the House of Representatives discussed the volunteer military as an alternative to the draft. By advancing the volunteer army, the political system was able to deflect attention away from the severe legitimation deficit that threatened the administrative systems. Bipartisan support was mounted to end conscription. Congressman Paren Mitchell (D, Md.) expressed the conviction that the legitimation crisis created by the draft had to be solved. Mitchell argued that an infusion of public support would be granted any administration who would end the draft: "We must now end the rhetoric and reassert our authority. Long hours and much labor has been invested in making all sides of the issue understandable to the American public and I strongly believe that there is overwhelming public support for a volunteer system."[66]

Congressman Guy Vander Jagt (R, Mich.) expressed similar sentiments for volunteer military legislation: "We must take advantage of the decreasing troop commitments to South Vietnam to reform our system of manpower requirements in a manner which will both meet the ideals of our free society and serve a higher measure of efficiency and effectiveness of our military operations.[67]

Kenneth Coffey observed that General Hershey and other supporters of a strong national defense capability should have seen the potential dangers in the challenge to Selective Service policies:

Indeed, the confrontation over draft reform kept the issue of the war and the draft in the public mind, with more and more citizens recognizing, as Theodore H. White explained, that "the draft could not work for which there was no consent, either of Congress or of the public, and which required so little manpower that choice for service became a matter of fate, bad luck, or trickery.[68]

Because the middle class opposed the draft, the military and political system was unable to sustain a subjective commitment in society's cultural institution. Claus Mueller argues that the *cultural strata* is the most politicized of any group in modern society. As Mueller notes, the cultural stratum is composed of writers, poets, social scientists, educators, publishers, civically involved lawyers, doctors, scientists, religious leaders as well as filmmakers, painters, and all other artists.[69] Moskos argued that the legitimacy crisis was led by a vanguard of the cultural and intellectual elite during the Vietnam War.[70] Without the support of this group, legitimacy could not be easily maintained. Mueller also thought that the cultural stratum was decisive for legitimacy:

> As studies of social change demonstrate, the political positions the cultural stratum take are crucial for the stability and the sustenance of legitimacy of the political system. This stratum's contribution, specifically of intellectuals, to stability or instability has been observed both by classical and modern social scientists. For Marx and Weber, whose theoretical perspectives were far apart, intellectuals serve to preserve or revise the images society has of itself.[71]

The volunteer military was implemented partly in response to the legitimation deficits of a rapidly disintegrating military apparatus. In 1971, members of the House of Representatives began plans to end the draft. By 1973 the draft was ended, and a volunteer military was in place. While the Vietnam War was a no-growth phase, during each year of the volunteer military, public support for the military as an institution grew. As Table 2.9 indicates, public opinion shifted dramatically after the end of the draft. By 1976 the number of persons who felt that military spending was too high decreased to 36 percent of the population. By February of 1980, Gallup reported that public confidence in the military as an institution had reached a 45-year high. As Table 2.9 documents, each year of the volunteer force was marked by a new infusion of public loyalty and confidence.

It is difficult to determine the degree to which the end of conscription contributed to the increase in public loyalty toward the military as an institution. Certainly the rise in public support from December of 1979 to January of 1980 reflected in part the Iranian hostage situation as well as the Soviet invasion of Afghanistan. But clearly the end of the draft and the switch to an all-volunteer army must have helped to regenerate the military's fund of legitimacy.

It is women who have made the military's strategy to regain legitimacy viable. To the extent that women have served as clientele in the military's "frontstage" presentation as a social welfare institution and to the extent that they have made the volunteer military strategy work, they

TABLE 2.9. Public Attitudes Toward Defense Spending
(1969–1980)

	Adequacy of Military Spending (%)			
	Too Little	Too Much	About Right	No Opinion
January 1980	49	14	24	13
December 1979	34	21	33	12
1977	27	23	40	10
1976	22	36	32	10
1974	12	44	32	10
1973	13	46	30	10
1971 (draft)	11	49	31	9
1969 (draft)	8	52	31	9

Source: George C. Gallup, The Gallup Opinion Index, Report No. 175 (February 1980), p. 2.

have helped the military rebound from an 11-year low point to a position of strength in the public eye.

Women have helped to legitimize the role of the military in American society. To the extent that the shift to the volunteer military has been responsible for the revitalization of the military's fund of legitimacy, women have contributed significantly to a new stage of legitimation solvency. Military women have been the reserve army of last resort who have helped to fill the ranks. Because they alleviate the problems of numbers, quality, social balance, social control, and cost, they have served the latent functions of strengthening military effectiveness.

During the volunteer years, the military has been able to replenish its legitimacy without total war. Because the attention of the cultural stratum has been deflected to other concerns, the military has weathered the legitimation crisis of the early 1970s. It is debatable whether the military could draft the requisite number of qualified male soldiers without resistance from the cultural stratum, even if there was another draft or another Vietnam-like venture. However, it is clear that, in the interim, women can be trained and controlled more easily than the available pool of high-risk males.

Until the draft can be reinstated, women can be used to foster the post–Vietnam War image of the Army as a social welfare institution. In the final section of this chapter, the functions that women fulfill in the enlisted culture of the all-volunteer military are explored. As we shall see, not only do women serve as a high quality surplus army at the institutional level, but they also provide individual male soldiers with important benefits.

The Uses of Women in Male Enlisted Culture

When women are introduced at the unit level, they provide previously all male groups with a convenient pool of marriage and sexual partners. It is particularly difficult for enlisted males to find an adequate number of women in an overseas setting. In West Germany, for example, enlisted men do not know the language and do not have the means to strike marriage contracts with local women.

In most garrison communities, single junior enlisted men are required to live in on-base barracks with their total institutional features. They are required to eat in the mess hall because, unlike married enlisted men, they may not claim separate rations. In addition, single junior enlisted men are subject to continuous military harassment in the form of unscheduled inspections, shakedowns, and urinalyses during their off-duty time. If these same men were to find a wife, their status would dramatically improve. Married men are eligible for off-post housing and food allowances and are free from the control and continual scrutiny of officers in charge of quarters. The *Army Times* reported that innovative junior enlisted men have found a solution to barracks life. Single males and females have developed a new form of "pseudo-marriage," in which they vow to stay together until one party to the "marriage" is reassigned to another base. In some of these alliances, partners never live together and view the marriage pragmatically as a means to receive attractive freedom and benefits. The "until death do us part" has been replaced with "until we ETS" (End of Tour of Service).[72]

While the "contract marriage" has obvious appeal for some men and women, an increasing proportion of military women are married to military men. In the Air Force alone, Pentagon officials estimated that 6,000 Air Force women—about 40 percent—are married to military men.[73] For the services as a whole, one in three women recruits finds a marriage partner in the military. By 1978, a recruiting slogan for first-term soldiers was, "Ask Your Wife About Re-enlisting!"

The evolution of dual career military marriages has also benefited the military. In some marriages, persons who may have been reluctant about finishing their term of service or reenlisting have chosen to remain in the military because of their partners. Most importantly, two-career couples are cheaper for the military than traditional marriages, since the dependents of two soldiers can be supported for the price of one. Williams envisions a new work-family system in the military:

As more and more women enter the military, we can expect to see increasing numbers of dual-military career families. It is no longer necessary for a women to leave the service if she becomes pregnant; thus we can predict more situations in which active duty couples have children, with the marital partners sharing in all required activities associated with the care of infants. It is no longer absurd to believe that at some time in the future that entire families—mother, father, and children—may be on active duty, simultaneously performing their required duties in the military while living together as a family unit.[74]

In summary, the critical functional perspective has been used to uncover eight latent functions of women in the volunteer military. Unpublished data and reports from the "backstage" area of Defense planners reveal that women serve the following purposes: (1) they shore up the Defense Department's image as an equal opportunity employer; (2) they serve as a reserve army of last resort; (3) because high quality females can be recruited at the same price as low quality males, women improve the quality of the services; (4) women soldiers improve the social mix of the services because they are more representative of a general youth population; in contrast, males are more likely to be married, of lower educational level, and have less aptitude for military jobs; (5) women save administrative time and money; they end up in the brig less often than their male counterparts and have much lower desertion, court martial, and disciplinary rates; they are also less likely to lose duty time to drug and alcohol abuse; (6) female military laborers are cheaper to recruit; because women help to cut costs, they help to stave off exponential manpower cost increases that threaten to induce a fiscal crisis for the military; (7) to the extent that women have made viable the strategy the military used to regain public support, they have replenished the military's fund of legitimacy; and (8) at the unit level, women serve as a reservoir of fictive and real marriage partners for male soldiers.

Thus, the real momentum behind the recent female expansion in the services has been their role in thwarting the internal crisis of the volunteer forces. For the contemporary U.S. military, internal crisis better explains female inclusion than does external crisis, which has historically and cross-culturally been associated with sex role dedifferentiation in organized armies.

Emerging Latent Functions?

In the early 1970s, the greatest interpersonal problems in the U.S. military were racially based. Human relations offices were created in every branch of the services to ease racial tensions. However, racial awareness seminars were inadequate to stave off fights between blacks and whites over such issues as the kind of music to be played on the enlisted club's jukebox. Cortright reported widespread racial unrest in the services in the early 1970s: "Given the large and steadily mounting percentage of non-whites within ranks, discriminatory conditions have inevitably led to frequent black rebellion. Indeed, while Detroit, Watts, and other cities quieted down in the late 1960s, Camp Lejeune, Mannheim, Long Binh, the Kitty Hawk, and countless other military bases exploded in black rebellion."[75]

The rising proportion of black entrants in the military has been one of the most widely discussed issues vis-à-vis the viability of the volunteer armed forces. Given the low educational level of white male entrants during the volunteer years, it could be expected that the structure of enlisted culture would polarize into black and white sectors. However, during the time in which the number of minority entrants doubled, racial tensions eased. Black-white confrontations within the military were reduced so significantly that by 1978, Secretary of the Army, Clifford Alexander Jr., and General Bernard W. Rogers warned of the dangers of "complacency" in a report on the Army's affirmative action program.[76]

The military clearly made a positive effort to reduce racial tensions with its human relations programs. Special efforts were made to recruit blacks for supervisory positions. The military fulfilled a positive function of providing social welfare to minorities redundant to the civilian economy. It is postulated here, however, that an emerging latent function of including more women in the services is the realignment of enlisted culture. Beginning in the mid-1970s, women have been increasingly assigned to nontraditional skills. The largest change has occurred in the combat-support jobs, where more and more women have integrated previously all-male domains.

It is hypothesized that women are replacing blacks as "flak-catchers" in enlisted culture. One of the unanticipated functions that women may be serving is to direct attention away from racial cleavages. Human relations offices in the U.S. Army in Europe reported in 1978 that racial discrimination complaints had decreased since the early 1970s by up to 500 percent in some units. During the same period, sexual harassment and sex discrimination complaints increased three to five times.[77]

There are many problems in making the argument that women have replaced blacks as "flak-catchers." There is a significant methodological problem discerning the relationship between reported and unreported incidents. Even if the reported incidence of sexual and racial conflicts were to demonstrate the inverse correlation that is hypothesized, there is a problem that the data could reflect "selective attention" from the Army Human Relations Office. In the early 1970s, Army counselors were trained to process racially related tensions. It wasn't until the late 1970s that "sex-role tensions" were defined as a social problem for the Army. A sharp increase in processing sex-role complaints would lead to a decrease in attention to racial problems. With these methodological caveats in mind, it is suggested that, when women are able to do traditionally male jobs successfully, the basis of masculinity is challenged. The presence of women in tough jobs casts doubt on whether military service really validates manhood.

A second source of sexual tension is the discrepancy in educational level between the sexes. Because women recruits score higher on military aptitude tests and are better educated, they threaten previously all-male domains. Women soldiers are excellent scapegoats because they can't fight back. Less than 0.5 percent of female soldiers are in the noncommissioned officer ranks. Thus, not only are women outnumbered, but they lack the organizational power to exercise influence and control over their social fate as token women in a male environment.

If male-female tension is the emerging crucible for the full expression of enlisted hostility, women are serving the latent function as "scapegoats." When black and white male soldiers realign the boundaries of enlisted culture to exclude women, they unwittingly develop mutual dependencies. Sex-role exclusivism is less dangerous to the military than are racial confrontations because women are not in a position to fight back.

ALL-MALE DRAFT REGISTRATION
AND EQUAL PROTECTION

Prior to 1971, the U.S. Supreme Court had never contested a legislative or administrative statute based on invidious gender classifications. *Bradwell v. Illinois*, 83 U.S. (16 Wall.) 130 (1873), was emblematic of early judicial attitudes toward women and work. *Bradwell* upheld a state statute that denied women the license to practice law. The concurring justices legitimated the different treatment of men and women on the basis of natural law: "The paramount destiny and mission of women are to fulfill the noble and benign offices of wife and mother. This is the law of the creator."[78]

Beginning with the case of *Reed* v. *Reed*, 404 U.S. 71 (1971), the Court began to extend the new equal protection to women. In *Reed*, a state law preferred males to females in the administration of intestate estates. The Court in *Reed* contended that it was impermissible to prefer male to female estate administrators. Such a distinction was arbitrary and not rationally related to any legislative objective. Since there was no good reason to discriminate against women, the statute was struck down. The standard

of judicial review was that gender classifications must bear some substantial relationship to legislative goals.[79]

Following Reed, the Court in the previously mentioned case of Frontiero
v. Richardson, 411 U.S. 677 (1973), held that dissimilar treatment for men
and women officers concerning dependent allowances was an evisceration
of women soldiers' due process guarantees under the Fifth Amendment.

Justice William Brennan, writing for the plurality in Frontiero, argued
that the government's differential treatment of men and women served no
purpose other than mere "administrative convenience." Any statutory
scheme that draws a sharp line between the sexes, according to Brennan,
involves the very kind of arbitrary legislative choice forbidden by the
Constitution. Brennan thought that women faced many special disabilities
as the result of their sex characteristics. Since sex bears no relation to ability
to perform or contribute to society, classifications based on sex are
inherently suspect.[80]

The hope that women could be integrated on an equal-status basis
into American society suffered a severe setback when, on June 26, 1981,
the Court upheld, by a vote of 6 to 3, the constitutionality of male-only draft
registration. In Rostker v. Goldberg, 453 U.S. _____ (1981), the Court rejected
arguments that it was unconstitutional to exclude women from draft
registration.

Justice William Rehnquist, in the majority opinion, deferred to
military policy arguments and rejected a due process challenge to the
exclusion of women from registration:

> The exemption of women from registration is not only sufficiently but
> closely related to Congress' purpose in authorizing registration. The fact that
> Congress and the Executive have decided that women could not serve in
> combat fully justifies Congress in not authorizing their registration, since the
> purpose of registration is to develop a pool of potential combat troops. As was
> the case in Schlesinger v. Ballard, "the gender classification is not invidious, but
> rather realistically reflects the fact that the sexes are not similarly situated" in
> this case. The Constitution requires that Congress treat similarly situated
> persons similarly, not that it engage in gestures of superficial equality.[81]

The most obvious consequence of Rostker v. Goldberg is the mandate
that the Defense Department has received to exclude women from the
draft on the basis of stereotyped distinctions. Rather than use classifications
based on ability, interest, or achievement, the Defense Department has
received judicial permission to employ the "quick and dirty" test of gender
to fill military jobs. To women in the military, Rostker supports the
proposition that women are merely temporary participants in the volunteer military and that they would be excluded as participants during times
of war.

For civilian women, *Rostker* is an erosion of the new equal protection principles that began with *Reed* v. *Reed*. The *Harvard Law Review*'s survey of the 1980–81 Supreme Court term described *Rostker* as follows: "In that respect, the Supreme Court's holding in *Rostker* is a major setback for women's rights. By abandoning the *Craig* test [intermediate scrutiny of gender classifications] here and deferring extensively to Congress, the Court has left untouched a congressional decision in one of the last bastions of 'traditional way[s] of thinking about women.' "[82]

The question of registering women for the draft has been the subject of national debate. Opposition to women in the draft has come from many sources. While token gains of military women in the 1970s have not been reversed by the Reagan administration, his Secretary of Defense, Caspar Weinberger, has frozen plans to further expand the number of women soldiers.[83] Officially, the Reagan administration is committed to the all-volunteer force. It is difficult to know what role military women will play in the future. Could military women be used to legitimate the return of the draft? Could the spectre of women in body bags be used to manipulate sex-role proscriptions against women in the military? An emerging latent function of military women may be to justify the return to conscription. George Gilder believes that the thought of women maimed, raped, or killed in combat is more than many men can stand:

> The primary motivation for a man to risk his life as a warrior or hunter is to protect women and children. Groups of men in warrior-hunter roles, whether literal or metaphorical, have a special kind of emotional character that sexually mixed groups cannot have. The entrance of women into the Army in large numbers—now about 64,000—will lower the Army's prestige in men's eyes since it is no longer exclusively male and the province of warriors and hunters.[84]

While the Defense Department has officially supported the inclusion of women in combat-support roles during the 1970s, many military men have been ambivalent or hostile to these policies. General William C. Westmoreland, former commander of the U.S. forces in Vietnam, said of women in combat, "Maybe you could find one woman in 10,000 who could lead in combat, but she would be a freak and we're not running a military academy for freaks... The pendulum has gone too far... They're asking women to do impossible things. I don't belive women can carry a pack, live in a foxhole, or go a week without taking a bath."[85]

General John K. Singlaub, former commander of troops in Korea, expressed the following view to Washington reporters upon the deployment of women to the 82d Airborne Division: "The presence of women in our combat units is perceived by our friends as well as by our enemies as a sign of weakness. The projected goal for our Army to be 12 percent women will be considered a weakening of that Army with a consequential reduction in the deterrent effect of that force."[86]

In a letter to supporters of the Pro-Life Amendment, C.S. White sought to muster public support to "help the women in our military services get out of combat roles":

> For instance did you know . . .
> —That the Green Berets' medics have been taught to do
> "coat-hanger abortions"? . . . They use No. 10 wire instead
> of regulation coat hanger because it's thinner and stiffer,
> which makes it better for cutting fetal tissue.
> —That a military officer, in an emergency, can order a
> woman under his command to get an abortion?
> —Those aren't all. For instance the United States is . . .
> the first country in the history of the world to order
> Army women to go on combat maneuvers and fix tank treads
> when they are known to be pregnant.
> . . . the first country in the history of the world to refuse
> to grant discharges to women in its military
> services for reasons of pregnancy.
> . . . The reason I'm telling you these things is that I don't like them any better than you do (now that you know them), and I'm trying to do something about them. I want to get laws passed to permit women to get discharges because of pregnancy and marriage, to prevent pregnant women from being exposed to the hazards of sea duty and other service under conditions that pregnancy makes a woman less able to handle . . . including combat.
> I'm an old-fashioned type. I don't much like the idea of women losing their hands, feet, eyes, and other things to the "effects of enemy fire."[87]

It is difficult to know the full implications of *Rostker* v. *Goldberg* in supporting the undercurrents of conservative resistance to social changes in the roles of women. It is also difficult to predict if the draft will be reinstituted in the 1980s. Secretary of Defense Weinberger has already lowered the Defense Department's recruiting goals for women. It is possible that the emerging decline in the use of women could be used to justify the return of the draft. Both institutional attitudes and public opinion may be receptive to the idea that military women detract from combat readiness. A letter to the editor of an Oregon newspaper raised the issue that the presence of women should shame the public into returning to the draft: "Are we becoming a sissified dronish society that men will permit women to take over their duties as protectors of the family?"[88]

In February of 1980 on the television program "Saturday Night Live," the theme of "Women in Combat" was satirized by comedian Bill Murray in his Weekend Update editorial: "I think it's a good idea that women go to war. Think of the advantages. If the Russians win the next war, we can say, 'So what, you just beat a bunch of girls.' "

It is too early to determine whether sex-role proscriptions can be used by the Defense Department to reverse female military participation, but the Defense Department can find latent functions for women whether or not there is a draft. If the volunteer military is retained, women will help to make it work because of their high quality. If the military's fund of legitimacy is replenished to the extent that the draft could be reinstituted without undue opposition from the cultural stratum, women could be used to justify male-only military service. In the interim, female inclusion will continue to stave off the crisis of the volunteer forces.

If the military is reversing itself in light of *Rostker* v. *Goldberg* and the recent cutbacks in female participation, the second-class status of military women may fulfill other latent functions in the future. Richard Cohen has argued that, if women are not included in the military as full participants, it will drop them to less than full citizenship:

> The whole thing would be silly if we weren't talking about the very serious matters of obligations to one's country. To say that men have such an obligation and women do not, relegates women to something less than full citizenship. It makes them the protected ones, wards of the state—provides them with an institutionalized parasol. As long as women do not have to shoulder the same obligations as men, they will not get the same respect as men—not from men anyway.[89]

NOTES

1. Department of Defense, *Women Serve Proudly* (Washington D.C., 1980).

2. Peter Berger and Thomas Luckmann, *The Social Construction of Reality* (Garden City: The Anchor Press, 1968).

3. Erving Goffman, *The Presentation of Self in Everyday Life* (Garden City: The Anchor Press, 1959).

4. Robert Merton, *Social Theory and Social Structures* (Glencoe, Ill.: The Free Press, 1968).

5. Herbert Gans, "The Functions of Poverty: The Poor Pay All," in John B. Williamson, Jerry F. Boren and Linda Evans, eds., *Social Problems: The Contemporary Debates* (Boston: Little, Brown, 1974), pp. 140–46.

6. Much of the Defense Department data reported in this chapter was requested through the Assistant Secretary of Defense's Office for Manpower, Reserve Affairs, and Logistics. Tabulations were derived from the All-Volunteer Force Data Base, March 1980. I was unable to receive 1981 data because Lawrence Korb, President Reagan's new Assistant Secretary of Defense for Manpower "froze" my data request. I was told by contacts within the Defense Department that data would not be forthcoming because Secretary Weinberger wanted his staff to "edit" the data before they are released to researchers.

7. Office of the Director, Women's Army Corps, "Addendum to ODWAC Notes" (Washington D.C., January 1978); the Women's Army Corps Office was eliminated in 1978 as a part of the movement to fully integrate women in the forces.

8. Bernard W. Rogers, Army Chief of Staff, *Army Times*, May 22, 1978.

9. The military trade periodicals included the following sources:

James C. Pearson (1st Lt.), "She Operates a Gas Station at 20,000 Feet," *Sergeants*, September 1980, p. 18.

Thomas L. Sack (Major), "They Are the First," *Air Force Magazine*, September 1980, pp. 154–55.

Editors, "35 Proposals Eyed (by Air Force Uniform Board): Skirts to Come Down!," *Air Force Times*, April 21, 1980, p. 3.

Editors, "Women Get More Specialties," *Air Force Times*, June 23, 1980, p. 3.

Editors, "Women to Get Centrifuge Tests at SAM," *Air Force Times*, November 17, 1980, p. 20.

Editors, "DACOWITS Gaining New Clout," *Air Force Times*, May 26, 1980, p. 15.

Editors, "DACOWITS—No Sexism in Recruiting Literature," *Air Force Times*, January 14, 1980, p. 17.

Marianne Lester, "What Happens When the Boss Is a Woman," *Air Force Times*, *Times Magazines*, (supplement), January 14, 1980, pp. 4–8.

Editors, "Women Denied Husband Care Get Break," *Air Force Times*, July 28, 1980, p. 2.

Ira C. Eaker (Lt. Gen., Ret.), "Women Graduates of the Academies," *Air Force Times*, June 16, 1980, pp. 19–20.

Judith H. Stiehm, "Women and the Combat Exemption," *Parameters* (June 1980): 51–59.

Robin Drew (SP4), Army's Hayes, First Black Woman Military Aviator in U.S. Forces, *USA Aviation Digest* (January 1980): inside back cover.

Thomas J. Gelli, "The Changing Face of Army Basic Training: More Flexible and Coeducational," *Defense Management Journal* (First Quarter, 1980): 22–29.

Bruce M. Bant (SGM), "The Army's Assault on Sexism," *Soldiers* (October 1980): 6–9.

Editors, "Women Marines in FMF Units," *Marine Corps Gazette* (June 1980): 4.

10. "A New Day and a New Age", *Stars and Stripes*, January 12, 1977.

11. Murray Kempton, "Winners and Losers at the 'Times,' " review of Harrison E. Salisbury, *Without Fear or Favor: The New York Times and Its Times*, in *The New York Review* (September 1980): 43.

12. Editors, *New York Times*, November 11, 1972.

13. Editors, *New York Times*, August 8, 1971.

14. These headlines appeared in the following *New York Times* issues: (1) August 8, 1972; (2) November 13, 1972; (3) November 8, 1972; (4) August 14, 1972; (5) September 12, 1972; and (6) August 9, 1972.

15. *New York Times*, January 23, December 12, and November 18, 1973; and July 26, March 25, and October 12, 1974.

16. *Boston Globe* articles appeared on the following dates: September 18, 1977; November 16, 1973; June 20, 1973; November 16, 1973; October 15, 1972; April 20, 1971; and December 12, 1972.

17. See, for example, *Washington Post* articles published on: September 10, 1975; April 23, 1972; February 9, 1972; and January 25, 1972.

18. Bernard Beck, "The Military as a Welfare Institution," in Charles C. Moskos, *Public Opinion and the Military Establishment* (Beverly Hills: Sage Publications, 1971), pp. 137–40.

19. Charles C. Moskos, "The Enlisted Ranks in the All-Volunteer Army," in John B. Keeley, ed., *The All-Volunteer Force and American Society* (Charlottesville, Va.: University of Virginia Press, 1978), pp. 39–60.

20. Department of Defense, Office of the Assistant Secretary of Defense for Manpower, Reserve Affairs, and Logistics, *Use of Women in the Military*, 2d ed. (Washington D.C.: Office of the Assistant Secretary of Defense, September 1978), p. 1.

21. Karl Marx, " The Eighteenth Brumaire of Louis Bonaparte (1851)," in Robert C. Tucker, *The Marx-Engels Reader* (New York: W. W. Norton, 1978), p. 613.

22. Frederick Engels, quoted in Michell Barrett, *Women's Oppression Today: Problems in Marxist Feminist Analysis* (London: Verso, 1977) p. 161.

23. E. P. Thompson, *The Making of the English Working Class* (New York: Pantheon, 1963), p. 414.

24. Heidi Hartman, "Captialism, Patriarchy, and Job Segregation by Sex," in Martha Blaxall and Barbara Reagon, eds., *Women and the Workplace* (Chicago: University of Chicago Press, 1978), pp. 166–67.

25. Department of Defense, *Use of Women in the Military*, p. 1.

26. Ibid. In the early years of the all-volunteer force, the female labor pool was considered to be a free recruiting market for the Army. No specific resources were allocated to attain female recruiting objectives. However, the effects over time of increasing annual female recruiting objectives, raising enlistment standards, requiring women to enlist into nontraditional skills, and a generally tougher recruiting environment in fiscal year 1978 and fiscal year 1979 caused the Army to fall short of its recruiting objectives. Management actions were taken and the market was broadened, for example, by lowering female selection scores from 50 to 31. Nevertheless the Army was still unable to meet the fiscal year 1979 recruiting objective of 19,400 no-prior-service females. The Army achieved only 17,226 or 88.8 percent of that objective. For fiscal year 1980, the Army has provided guidance that the enlistment criteria for both men and women would be the same. This change will significantly enlarge the female market. See "Women in the Military: Hearings before the Military Personnel Subcommittee," Committee on Armed Services, U.S. House of Representatives, February 11, 1980, p. 114.

27. Jay Finnegan, "Worst Volunteer Recruiting: Army Short 16, 380," *Army Times*, October 22, 1979, p. 1.

28. Editors, "Average GI Reads at 9th Grade Level," *Army Times*, July 18, 1977, p. 1.

29. Department of Defense, Assistant Secretary of Defense for Manpower, Reserve Affairs, and Logistics, unpublished tabulations (March 1980).

30. *Army Times*, July 17, 1980, p. 1.

31. Ibid.; see also Andy Plattner, "More Recruits are 'Dummies,' " *Army Times*, March 10, 1980.

32. Ibid.

33. Robert F. McNown et al., *Economic Analysis of the All-Volunteer Force* (Boulder, Colo.: Discussion Papers in Economics, March 1980); see also Clifford Theis, "A Commentary on the Economic Analysis of the All-Volunteer Force," unpublished paper, Boston College, Department of Economics (January 1981).

34. Morris Janowitz and Charles C. Moskos Jr., "Racial Composition in the All-Volunteer Force: Policy Alternatives," *Armed Forces and Society* (1974): 109–23.

35. ABC Network, "The American Army: A Shocking State of Readiness," Thursday evening, April 20, 1978.

36. Editors, "Some COs Say the All-Vol Stinks," *Army Times*, May 9, 1977, p. 1.

37. Ibid.

38. Moskos, "Enlisted Ranks in All-Volunteer Army," p. 44.

39. Martin Binkin and Shirley J. Bach, *Women and the Military* (Washington, D.C.: The Brookings Institute, 1977), p. 56, Table 6-1.

It is important to observe 80% of the Army's sole parents are *men*. Soldiers on active duty can be involuntarily separated if the sole parent responsibilities cause them to be repeatedly absent, unable to perform prescribed duties, or not available for worldwide assignment. Policy changes effective in January of 1979 require soldiers who become sole parents while on active duty to be counseled by their commanders and to prepare a dependent care plan. See "Women in the Military: Hearings before the Military Personnel Subcommittee," p. 111.

40. Department of Defense Report System (RCS: DD-M (A) 1454, (unpublished tabulations, December 1978). High school dropout males constitute the major proportion of social control problems using any measure. In the second quarter of 1974, 65% of the Army

prisoners in correctional facilities lacked the high school diploma. In the same reporting period, 60% of the AWOL (absent without leave) soldiers were dropouts. Finally, 66% of the deserters were also in the high school dropout category.

41. General Bernard W. Rogers, Hearings for Reinstitution of Procedures for Registration under the Military Selective Service Act before the U.S. Senate Subcommittee on Manpower and Personnel, March 13, 1979, p. 50.

42. Editors, "Study Shows Extent of Drug, Alcohol Use," Army Times, December 15, 1980.

43. Arthur D. Little, "Drug Study," cited in Hearings on the Status of the All-Volunteer Force before the U.S. Senate Subcommittee on Manpower and Personnel, June 20, 1978, Appendix.

44. Binkin and Bach, Women and the Military p. 63. For a discussion of official military policy toward pregnancy, see "Women in the Military: Hearings before the Military Personnel Subcommittee", pp. 110–11.

In general, the Army views pregnancy as a temporary medical disability and not as a social control issue. The services do not have reliable data on the number of persons who are pregnant at any given time. Experience data show that the number of pregnant women soldiers (Army only) ranges from 3,000 to 3,500 worldwide, of which 1,600 to 1,700 are in Europe. Effective January 1, 1980, a policy approved by the Secretary of the Army will be implemented to selectively evacuate pregnant service members from overseas commands if general noncombatant evacuation is ordered.

45. James O'Connor, The Fiscal Crisis of the State (New York: St. Martin's Press, 1973), Introduction, p. 9.

46. Emma Rothschild, "Boom and Bust," review of Department of Defense, Annual Report, Fiscal Year 1981, in The New York Review of Books, April 3, 1980 p. 31.

47. Ibid.; see also "Contractors: The Top Ten," New York Times, January 11, 1981. The net value of government contracts for General Dynamics was 3.5 billion. For Tenneco, Raytheon, Grumman, Boeing, Hughes Aircraft, General Electric, United Technologies, and McDonnell Douglas, the value of defense contracts ranged from 1.0 to 3.2 billion dollars.

48. Martin Nolan, "American Defense Spending," review of James Fallow, American Defense Spending, in The New York Times Book Review, June 28, 1981, p. 9.

49. Testimony by Admiral Baldwin, U.S. Navy, Senate Subcommittee Hearings on Department of Defense Authorization for Appropriations for Fiscal Year 1980, Committee on Armed Services, U.S. Senate, Part 4, Subcommittee on Manpower and Personnel, April 4, 1979, p. 1,857.

50. Robert Handberg and Robert Bledsoe, "Shifting Patterns in the American Military Budget: An Overview," The Journal of Strategic Studies (December 1979): 349.

51. Senator Sam Nunn, Senate Subcommittee on The Cost of the All-Volunteer Force, U.S. Senate Subcommittee on Manpower and Personnel of the Committee on Armed Services, United States Senate, February 6, 1978, p. 54.

52. General Louis H. Wilson, Senate Subcommittee on the All-Volunteer Force, pp. 33–34.

53. General Bernard W. Rogers, Senate Subcommittee on the All-Volunteer Force, p. 28.

54. Admiral James L. Holloway, Senate Subcommittee on the All-Volunteer Force, p. 32.

55. Department of Defense, Use of Women in the Military, p. 1.

56. Adapted from Binkin and Bach, Women and the Military, Chap. 6, pp. 53–71.

57. Ibid., p. 71.

58. Guenther Roth and Claus Wittlich, Max Weber's Economy and Society: An Outline of Interpretative Sociology (New York: Bedminister, 1968), vol. 1, chap. 3, "The Types of Legitimate Domination," pp. 212–13.

59. Jürgen Habermas, "Legitimation Problems in the Modern State," essay in Communication and the Evolution of Society (Boston: Beacon Press, 1979), pp. 178–79.

60. Jacques Van Doorn, *The Soldier and Social Change: Comparative Studies in the History and Sociology of the Military* (Beverly Hills: Sage Publications, 1975), pp. 87, 98.

61. Jürgen Habermas, *Legitimation Crisis*, trans. Thomas McCarthy (Boston: Beacon Press, 1973), see Part 2.

62. George H. Gallup, *The Gallup Opinion Index* (February 1980), p. 9.

63. David Cortright, *Soldiers in Revolt: The American Military Today* (New York: Anchor, 1975); these incidents were drawn from Chapters One through Five.

64. Morris Janowitz, cited by Cortright, *Soldiers in Revolt*, p. 1.

65. Moskos, *Public Opinion and the Military Establishment*, Introduction, pp. xi–xiii.

66. Hon. Parren J. Mitchell (D, Md.), Testimony given in hearings on the Extension of the Draft and Bills Related to the Voluntary Force Concept and Authorization of Strength Levels, U.S. House of Representatives, Committee on Armed Services, Ninety-Second Congress, First Session, February 23, 1971.

67. Hon. Guy Vander Jagt, Hearings on the Extension of the Draft.

68. Kenneth Coffey, *Strategic Implications of the All-Volunteer Force: The Convention Defense of Central Europe* (Chapel Hill: University of North Carolina Press, 1978), p. 32.

69. Claus Mueller, *The Politics of Communication: A Study in the Political Sociology of Language, Socialization, and Legitimation* (New York: Oxford, 1973), p. 146.

70. Moskos, *Public Opinion and the Military Establishment*, pp. 271–72.

71. Mueller, *Politics of Communication*, pp. 146–47.

72. Editors, "Until ETS Does Us Part," *Army Times*, December 5, 1977, p. 1.

73. John W. Williams, "Dual-Career Military Families," in Edna J. Hunter, ed., *Military Families: Adaptation to Change* (New York: Praeger, 1978), p. 109.

74. Ibid.

75. Cortright, *Soldiers in Revolt*, pp. 155–59.

76. Quoted by Don Hirst, "Racial Tensions Ease in Military," *Army Times*, May 1, 1978.

77. Estimates were given to me in January of 1978 by the Human Relations Office, U.S. Army in Europe.

78. Bradwell v. Illinois, 83 U.S. (16 Wall.) 131 (1873).

79. Reed v. Reed, 404 U.S. 71 (1971).

80. Frontiero v. Richardson, 411 U.S. 677 (1973).

81. Rostker v. Goldberg, 453 U.S. ___ (1981).

82. The Supreme Court 1980–81 Term," *Harvard Law Review*, 95: 1 (November 1981): 171.

83. In the summer of 1981, I was denied access to data from the Assistant Secretary of Defense's office on the grounds that policies concerning the use of women were being reviewed.

84. George Gilder, quoted by the *Army Times*, April 7, 1980, p. 1.

85. General William C. Westmoreland, quoted in Binkin and Bach, *Women and the Military*, p. 50.

86. General John K. Singlaub, quoted by Jay Finnegan in "Singlaub Blasts Women," *Army Times*, July 1978, p. 1.

87. The letter signed by "Graham A. Bell" was sent in care of C. S. White, Esquire, Arlington, Virginia; a copy of this letter is available at the Arthur and Elizabeth Schlesinger Library, Harvard University, filed under Military Women in the clippings file.

88. Letter to the Editor, *Daily Oregonian*, February 2, 1978.

89. Richard Cohen, "It Drops Women to Less than Full Citizenship," *Boston Globe*, July 1, 1981.

Chapter Three

THE KHAKI-COLLAR WOMEN OF COMPANY C: THE SETTING AND BACKGROUND FOR THE STUDY OF FEMALE ENLISTED LIFE

The military community, which I will call Khaki Town, consists of four American military installations situated in West Germany, one hour by car east of the French border. Located one-half hour's drive from the nearest autobahn, this chiefly agricultural area has been continuously occupied by military forces since the late 1930s, when 22,000 acres were seized by the Army of the Third Reich for use as a tank battalion training grounds. Within a half hour of Khaki Town, General Rommel trained and inspected his elite tank corps. In 1945, the area was assigned to the French in the postwar occupation of Germany.

Today, nearly one in three persons within a twenty-five-mile radius of Khaki Town is an American soldier. The installations themselves are islands of American military culture amidst some of the finest farm and wine-producing land in West Germany. Since the early 1950s, when Americans assumed control of the area, the garrison community has evolved into a firmly entrenched outpost of American military culture. Khaki Town military units provide communications support for the more than 234,000 U.S. troops in Europe; the installations are also the center for tactical communications warfare. In addition, units of combat troops share the garrison with Signal Corps units.

The "Welcome to Khaki Town" orientation guide prepared by the Army Community Services Auxiliary states that large garrisons have occupied Khaki Town since 1,000 B.C.:

The Great Legions marched through the area and the Franks and Germans fought for its rule constantly. First burned by Croatian soldiers during the Thirty Years War, Khaki Town suffered the same fate twice more, in 1678 by Lothrenglan soldiers and in 1800 when it was almost totally destroyed.

Involved in World War II, the grounds were confiscated by Americans. With the presence of the U.S. Forces came job opportunities for the Germans.[1]

In this chapter I will describe the community setting of Khaki Town and the nature of the work performed by its soldiers. Khaki Town is described as a "garrison community," which isolates the American military community from German society. In addition, this chapter will compare the background characteristics of females and males who work together in 15 Signal Corps companies.

In order to study the social role of the female soldier, it is necessary to examine the culture in which both female and male soldiers live and work. Everett Hughes has commented that the study of ethnic relations must involve both the dominant and the minority group. To paraphrase Hughes, "If only women soldiers were studied, it would be similar to watching only one fighter in a boxing match!"[2] This chapter will attempt to distinguish which of the problems that military women face are due to sex-role tensions and which are due to the way life is organized in the Army.

KHAKI TOWN: THE SETTING

Wolfman Jack, the disc jockey of American Graffiti fame goes on the air every night at 9:00 following the news on the Armed Forces network. He broadcasts for the U.S. Army, a job he has performed for years. "The Wolfman" appeals to soldiers who speak in the restricted code of enlisted culture. He offers simplistic platitudes, military information, and an idealized view of the GIs' world and opportunities. His message resonates with the terms that only soldiers understand. He rehammers the clichés of military slang and colloquial speech along with words that are easily understood about the necessity to reenlist. In the early 1970s, he adopted jive talk and soul records: "Black is Beautiful, Man!" Today, he speaks in all of the tongues of enlisted culture:

When you all or yer loved ones, need civilian medical care, don't you worry. The services have worked out a program to help you. CHAMPUS. CHAMPUS is there to help you.
Take it from your old Uncle Wolfman [sinister chuckle], if your time is almost up, then it's time to reconsider, re-evaluate, re-enlist! Man *that* is the smart thing to do![3]

A stranger visiting West Germany for the first time is struck by the extent of the American military presence there. In southern Germany where Khaki Town is located, there are well over 200 American bases, and there are over 234,000 American soldiers and an additional 300,000 family members of soldiers living in West Germany. Nearly every German town over 5,000 has at least one American military attachment or "Kaserne," as termed by the Germans.

Khaki Town and other overseas bases were characterized as "boom-towns" by Charles Moskos in his study of the American enlisted man.[4] Charlotte Wolf variously referred to the American overseas military communities as "ethnic communal enclaves," "the gilded ghetto," "small alien islands of foreign culture," and "Little Americas" before settling on the term, "garrison community."[5]

The qualities of the garrison community were defined in the following way by Wolf in her study of the American base in Turkey:

> In these respects, the community in Ankara is not a microcosmic duplication of American life as lived in the United States, it is not a miniature of American society. It is not only alien to the Turkish world outside of it, but in many ways it is alien to the American society, as well. With the subordination of institutions and social values to military considerations, its ethos is that of the garrison community.[6]

As in the base described by Wolf, Americans living in Khaki Town are fully immersed in military life. In Khaki Town there was the story, perhaps apocryphal, of an officer who claimed that he never ventured off base during his three-year tour of Germany, and, in fact, it is entirely possible to conduct all normal business within the "recipe community."

Each base has similar facilities and similar routines. A person stationed in Khaki Town can shop at its newly constructed post exchange and commissary, which has the élan of a Star, Kroeger, or Piggly Wiggly supermarket chain. Budweiser and Michelob outsell Heineken and Löwenbrau at military Class V liquor stores in Europe. Military personnel and their families use their identification cards (IDs) as entrée to military doctors, chaplains, barbers, veterinarians, lawyers, and dentists. Residents support Army base football teams such as the Mad Dogs of Company C for the base's version of the Super Bowl. On some bases, intramural games are broadcast on the local radio stations of the Armed Forces radio network. In the spring and summer, Little League begins for the sons and daughters of soldiers, whether they be in Korea, Germany, or the Azores. Taped television serials such as "General Hospital" and "Soap" are broadcast throughout the world by the Armed Forces television network (AFN-TV).

There are only superficial differences among military installations whether they are in Brindisi, Italy; Karamursel, Turkey; or Hohenfels, West Germany. In Aviano, Italy, a smattering of Spanish architecture may be found, but the base is surrounded by the ubiquitous wall: barbed wire and military police guards. Inside the walls, soldiers buy the standard products in the familiar post exchange and commissary, receive the standard cold pack in the clinic, and live in quarters policed and maintained by the Department of Defense. Even the silverware and totally institutional plates are the same in the Frankfurt Army and Air Force Exchange Service (AAFES) cafeteria as they are in Khaki Town. There is a concerted effort to make each installation as interchangeable as the personnel who, on the average, stay at one base for only two years. Like Ford Motor parts, soldiers and their families are expected to plug in and plug out of their recipe communities with a minimum of interference with thier military jobs.

Each base tries to make the military cliché, "I found a home in the service," come true. Each recipe community has the same barracks, bowling alleys, crafts shops, all-faiths chapels, recreation centers, and nine-hole golf courses. Except for superficial interbase differences, each base offers the same undistinguished "home in the service."

The central facility of every base is the post exchange or PX. Adjacent to every PX is the ubiquitous Armed Forces fast-food cafeteria. Persons gather there for steak night every Tuesday, a major social event for military families. Overseas soldiers refer to the United States as the "Big PX." The PX is both a physical and symbolic boundary separating the overseas American soldier from the outside world. While German civilians can work on base in the cafeteria or in the motor pool, they cannot shop in the PX. PX privileges are denied to outsiders. For those who are qualified for the ID card, the PX is the closest thing to shopping in the United States.

Physically, the PX is often as large as a K-Mart or Korvette's; yet it is a general store offering a much wider variety of products and services than the ordinary chain store. An American soldier can order a Plymouth or a Ford from the PX. An American stationed abroad can buy a Black Forest cuckoo clock, crystal, or a Spanish sword in the PX, thus avoiding embarrassing encounters in a local language that is not understood. The PX offers discount prices in contrast to the local economies in which bases are located. Given the weakness of the dollar, many soldiers and their families do not have the option to shop in local German markets.

Sometimes low prices are maintained artificially at enormous expense to the government. It is reputed that "iceberg" lettuce is flown in weekly from California at $5 per head. The food commissaries are managed centrally but supervised by junior officers at the local base level. Service people are exhorted to buy American produce because it is cheaper and more reliable than local produce. However, in Khaki Town, the opposite was true. Produce was both cheaper and of higher quality in the local farmer's market. However, for most sundries, the PX's prices were lower and it was more convenient than excursions into strange host cultures.

In Khaki Town, long lines form at the American Express Banking

concession on payday. American Express has a monopoly on banking services on most bases in southern Germany. Unlike the Americans depicted
in the Company's ads, soldiers rarely purchase traveler's checks. The bulk
of American Express business is routine. Dollars are converted to deutsch
marks for rent and telephone bills if the soldier and his family live in the
Germany economy. Payroll checks are cashed. People sign up for the tours
for military personnel that American Express regularly offers to such spots
as Lourdes, Ephesus, and the Black Forest. All of these transactions are
carefully monitored by a military policeman with a M-16. Interestingly,
soldiers who have American Express cards from military installations are
not allowed the ordinary privileges of regular card carriers. The military
branches of American Express give fewer services to the soldier. Significantly, civilian American Express branches in European cities do not
honor military American Express cards.

Rank is a precise indicator of privilege on a military base. For officers,
the base is the America of middle-class memories: Sunday brunches at the
"O" Club (Officer's Club), Muzak in the golf shack, and polite policemen.
For the noncommissioned officer, there is bingo at the NCO Club, a
modest apartment or duplex, and softball on Saturday afternoons. Rank is
the absolute determinant of status, demeanor, and social distance as well
as home style. Rank determines each soldier's place in the military
community's matrix. There are a few exceptions to this system, that is, a
senior NCO may have more informal status in the work group than an
ROTC second lieutenant. All children go to the same "dependent's school."
Rank tends to replace other divisions commonly found in civilian society.
There is relatively little stratification by religion. The all-purpose chapel
serves the three standard faiths. There is less racial segregation both on and
off duty on military bases than in civilian society.

Recreation is inexpensive and accessible to all. In Khaki Town, there
are three movie theatres, four gymnasiums, a library, an educational
center, a stock-car racing track, a ceramics shop, a wood craft shop, two
swimming pools, two bowling alleys, and three recreation centers. Before
each movie at the Khaki Town theatres, all personnel are required to stand
for the national anthem.

Commanders, especially on overseas bases, have vast discretionary
authority, often exercising more control over the military community than
political machines, such as Mayor Daly in Chicago or Mayor Curley in
Boston. Overseas soldiers are free to locate their own apartment, but they
must receive command approval for the apartment rental contract or face
official military reprimand. The *Bulletin* of the Khaki Town Housing
Referral Office issued the following warning to the military community:
"Read the Off-Limits list carefully and don't deal with landlords upon
which restrictive sanctions have been imposed." In military society,

individuals who rent from unscrupulous landlords are themselves subject to punitive action through the Uniform Code of Military Justice!

Garrison life has features of the absolutist state. On one base where I resided, there were several complaints made to the commander about unleashed dogs. The base commander ordered that all unleashed dogs be shot on sight! A base commander has the authority to order seach and seizures, declare any dependent, civilian, or soldier *persona non grata*, or even to order a soldier and his or her family back to the United States.

Governed by the base commander, soldiers, civilians, and their families work, play, sleep, and reproduce under the same overall plan in the recipe community. Because of a severe housing shortage in West Germany, many junior enlisted personnel and noncommissioned officers and their families were compelled to live off base. However, this did not mean that these person were not under the same plan. Most off-base residents spent the majority of their on- and off-duty time on base. It was common, for example, to see young wives of junior enlisted men, afraid to be in their off-base apartments alone, spend their husband's work day playing cards in the cafeteria or watching reruns on the television at the recreation center. Families who lived in the Germany economy were required to have German telephone service so that they could be contacted during alerts, special details, field exercises, or invasion by the Soviets. Continual information regarding base activities was available through the local affiliate of the Armed Forces radio and television network, which was the only English language broadcast in the country. Even the milk cartons purchased at the commissary contained Wolfman Jack's message: "Re-consider, Re-evaluate, and Re-enlist!"

Barracks Life

Unmarried and lower ranked enlisted soldiers do not have the choice of whether to live on or off base. In Khaki Town, they were forced to live in barracks constructed in the 1930s by the Army of the Third Reich. These aesthetically shabby buildings were "Kaserne" housing intended to be temporary quarters for the duration of World War II.

My short visits in January of 1978 to the enlisted barracks revealed poor living conditions. While Khaki Town actually encompasses four installations, there was little variation in the housing conditions, regardless of the base. The following observations are from five visits to two barracks in the spring and summer of 1978.

Toilets were overflowing, clogged with debris, including rolls of toilet paper, cigarette butts, and beer cans. I observed runoff from the toilets, including feces, in the shower drain. In one toilet stall, (door missing) an individual had written "Fuck the Army" on the wall, using feces.

The heating system appeared to be inadequate, with little control over the distribution of heat. In some first floor rooms, the temperature was below 60 degrees; in other rooms, saunalike conditions prevailed. Doors were damaged reportedly by an individual named "Mad Dog," who ran amuck through the first floor with an SS saber that he drove through the doors. Another individual nicknamed "Ape-Shit" reputedly broke two doors with his fists. Although the floors were well polished and the interior covered with at least eighteen layers of drab olive and yellow paint, the building appeared to be structurally unsound. Major repairs were urgently needed on rotting windows, stairs, and the roof. Plaster hung precariously from the ceilings. Stair railings were rotten and broken in places. Windows could not be lowered or raised. Some windows were painted into place, but were seemingly unsecured by the frame. The last major repairs were conducted in the early 1970s as a part of the all-volunteer Army publicity campaign to improve living conditions.

Conditions were crowded, with three to six individuals to a room. There were no partitions or other boundaries separating individual living areas. Decor consisted of cheap tapestries, nude pinups from "girlie" magazines, psychedelic posters, and beer signs. Periodically, there were disputes between the occupants and inspecting officers as to the propriety of some of the posters, as "girlie" posters were forbidden by military regulations. The solution of the occupants was to remove potential contraband several days prior to and after announced inspections, and conflicts arose chiefly during unannounced barrack shakedowns.

There were few books in evidence. The only reading materials openly displayed were the Armed Force's unofficial *Stars and Stripes* newspaper, Mickey Spillane-type thrillers, pornographic magazines, and comic books. Comic books, particularly adventure and fantasy types, were the most widely displayed. *Stars and Stripes* bookstore employees in Khaki Town estimated that comic books were the best selling reading materials in the store. Significantly, comic books sold to enlisted men exceeded the sales to dependent children of soldiers.

Although I was not permitted to visit female enlisted quarters in Khaki Town, the following comments from unstructured interviews in January 1978 revealed that women, too, lived in substandard conditions:

People in the barracks are terribly discriminated against as far as privacy and overall living. Living conditions are terrible here. There needs to be more consideration for living facilities. Conditions here are shameful.

Our living quarters are terrible. We lack minimal privacy. We should have private rooms or apartment-style arrangements.

We should have fewer inspections of personal areas. There should be no shakedowns except for the purpose of recovering stolen property. We should really live in our own apartment away from the barracks. We should be given separate rations instead of mess hall meal cards. Women cannot take care of their special hygiene problems because there are no bathtubs in the units. NCOs have too much to say about our personal living business.

We in the barracks are repeatedly subjected to unnecessary interferences. I would like to live off post so I can resume life as a human being instead of being locked up like an animal.

I would move out of the billets or change barrack conditions for lower enlisted persons. We are crowded, lack privacy, and are subject to petty cleanup details. Single people get shafted by the Army in the barracks.

The total institutional features of Khaki Town barracks have their antecedents in the 19th century factories of towns such as Lawrence, Lynn, Lowell, and Waltham, Massachusetts. In the cotton and shoe industries, workers lived in barrack-like dwellings where they could be kept under continual scrutiny by employers. During the International Labor Union's organizational efforts, barracks and mills were patrolled by men with revolvers who were to shoot union organizers if they approached. Khaki Town barracks are patrolled by the military police and are under the arbitrary control of the base commander. The rationale for maintaining barracks living for junior enlisted persons is to keep them on base as much as possible. More continuous control can be maintained when the boundaries between work and private life are blurred. In a similar way, the barracks of 19th century Massachusetts company towns controlled the workers. As a 19th century labor historian described it, "Large dwellings were built in all the mill-yards for the knobstick spinners to reside in, because the employers were afraid to have them outside the mills."[7] In Khaki Town and on other bases, the Army feels that it is more rational to keep young enlisted soldiers on a short leash. By restricting contact with the outside, soldiers are continuously subject to military discipline and domination.

The Job: The Signal Corps

While soldiers stationed in the Khaki Town military community had a variety of occupations, the Signal Corps was the single most important component. Khaki Town was known by soldiers in Europe as having two distinctive characteristics. First, Khaki Town maintains the largest mortuary and cold storage area in Western Europe. The bodies of soldiers, civilians, and others attached to the American community are prepared and stored before being returned to the United States for burial, but Khaki

Town's distinctive ethos is as the center of telecommunications for the U.S. Army in Europe. The following excerpt from the Signal Corps' service magazine, *Army Communicator*, conveyed the importance of Khaki Town's Signal Corps work to the other military units in Europe: "Khaki Town's a busy place. The ____ Signal Corps is spread over 5,200 square kilometers and works with all Signal equipment found in the command."[8]

The Threat

> From my mother's sleep I fell into the State, and I hunched into its belly till my wet fur froze. Six miles from earth, loosed from its dream of life, I woke to black flak and the nightmare fighters. When I died they washed me out of the turret with a hose.
>
> —Randall Jarrell, 1945

The Signal Corps is an organic part of armored, infantry, and mechanized divisions. The battalion is part of the combined arms team and provides communications combat support for the division.[9] In general war, Signal Corps personnel would be killed from nuclear weapons, chemical, biological, and radiological agents. In limited war, Signal Corps personnel would be in the midst of action. If the Warsaw Pact tanks rolled over the East German border, Signal Corps units would provide tactical communications support.

In some Khaki Town military offices, there are large posters of muscular Soviet soldiers poised for attack, ready upon command to enter their tank turrets. The caption, "He's ready, Are you?" symbolizes the "threat" that is constantly mentioned in command briefings, conversations, and advertisements on the Armed Forces network. The Soviet threat is stressed in the orientation booklet, *Why We Are Here*, which each soldier receives upon his assignment:

> The Soviets have been building, in every category of military force, a powerful series of strategic and tactical weapons systems. Their military capabilities—as demonstrated by Soviet and Warsaw Pact land, sea, and air exercises give cause for disquiet by virtue of the moderness of their equipment, their increased tactical and strategic mobility, their preponderance in front-line divisions and armor, as well as their increased activity.[10]

All civilian and military personnel and their families are required to attend an orientation session when they arrive in Khaki Town. Included in this session are rules and regulations concerning the base as well as a talk on "the threat." In an orientation session that I attended, the officer in charge grimly observed:

If the Ruskies come over that border [pointing to a map] we will take the following action. First, you [civilians and soldiers' dependents] will be alerted by the base commander as to which flights you will take home. This will take place in an orderly and expeditious fashion. You will be transported at military expense to Rhein-Main [air base outside of Frankfurt]. So you should always have your passports and papers ready at hand in event of emergency.

[At this point the officer was interrupted by an astonishingly obese woman in the back of the room seated with her two preschool children.] "What about our dogs and cats? Will they also be flown at military expense?"

Without blinking, the officer said in a slow and deliberate tone: "No, your pets will have to stay." At that point, there were several groans and loud weeping from the woman. She wailed in a muffled tone, "My poor, poor Fifi!"

The evacuation of military and civilian dependents would be no small accomplishment, as there were over 300,000 family members of military personnel in Germany alone in 1978. The threat of Soviet invasion and ultimate nuclear war was nearly universally felt by military personnel in Khaki Town. In the questionnaire (Appendix B) that I administered to Khaki Town's soldiers in the spring of 1978, to be described later in this chapter, 71.2 percent of the 141 male soldiers either strongly agreed or agreed with the statement that "Thermonuclear war is likely"; 48 out of 91 female soldiers, or 53 percent, agreed or strongly agreed with this statement.

The imminence of the Soviet threat is continually reinforced by posters, radio advertisements, orientation sessions, and field exercises. The orientation booklet continues:

You are one of about 191,000 U.S. Army Europe soldiers here to defend the United States as far forward as possible. The United States sees Western Europe as a partner in promoting political values and social and economic ideas, while Western Europe turns to the U.S. for leadership...
The basic mission of your command is to maintain a combat-ready force...How are we defending our homeland by stationing forces in Europe? Our presence in Europe is both a warning and a commitment from our country to other free world countries that America can be counted on to support freedom and fight aggression if war should occur...You form the standard by which our allies measure their own military and political commitments to security.[11]

Soldiers in Khaki Town did not always appear poised for attack. American soldiers, especially "heads" and "goons" expressed quite an opposite mood when off duty in the German towns amidst Khaki Town. It was a common sight to see junior enlisted personnel wearing "Fuck the Army" or "Reefer Madness" T-shirts while walking the streets with stereo tape players blasting songs such as "Daddy Kool."

It was common to see groups of male GIs leering at German females and elderly German couples staring back at the GIs. For the German civilians who operated shops in the villages amidst Khaki Town, the GI represented an easy prey. Prostitutes waited in Mercedes outside Army posts on payday. Many soldiers preferred to find women in the Eros Center of Khaki Town. The Eros Center was a legally operated sex hotel in which there were floors of women in cubicles. For 40 deutsch marks ($25) a soldier could have a woman for 30 minutes. A typical weekend for other enlisted men was a trip to Nuremberg, where most soldiers stayed at the military operated Bavarian-American Hotel (BA Hotel). The BA was within easy walking distance of the Wall (prostitution section) and also of McDonald's where men could find women and Big Macs only 350 feet apart.

A German resident of Khaki Town once told me, "You Americans have taken crime off the streets and sent it to Germany." While it is not the purpose here to assess German-American interactions, it should be observed that American soldiers did not experience German society either as tourists or as potential immigrants. Most U.S. soldiers were thought of as outcasts by most Germans. A common expression was that GIs and guest-workers (gastarbeiters) were the only poor people in Germany. Few soldiers experienced German culture in a positive, sustained way. Set apart from the Germans as pariahs, soldiers' lives revolved around the garrison community. The current status of the GI in Germany is the reverse of the situation immediately after World War II. Then American soldiers were among the only "rich" persons in West Germany.

The work in Signal Corps military occupations is difficult and tedious. Because these units support armored and infantry divisions, Signal Corps soldiers participate in extensive war games. According to the Department of Army field manual on the Signal Corps, the following tasks and capabilities are to be performed by soldiers in that specialty:

1. Command multichannel telephone and teletypewriter circuits from echelons of division headquarters to division artillery; support command, aviation battalion, and other major subordinate units.
2. Internal communication facilities for command posts.
3. Internal communication facilities for support of command post and forward area signal centers.
4. Field wire and/or cable construction from support command posts to forward areas of signal centers.
5. Radio teletypewriter terminal operation and maintenance in designated radio net areas.

6. Division motor messenger service.
7. Photography for the division.
8. Direct cryptologistics support of the division.
9. Radio wire integration for all echelons.[12]

Since the Signal Corps is considered to be a combat-support activity, its members are required to be trained with weapons. The following statement from the *Signal Corps' Field Manual* affirms the combat support role: "Each individual of the signal battalion is trained to fight as an infantryman when required. The battalion, therefore, has some capability of defending itself against hostile ground attack."[13]

WHY THE SIGNAL CORPS WAS CHOSEN
FOR THIS STUDY

Beginning in 1973, the U.S. Army opened most combat-support roles to women.[14] In January of 1976, directives from the Department of the Army required all women soldiers to qualify for training with the M-16 rifle.[15] Because women were increasingly assigned to the military police, signal corps, transportation, and other field units, training with weapons became necessary in order for women to defend themselves and their outfits in emergency situations. At the time of the study, 46,000 women had enlisted in the Army; 5 percent of these women were in combat-support units such as the Signal Corps. The general expansion of women in the military that started in 1973 increasingly included women soldiers in traditionally male areas. This trend reflected and paralleled the recruiters' inability to find enough male accessions to fill these jobs.

In 1975, the first women were sent to Khaki Town to be integrated into previously all-male Signal Corps units. From all accounts, the experience of the first women was largely negative. From 1975 to the period of the study in 1978, nearly 300 women had been assigned to field and labor-intensive military jobs. Compared with previous assignments for women soldiers were expected to live in tents and experience combatlike volved from 30 to 60 days of field exercises each year, during which women soldiers were expected to live in tends and experience combatlike conditions in the same fashion as men. During war games, women were expected to assemble heavy telecommunications antennas, carry tool chests, change tires on two and a half ton trucks, and use electronic equipment in rough terrain, often in inclement weather and conditions of wind, rain, or snow.

The study of how women adapted to Signal Corps jobs in Khaki Town is interesting because combat-support jobs involved more physical and psychological demands than jobs in administration and nursing. The consequences of female military participation in previously masculine domains has important implications for the study of both military and blue-collar women.

In the spring and summer of 1978, I conducted both structured and unstructured interviews with 91 female soldiers and 141 male soldiers assigned to Signal Corps companies. The goal of this study was to explore in depth insights into the world views of the respondents. The goal of the field work was to gain from both male and female soldiers an understanding of the actions and events concerning female participation in Khaki Town.

To supplement the unstructured interviews and observations, each soldier answered a questionnaire that assessed the following areas: (1) background information about the respondent and family, (2) attitudes toward specific military job characteristics, (3) sex-role attitudes and perceptions of military women, and (4) perception of the seriousness of social problems of military life. (The questionnaire appears in Appendix B.) Together the field notes, questionnaires, and observations serve as an ethnographic record of life in Khaki Town in the spring of 1978.

THE MEN AND WOMEN OF KHAKI TOWN: THEIR BACKGROUND

Results from this sample support Moskos' 1978 Congressional testimony that the enlisted Army diverges widely from civilian society in social representativeness.[16] For both sexes, respondents were disproportionately Southern, and of minority race and lower social class origin. Both sexes were more likely than the U.S. population as a whole to identify themselves as members of nonstandard Protestant religious groups such as the Nazarenes and African-Methodists versus standard Protestant or Catholic religions. Although the majority of the sample identified themselves as members of the working or lower middle class at age 16, 16.3 percent of the females and 46 percent of the males identified their class of origin as lower or upper lower class.

Finally, the females in this sample were younger than the males and had a lower modal rank. The modal rank for males was a sergeant or sergeant first class (E-5 or E-6), while the modal rank for females was corporal (E-4); 21 (23 percent) of the females were in supervisory positions (E-5 or E-6), as compared with 74 percent of the males. However, the junior noncommisioned officers (E-5 or E-6) were often only supervisors at the team or platoon level. A team in Khaki Town ranged from 5 to 10 persons, while platoons averaged 20 persons. Senior non-

TABLE 3.1. Background Characteristics of Khaki Town's Men and Women

	Females (91)(%)	Males (141)(%)
1. Region of the country		
East	15 (16.5)	22 (15.6)
Midwest	17 (18.7)	18 (12.8)
South	31 (34)	76 (53.9)
West	28 (30.8)	25 (17.7)
2. Race		
Caucasian	60 (66)	96 (68)
Black	25 (27.5)	36 (25.5)
Hispanic	6 (6.5)	9 (6.4)
3. Social class		
Lower lower	11 (12.8)	48 (35.6)
Upper lower	3 (3.5)	14 (10.4)
Working	12 (14.0)	13 (9.6)
Lower middle	22 (25.6)	19 (13.5)
Middle	28 (32.6)	32 (22.7)
Upper middle to upper	15 (16.5)	15 (10.6)
4. Religious preference		
Standard Protestant	21 (23.1)	14 (9.9)
Catholic	13 (14.3)	25 (17.7)
Nondenominational	41 (45.1)	77 (54.6)
None	16 (17.6)	25 (17.7)
5. Age		
18–20	29 (31.9)	0 (0)
21–24	33 (36.3)	34 (24.1)
24–29	21 (23.1)	44 (31.2)
Above 30	8 (8.8)	63 (44.7)
6. Rank		
E-1—E-3 (privates)	30 (33)	0 (0)
E-4 (corporals)	40 (44)	10 (7.1)
E-5—E-6 (junior noncommisioned officers)	21 (23)	104 (74)
E-8—E-9 (senior noncommisioned officers)	0 (0)	25 (17.7)

Source: Women in the Military Questionnaire (Appendix B), Spring 1978 (compiled by the author).

commissioned officers (E-7 to E-9) would be classified exclusively as supervisors and would be responsible for groups from 50 to 100 persons; 18 percent of the males were senior noncommissioned officers (NCOs). There were no female senior NCOs in the sample.

While the sample does not contain adequate numbers of female noncommissioned officers, it accurately reflects an Army-wide problem of few noncommissioned female officers. In 1976, the Department of the Army reported that less than 1 percent of its enlisted females held senior noncommissioned positions; 15 percent of the females in the Army were in the junior noncommissioned officer ranks (E-5 or E-6). Thirty-five percent of the females were in the corporal rank (E-4), while 48 percent were in the private grades (E-1, recruit; E-2, private; and E-3, private first class). Table 3.1 reflects a reasonably representative distribution of females in the enlisted ranks when compared with Army-wide statistics. For males, the sample is skewed toward junior NCO ranks. The modal rank for males in the sample was E-5 as compared with E-4 for the Army as a whole. Because males in the study had a higher rank than females, there are problems in separating the effects of sex differences alone from the effects differences in rank. However, this study seeks to develop analytical rather than statistical generalizations. The soldiers who were studied constituted a natural work setting that generally paralleled what might be found in an Army-wide study.

While all soldiers were actually trained in telecommunications work, only 55 of the 91 women soldiers were performing such duties at the time of the study. Of the women, 27 were assigned out of their primary military occupation to traditionally female work in the medical and clerical areas (pink-collar military jobs). Ten other women were first-line supervisors and performed "khaki-collar" Signal Corps work as a part of their job. Most of the males were line supervisors who also performed khaki-collar work.

Soldiers of both sexes participated in the following kinds of activities when assigned to communications units: (1) maintenance of trucks, vans, and generators; (2) installation of telephone cable, field switchboards, and tactical communications equipment; (3) operation of radios, switchboards, and generators in "war games"; and (4) preparation of teletype communications equipment for actual wars.

The Women of Khaki Town

Previous Civilian Jobs and Attitudes toward Enlistment

One generalization that can be made, based on a comparison of males' and females' previous civilian jobs with the actual military jobs held in Khaki Town, is that a sex difference exists. Males tended to have held

TABLE 3.2. Signal Corps Jobs Held by the Soldiers of Khaki Town

	Males	Females
I. Khaki-collar specialties		
(truck maintenance, wheel vehicle mechanic, general mechanic, generator mechanic, radio equipment maintenance, microwave systems repair, wiremen, linemen, machinist, multichannel radio communications, carrier operator, military security, voice interceptor, miscellaneous jobs in telecommunications)	29	55
II. Pink-collar specialties		
(clerk-typist, training, drug-alcohol, reenlistment counseling, switchboard operator in garrison, training clerk, cook, personnel management, supply dispatcher, radio operations in garrison, equal opportunity office)	4	27
III. Exclusive supervisors		
(first-line squad, platoon, and company supervisors)	108	9
Total	141	91

Source: Women in the Military Questionnaire (Appendix B), Spring 1978 (compiled by the author).

unskilled and semiskilled blue-collar jobs in the civilian economy while females made the transition from predominantly service jobs.

Table 3.3 lists all of the previous jobs held by Khaki Town's female soldiers. An inspection of this table reveals that many were discouraged workers or workers able to find only seasonal or part-time employment. Discouraged workers are classified as workers who have looked for work but could not find a job or who believe there is no work available. Because discouraged workers do not actively seek employment since they feel they lack the necessary skills, they are not included in the unemployment statistics. Part-time employees who believe there is no full-time work available or those who feel they lack the necessary skills for satisfying employment can also be considered "discouraged" workers. For the years 1975–77, when most of the women in the sample were recruited, the overall jobless rate in the United States averaged 16.7 percent for single females between the ages of 18 and 25.[17]

Therefore, a reasonable case could be made that the women in the

TABLE 3.3.   Job Histories of Khaki Town's Army Women

Respondent No.	All Jobs in Chronological Order Prior to Enlistment in the Army
001	Waitress, secretary
002	Credit collector, secretary
003	Cook, Woolworth's saleslady
004	Volunteer work, lifeguard, Brownie leader
005	Waitress, secretary, credit collector, assistant retail manager
006	Sewing factory worker, college dining facility worker
007	Car hop at A&W root beer stand, salesclerk, babysitter
008	Clerk-typist, social worker's assistant, assembly-line worker
009	Roller rink manager, disc jockey at small radio station
010	Salesgirl, typist, clerk
011	Jewelry store polisher, machinist
012	Store clerk, mail and duplicating room clerk
013	Farm worker
014	Key punch operator, summer resort assistant, tutor
015	Cook, clerical worker
016	Taco Bell cook, Jack-in-the-Box waitress, factory work, secretary, farm work
017	High school teacher, restaurant hostess
018	Secretarial work, temporary worker, part-time work as office worker
019	Enlisted immediately after high school
020	Printer's assistant, waitress
021	Waitress, nurses' aide, office clerk
022	Waitress, cook, factory worker in Standard Mills, Thatcher Carpet factory worker
023	Librarian assistant, salesperson, hostess in night club
024	Salesclerk, hospital clerk
025	Cashier, dishwasher, sales clerk
026	Tropical fish store clerk, department store clerk
027	Craft instructor, librarian assistant, recreational aide
028	Nurses' aide, veterinarian's assistant
029	Blueprint assistant, accounting clerk, typist
030	Typist
031	Typist, barmaid, retail sales
032	Office jobs, accounting clerk, typist

033	Customer relations in small industry and bank teller, shampoo girl, inventory girl for department store, waitress, short-order cook, tutor, salesclerk, credit bureau reporter
034	Shampoo girl, beautician
035	X-ray technician
036	Farm worker, cashier, housewife
037	Laundry worker, waitress, worked with handicapped children, public sales, truck driver, motor-route operator
038	Factory work, unemployment
039	Farm work; teacher's aide; folder, cutter, and packer in factory; gas pumper; secretary
040	Single mother
041	Dishwasher, food handler, key-punch operator, nightclub performer
042	Babysitter, housekeeper, waitress, assistant manager of department store
043	Waitress, coach of high school gymnastics team
044	Factory worker, housewife, sales person, cocktail waitress
045	Day-care center worker
046	Waitress, housekeeper, bus girl
047	Cook, waitress, salesclerk, teacher's aide, department store advertiser
048	Typist
049	Teller and janitor in movie theatre, babysitter
050	Sander of furniture, waitress, babysitter
051	Unemployed, part-time babysitting
052	Unemployed
053	Clerk and sales
054	Unemployed from factory work, part-time babysitter
055	Food service worker
056	Unemployed; previous job, assembly work
057	Page in public library, medical records specialist, insurance clerk, cashier in medical clinic
058	Helper in lumber store, clerk
059	Waitress
060	Never employed, enlisted a year after high school graduation
061	Waitress

Continued

TABLE 3.3 *(continued)*

Respondent No.	All Jobs in Chronological Order Prior to Enlistment in the Army
062	Secretary, waitress
063	Waitress
064	Cleaned offices, babysitting
065	Neighborhood Youth Corps, hamburger stand, television repair, librarian assistant
066	Custodian in school, unemployment
067	Cosmetology, dental assistant, dispatcher for state highway patrol
068	Potato chip company
069	Enrolled immediately after high school
070	College student
071	Butcher, typist, cashier
072	Short-order cook in hamburger joint, bookkeeper, typist
073	Telephone sales solicitor, barmaid
074	Secretary
075	Full-time student at community college
076	Computer operator
077	Factory work, sales work, nurses' aide
078	Waitress, cashier
079	Tour guide, clerk-typist, teachers' aide
080	Cashier at grocery store, drug store, hardware store; assistant manager of Rexall Drug Store
081	Hotel maid, clerk, cashier
082	Pizza Hut and Howard Johnson's waitress cocktail waitress, performer in nightclub
083	Cashier, cook
084	Laundress
085	Waitress
086	Never employed
087	Teacher, job interviewer, job counselor, sewer inspector, stocking model, file clerk, research assistant
088	Farm worker, factory work, typist
089	Night operator for doctor's answering service, emergency room receptionist, admitting clerk, cashier at hospital
090	Enrolled immediately after high school
091	Factory work, unemployment

Source: Compiled by the author.

sample were predominantly economic conscripts. While the background statistics are helpful in constructing broad patterns of social origin, it is necessary to turn to unstructured interviews to learn in detail why these women chose to join the Army. Was it true that women were attracted by military ad compaigns or did they enter the Army only after all else had failed? Did the women view the military as an equal opportunity employer or as an employer of last resort?

Previous Employment Opportunities

Unstructured interviews with the female soldiers of Khaki Town substantiate the claim that many were "economic conscripts." With little prospect for advancement, many thought the military would offer them steady employment and a career. This pattern is evident in the following comments. From an administrative clerk from Reno, Nevada:

> My only previous jobs were knick-knack jobs. I worked as a carhop at A & W, as a part-time sales clerk at Woolworth's and as a babysitter. I thought that I would have a real job if I enlisted. I was excited about the prospect of a real job.

A microwave systems repair person from Jamestown, New York recalls her motives for joining in this way:

> I wanted to go in because I wanted a job, any job. My mother did not want me to because I would be doing a man's job. I didn't care. I just wanted a job.

That women saw the military as a means of obtaining steady employment was evident from the following recollections of radio repair persons from Texas and Georgia:

> I wanted to get away from a boring small town with no job. Our town was near the one shot in the "Last Picture Show," so you can get the feeling that there was little future for me there.

> I really didn't do anything. After high school I did some babysitting. That's about all. Thought I'd try the military.

Other women in the sample had been able to find steady employment in the secondary or tertiary sectors. However, these women felt that there was little opportunity in these jobs. For these women, enlistment in the Army with the promise of educational and training benefits was an attractive alternative to a monotonous and demeaning job. From a 28-year-old sergeant from Alabama:

I worked at a jewelry store polishing jewelry on a machine. I thought that there was more I should get from life than that.

A switchboard operator from North Carolina who was a corporal reiterated similarly:

I had previously worked in a sewing factory and hated it. Next, I worked in a college dining facility at North Carolina State University and felt humiliated by that line of work. I joined the Army so I could work at something where I would amount to something.

The words of a 24-year-old squad supervisor from Washington State, who had worked in sales before joining, are also expressive of the theme that women soldiers' previous employment was without career lines:

I wanted to change my life and to learn more about people. I wanted a change in pace where I could have a chance to perform a job. My ex-civilian boss encouraged me to join the military. He said that "a bright girl like you shouldn't be doing this type of work and the military might just be the place for you." The Army offered schooling and travel. The parents couldn't afford any money for these things, so I joined.

The women's persistence in seeking employment was evident from both the list of their previous jobs and their descriptions of their job histories. A 23-year-old radio repair person from Wilmington, Delaware, was one who managed to find temporary work in a number of low-paying areas:

Previously, I worked as a laundry drudge, a waitress, a truck driver, and gas station attendant. I wasn't afraid of hard work. I also worked as a telephone solicitor for pots and pans. I never found a job with a future. My parents didn't want me to join because they thought I would become a man. I told them I didn't really have a choice. At least the Army was some type of career.

A female staff sergeant from rural North Carolina was another woman whose work history included a series of routine, monotonous jobs. She joined the Army in the hopes of finding greater life chances:

I worked as a farmer, folder, cutter, and packer. Neither farm work or factory work gave me any pay or respect. I even tried pumping gas. The result from all of these jobs was that I wanted a change. I was very bored and thought the Army would be a real job with a real challenge.

A 40-year-old sergeant from West Virginia had previously worked for a potato chip factory and at Shakey's Pizza Parlor. Her words spotlight the limited choices that many enlisted women in the sample experienced in civilian life:

> I suppose that I could have got married and found someone to support me. But no, I had pride. I worked at anything I could find because I wanted to. I joined the military because I wanted something more rewarding and challenging and something which would give me job security. In my previous jobs, I used only a small portion of my intelligence. I thought that maybe I could do better if I joined the Army.

When women were asked to list their reasons for joining the Army in the structured questionnaire, the following factors were listed most frequently as the reason for enlistment:

1. Education or training, 30 (33 percent)
2. Money or job, 21 (23 percent)
3. Travel, 10 (11 percent)
4. Personal growth, 10 (11 percent)
5. Negative reasons, such as boredom, 6 (7 percent)
6. Patriotism, 4 (4 percent)
7. New experience, 4 (4 percent)
8. Peer pressure, 1 (1 percent)
9. No one reason or didn't know, 5 (6 percent)

The unstructured interviews confirmed the findings of the structured questionnaire. Table 3.4 lists reasons given by Army women for their enlistment, derived from the unstructured interviews. Women in this sample joined the Army only after they were unable to hold their own in the civilian economy. The women of Khaki Town were from predominantly lower and working class families. A young woman from Clifty, Arkansas, or Humboldt, Minnesota, with limited resources for education or a decent job might find the idea of equal pay for equal work in the military attractive. Advertisements picturing travels to Munich, Rome, and Cannes proferred a more attractive future than life on the assembly line, in a small town, or in an early marriage. Army women were aware of their dispensability in a developed economy. In a sense, military service was a last resort. To many of the women in the sample, enlistment was also an escape from the welfare rolls. James O'Connor characterizes the limited life chances of unskilled labor-power, as derived from membership in a surplus population:

> Unable to gain employment in the monopoly industries by offering their laborpower at lower than going wage rates (and victimized by sexism and

TABLE 3.4. Why Khaki Town Women Joined the Army

001	Travel, GI bill
002	Education and independence
003	Education, travel, and self-discipline
004	Search for independence
005	Travel, to get away from home, to get to meet new people
006	To make something of my life
007	Looked for a significant job, pay, equal rights
008	To find a steady paycheck, to use my brain
009	Benefits, a challenge, opportunities, satisfaction
010	Education
011	Travel, education
012	Money and a good time
013	Travel, new experiences
014	Travel, GI bill
015	Education, independence
016	Education, travel, and self-discipline
017	Travel, to get away from home
018	To make something of my life and to be happy
019	GI bill, benefits
020	Good pay, security
021	Pride in the military, a chance to prove myself
022	GI bill, leadership potential, and personal development
023	Travel and a need for change in my life
024	Freedom from a bad marriage, a new life
025	A chance to improve myself and to meet new people
026	Freedom from home, desire for responsibility
027	Not able to find a job on the outside, benefits
028	Training, travel, and military benefits
029	For a career and to further my education
030	To gain a skill, to better myself
031	To do something different, to better myself
032	Temporary insanity
033	A job, benefits, travel opportunities, to learn about different people
034	Because I wanted to serve my country
035	Educational opportunity
036	Educational opportunity
037	To travel and to live in Europe
038	Responsibility and freedom
039	Education and benefits
040	To change my life, try something different
041	For a job

042	Tired of my civilian job
043	My recruiter
044	Travel, education
045	To obtain a college degree
046	Educational benefits, GI bill
047	Education, travel, and experience
048	Dissatisfied with the lack of challenge in my life, no job on the outside
049	An opportunity to improve myself
050	In order to change my life
051	To see Europe, military benefits
052	In order to go to college on duty, travel
053	Escape from a small town
054	Independent living situation
055	To find a career
056	A chance to improve myself
057	Travel, to see new places and meet new people
058	To find a job, to find happiness, to be independent
059	Not too sure why I joined, maybe my recruiter lied to me
060	A chance for a steady paycheck, a job
061	Travel and change
062	Had no skills, wanted a job
063	Like the old movies about the military, Dad talked me into it
064	Freedom from home
065	Desire for responsibility
066	A chance to leave home
067	Desire to meet new people and see new places
068	Travel, education, benefits
069	Training, travel, the GI bill
070	For a career, to further education
071	To further my education, benefits
072	Was looking for a challenge and a way to serve my country
073	No job or experience, nothing left to do
074	Good pay, benefits, secure job, a chance to better my life
075	Military life seemed attractive
076	Skills, training, education
077	To get dental work done, benefits
078	Uncertain, don't know why I joined
079	Career and school
080	To get money for college

Continued

TABLE 3.4 (continued)

081	Thought I would enjoy military life
082	Travel and education
083	Couldn't make enough money for my own apartment on the outside, military pay
084	GI bill, I was only 18 and didn't think about joining long enough
085	GI bill, travel
086	To get job experience and education
087	To escape from a bad marriage
088	Travel, education
089	To learn a skill
090	Advancement, freedom from parents
091	Education and housing loans after my term

Source: Compiled by the author.

racism), and unemployed, under-employed, or employed at low wages in competitive industries, the surplus population increasingly becomes dependent on the state.[18]

"They'll Turn You into a Man": The Parents' View

Women were asked to recollect their parents' attitudes toward their enlistment. The question was advanced in order to determine the amount of support that women received from their families for their decision to enlist in the Army. Did parents perceive the Army as "a great place to start" or did they feel that the Army "was no place for a woman"?

For 19 women, both parents were negative and unable to support their daughters' decisions to enlist, according to unstructured interviews. In ten other cases, the father was supportive while the mother was either neutral or negative concerning the enlistment decision. In 14 cases, the mother was supportive while the father was either neutral or negative to their daughter's decision to join the Army; 14 other women reported that both parents were primarily supportive of their decisions to enlist.

In addition, eight women replied that they enlisted without consulting either parent, three women stated that they were raised in orphanages, three women reported that they were residents of detention or foster homes, four women reported that their parents didn't care either way, and four women stated that their parents favored enlistment but preferred that their daughters had joined the Air Force or Navy. The remaining 15 women indicated that their parents were either dead or unaware of their enlistment, or they could not recall their parents' views.

For many women, limited family resources were a definite factor in their enlistment decision. Some women felt compelled to join so that there would be "one less mouth to feed." Given this pattern, enlistment for many women must have been a choice reflective of the dual problems of limited job opportunities and limited family resources. A telecommunications specialist from Wisconsin expressed her family's support of her decision in this way:

> My oldest brother influenced me when he said, "The only way to get out of Madison is to join the military." I had worked at Kentucky Fried Chicken and made signs for department stores, but it wasn't enough to finance my college education. I made it through two years of college, but was tired of the hassle. My parents couldn't help me. They didn't have much money and other kids at home needed them. I just couldn't see living under them any longer. My parents were the first to mention the military to me, even before my brother did. One June, Dad came into the kitchen and right out of nowhere said, "Why don't you join the military?" I told him, I didn't want anything to do with no military, but I checked it out secretly. I liked my recruiter, and here I am in the Army.

A telecommunications specialist chose to accent the positive when she spoke about her parents' attitudes:

> Dad thought the military would give me a chance to travel and see the world. He had been in World War II and loved it. While I was growing up, he used to tell me and my brother his war stories over and over again. I don't think he really wanted his little girl to leave home, but on the other hand, he was happy for me to have the opportunity to serve. I joined the Army less than a month after high school graduation.

Recollections of other women remembering positive family attitudes included the following:

> My parents were enthusiastic. They encouraged me to join . . . They thought I could get more education with the help of military benefits.

> My parents believed it would be an excellent opportunity for positive personal growth.

> Mother encouraged me. I was closer to mother. My father wasn't around much when I was growing up. I didn't ask his advice.

> My parents were proud.

> My father was proud of my decision.

My fiancé, then my mother encouraged me. My mother was proud. My father had died by the time I signed up.

My parents thought it was wonderful that I would get to travel and get additional schooling.

Other Parental Fears

Two patterns of parental resistance to the enlistment of their daughters were found. First, parents felt that the Army would make a man out of their daughter. Sex-role strains were a major source of concern. Secondly, some parents also feared that the Army was an occupation that would retard their daughter's education and development.

Sex-role concerns were by far the most frequent source of parental opposition, as expressed to these women:

Dad didn't approve because he thought I was too feminine to adapt to the military way of life.

They thought the Army was unsuitable for a woman.

They believed the Army was a man's world. My mother didn't want me to go in because she said it was a man's job.

Mom cried 'cuz her "baby" was leaving.

My father opposed the idea. I was closer to my mother, though. His fears were for his little girl. He wasn't around while I was growing up. He tried to enter into my life then, but I told him, "I don't want your advice. You keep your trap out of it."

My parents told me, "It was your mistake. Women should have women's jobs."

Dad didn't want me to join because of the men that would be trying to jump on my body!

My parents had fears at first about me going because of certain groups of guys who would hound me and try to jump on my bones.

My parents said that I lacked self-respect and would sleep with every man and give the family a bad name.

My parents let me know that it wasn't their choice that I join the Army with all of those men.

A second pattern of opposition was concern that the Army would be a waste of their daughters' skills and talents. The following accounts are representative of this theme:

> Father thought I would be wasting my life, but he said he would stand behind my decision.

Another corporal recalled that her parents had let her know that it wasn't their desire to see her wasting her education by "rotting away in the Army." A radio operator expressed a similar view:

> My parents let me know it wasn't their choice, but they are in general happy if I am.

Other parental patterns not specifically reflective of either sex-role or talent dissipation fears were broadly representative of the ambivalence of families:

> My parents opposed the idea, but I was on my own and they respected my independence.

> I didn't tell my parents until after I joined. They were not thrilled with the prospect of having a daughter in combat boots!

> My parents were uncertain as to the Army, but it was a great relief to have me out of the house.

> Dad was unsure, but wanted me to do whatever would make me happy.

> It took my mother a long time to accept my decision. My father said he would stand behind me, no matter what.

Still other women appeared to have other sources of parental reluctance:

> The Lord told me to join. He supported me, but my parents were upset.

> Both my parents opposed my enlistment, but since I've joined, they've both died of cancer. Before their deaths, my brother and sister managed to get me written out of the will. I haven't heard from anyone in my family since.

> I don't really know what my parents had in mind for me. I could never find a decent job before joining. They didn't encourage me and they didn't stop me. They told me it was all right by them if I joined the Army.

No one encouraged me to join the Army. My parents attitude was 'comsi-comsa'. Now they like the idea that their daughter is a sergeant, wow!

The accounts of civilian jobs and family attitudes are useful for their portrayal of these women's prior opportunities. Not surprisingly, however, the males of Khaki Town were also from predominantly lower and working class origins.

The Men of Khaki Town

We all know that today's Army is better trained, better equipped, and better paid than ever before. But we sometimes forget that an army is only as good as its people. We're doing our best to bring in the best people. We should all be doing our best to keep them.
— Army recruitment advertisement, July 1977

A number of sources, including structured questionnaires, unstructured interviews, and field observations, confirmed that many of Khaki Town's male soldiers were from lower and working class origins. Table 3.5 lists all previous jobs held by male soldiers prior to enlistment. The men in this sample had a pattern of sporadic employment in secondary and tertiary sectors, similar to the women. Unstructured interviews with the men confirmed the same chronology of unfulfilled expectations with civilian jobs.

From a 27-year-old first sergeant, who was the son of assembly line workers at General Motors:

I couldn't find a job before entering the military. My parents' attitude was both good and bad toward my enlistment. My father encouraged me after I told him I was joining. My mother didn't like it, but not enough to stop me. I was 18 and didn't need no signatures.

A 36-year-old platoon sergeant from the Appalachian region, whose father had been a noncommisioned officer during World War II, described his family in this way:

I had twelve brothers and sisters. I was the tenth. No one encouraged me to join. In fact, I even had a pretty good job pasteurizing milk for a while. Dad liked the idea. I joined to get away from the mountain way of living.

In the same vein, a 26-year-old squad leader from Queens, New York, said:

When I joined the military, it made my parents somewhat unhappy but they

TABLE 3.5. Job Histories of Khaki Town's Army Men

Respondent No.	All Jobs in Chronological Order Prior to Enlistment in the Army
001	General Motors assembly worker
002	Full-time student, cook
003	Enlisted after high school
004	Salesclerk, pinsetter in bowling alley
005	Insurance sales
006	Enlisted after high school
007	Enlisted after high school
008	Enlisted after high school
009	Fisherman, bank teller, meter man
010	Tractor mechanic
011	Enlisted after high school
012	No prior jobs, high school dropout
013	Cook
014	Painter, barber, assembly line worker, salesman of men's wigs
015	Enlisted after high school
016	Enlisted after high school
017	Enlisted after high school
018	Enlisted after high school
019	Enlisted after high school
020	Pharmaceutical assistant, grocery assistant manager, sales representative
021	Enlisted after high school
022	Janitor
023	Enlisted after high school
024	Enlisted after two years of college
025	Superintendent in cemetery, mechanic, shipping foreman in factory
026	Enlisted after high school
027	Laborer in oil fields
028	Ranch hand, meat packing, college student
029	No prior jobs, college student
030	Milk pasteurizer
031	Gas station attendant, ranch hand, factory worker
032	Factory worker
033	Assembly line
034	Dispatcher for a trucking company, trucker

Continued

TABLE 3.5 *(continued)*

Respondent No.	All Jobs in Chronological Order Prior to Enlistment in the Army
035	Enlisted after high school
036	Enlisted after high school
037	Laborer
038	Dishwasher, butcher, machine shop apprentice
039	Dishwasher, plumber
040	Loafer, dock worker, bookie, student
041	Landscaper
042	College student
043	Enlisted after high school
044	Enlisted after high school
045	Enlisted after high school
046	Enlisted after high school
047	Roofer
048	Farm laborer
049	Gas station attendant
050	Cook, gas station attendant
051	Lawn mower
052	Gas station attendant
053	Clerk, sales
054	Construction
055	Welder
056	Bricklayer, assembled trailers
057	No prior job, unemployed after high school
058	Farm laborer
059	Sugar beet weeder, harvester of tomatoes
060	Shipping and receiving supervisor, tractor trailer driver
061	National Guard
062	Shop clerk, factory work, laborer for Ohio State Highway Department
063	High school student, mechanic
064	Enlisted after high school
065	Part-time work as service station attendant
066	Truck driver, printer, shipping clerk
067	Taxi driver, laborer, bum
068	Painter
069	Cement work
070	Factory work
071	Farm laborer

072	Enlisted after high school
073	Enlisted after high school
074	Enlisted after high school
075	Nurses' aide, orderly
076	Enlisted after high school
077	Enlisted after high school
078	Waiter, dishwasher
079	Office clerk
080	Enlisted after high school
081	Enlisted after high school
082	Landscaping
083	Factory work, assembly line work
084	Truck driver, laborer
085	Laborer
086	Enlisted after high school
087	Enlisted after high school
088	Enlisted after high school
089	Enlisted after high school
090	Harvester
091	Mechanic
092	Factory worker, food services worker
093	Cook
094	Gas station attendant
095	Enlisted after high school
096	Enlisted after high school
097	Foundry worker
098	Enlisted after high school
099	Bricklayer, construction worker
100	Potato warehouse
101	Carry-out boy
102	Laborer
103	Lawn mower
104	Auto-body work, mechanic, painter
105	Supermarket carry-out boy
106	Enlisted after high school
107	Poultry factory
108	Stock manager
109	Enlisted after high school
110	Shop clerk
111	Enlisted after high school
112	Burglar
113	Enlisted after high school

Continued

TABLE 3.5 *(continued)*

Respondent No.	All Jobs in Chronological Order Prior to Enlistment in the Army
114	Enlisted after detention home
115	Farm work
116	Enlisted after high school
117	Handyman
118	Fisherman
119	Mechanic, factory work, construction
120	Enlisted after high school
121	Bank teller
122	Worked on cars, McDonald's sales clerk
123	No prior job, unemployment after high school
124	Construction
125	Enlisted after high school
126	Neighborhood Youth Corps
127	Carry-out boy, clerk
128	Ranch hand
129	Ranch hand
130	Food services
131	Enlisted after high school
132	Enlisted after high school
133	Mining
134	Enlisted after high school
135	Construction work
136	Enlisted after junior college
137	Enlisted after high school
138	Enlisted after high school
139	Worked for contractor in construction jobs
140	Odds and ends types of jobs
141	Enlisted after high school

Note: It should be noted that "enlisted after high school" does not mean that the respondent graduated from high school. It means that the respondent attended high school.

Source: Compiled by the author.

got used to the idea. I was a factory worker on an assembly line, a clerk in a transportation company, a dispatcher. . . . I did a little bit of everything. Nothing special.

When Army males spoke of their prior work histories, they revealed their vulnerability and low status in their civilian jobs. From a staff sergeant from Georgia:

I was a nobody. I worked as a cook and gas station attendant before. A friend encouraged me to join, then he backed out at the last moment. I'm here and he's not!

From a supply clerk from California:

I joined to find a job. I just wanted some freedom from always worrying about the next paycheck or whether I'd still be working the next week.

When men were asked to list their reasons for joining the Army, they tended to give more patriotic or normative reasons than did women soldiers. However, as in the case of the women, men also joined for calculative reasons. The military, to these men at the time, offered more advantages than civilian jobs. The following reasons were stated by men for their Army enlistment:

1. Patriotism and love of country, 42 (30 percent)
2. Money or job, 42 (30 percent)
3. Peer pressure, 17 (12 percent)
4. Personal growth, 9 (6 percent)
5. Negative reasons such as boredom, 6 (4 percent)
6. Experience, 5 (4 percent)
7. Travel, 5 (4 percent)
8. Didn't know or no response, 12 (9 percent)

The sample of Khaki Town soldiers studied was similar to those studied by Charles Moskos in his stays with Army units in Germany and the United States:

I am even more impressed by what I do not find in line units—urban and suburban, white soldiers of middle class origins. In other words, the all-volunteer Army is attracting not only a disproportionate number of minorities, but also an unrepresentative segment of white youth, who, if anything, are even less characteristic of the broader social mix than our minority soldiers.[19]

THE THEORY OF HIS ARMY AND HER ARMY

Jessie Bernard provided the impetus for studying the differences between the army experiences of men and women. In her study entitled *The Future of Marriage,* Bernard discovered that in every marriage, there were actually two marriages, his and hers—two distinct interpretations of the same marriage. In her survey of the marital satisfaction literature, she discovered a pattern of findings that constituted the basis for the different realities of marriage for men and for women. Marriage, in general, was beneficial for men and hazardous for women.[20]

In a similar vein, the concept of His Army and Her Army is used to explore differences in military experience for male and female soldiers. This theory will be used to describe sex differences in adjustment versus two views of the male-female soldier relationship.

What does it mean to be a female in a predominantly male work setting? Which problems of Her Army are due to men and which are due to the Army as an occupation? In the next chapter, I will argue that female soldiers experience problems peculiar to their sex because they are tokens in a work setting with a sex ratio highly skewed in favor of the males. Her Army then, has the problem of occupying a marginal position in an enlisted culture, a position of status contradiction. Past research on female tokenism has been conducted in high status organizations such as corporations and law schools, but what happens when women are tokens in a low-status organization such as the Army?

For males, the Army is a quasi-occupation that makes excessive demands on time, family, and identity. The occupation is not just another job. It is a task-oriented, total institution that extracts compliance from its enlisted members. His Army is a "special society" in which work is done under a rational plan within a symbiotic community that is cut off from civilian society. In its recruiting slogan, the Army says, "This is the Army. It's not just a job, it's an adventure!" The Army *is* more than an ordinary occupation, as we shall see. It is a coercive social institution that uses domination to "tame the troops."

Because females are both token women and soldiers, Her Army is all of the problems of being a low-ranked soldier, coupled with the problems of sexism.

Observations and interviews in Khaki Town confirmed that both sexes faced multiple stresses in their respective roles. Soldiers of both sexes who spoke with me were particularly bitter about overseas living conditions. Common problems of both sexes also included dissatisfaction with excessive field duty, military harassment, work-family interference, and complaints about services provided by the military. A military social stressors index was compiled from observations and interviews. For each

TABLE 3.6. Social Stressors in Khaki Town: Sex Differences

	Male	Female	Kendall's Tau
1. Child-care facilities	20.7% (29)	16.7% (15)	p < .05
2. Adequate money	35.5% (50)	26.4% (24)	n.s.
3. Educational opportunities	31.9% (45)	(38.5%) (35)	n.s.
4. Military occupational specialty (assignment out of trained area)	25.5% (36)	23.1% (21)	n.s.
5. Sexism (general)	24.1% (34)	34.1% (31)	p < .0001
6. Intimate relations	24.8% (35)	36.3% (33)	n.s.
7. Military medical care	41.2% (58)	30.8% (28)	n.s.
8. Overseas assignment	39.7% (56)	30.8% (28)	n.s.
9. Opportunity for advancement	24.9% (35)	27.5% (25)	p < .05
10. Sexist attitudes and institutional sexism	18.4% (26)	39.6% (36)	p < .0001
11. Male atmosphere of work setting	12.7% (18)	27.5% (25)	p < .001
12. Military justice system	26.9% (38)	34.1% (31)	n.s.
13. Inadequate living conditions	56.8% (80)	52.8% (48)	n.s.
14. Not using talent at work	48.2% (68)	46.2% (42)	n.s.
15. Lack of courtesy and remarks from co-workers	24.9% (35)	48.4% (44)	p < .0001
16. Interference with off-duty life	32.6% (46)	51.7% (47)	p < .0001
17. Poor reception to suggestions	24.1% (34)	23.1% (21)	n.s.
18. Sexist attitudes of immediate supervisor	16.3% (23)	28.6% (26)	p < .0001
19. Lack of trust in immediate work group	23.4% (33)	29.7% (27)	p < .05
20. Training for combat	24.1% (34)	30.8% (28)	p < .05
21. Job pressure	22.0% (31)	33.0% (30)	p < .05
22. Little credit for good work	29.1% (41)	40.7% (37)	p < .05

Note: The percentages indicate those reporting the problem as major or so serious that they would leave the Army because of it.

Source: Women in the Military Questionnaire (Appendix B), Spring 1978 (compiled by the author).

of the 22 stressors, respondents were asked: "How much of a problem is the following for you as a military person?" Possible answers were: (1) not applicable, (2) caused me to consider leaving the military, (3) a major concern, (4) a minor concern, and (5) no problem. (See Appendix B.)

The percentages reported in Table 3.6 represent soldiers reporting that a problem was a major concern or so serious that they would consider leaving the military because of it. As revealed in this table, military life was difficult for both males and females at the enlisted level; both groups reported a number of severe social stressors. For males, child care and overseas assignments were perceived to be more serious problems than for females. For females, the areas of sexism, opportunity for advancement, institutional sexism, the male atmosphere of the work setting, the lack of courtesy, interferences with off-duty life, the sexist attitudes of immediate supervisors, the lack of trust in the immediate work group, training for combat, job pressure, and little credit for good work were more likely to be listed as serious problems than with their male counterparts.

The most significant aspect of Table 3.6 is the finding that both sexes experienced multiple social problems. Inadequate living conditions, the underutilization of talent, and the problem of establishing intimacy were problems for both sexes. The issues of military justice, inadequate facilities, and poor conditions were indicators of encroachment on the well-being of both males and females. In the next chapters, I will further develop the theory of His Army and Her Army.

NOTES

1. Army Community Services Auxiliary, "Welcome to *Khaki Town*" (October 1977); Khaki Town is my name for the garrison community that is described in this study.

2. Everett C. Hughes, *Where People Meet* (Glencoe, Ill.: The Free Press, 1952); my paraphrase is from a conversation with Everett Hughes at Boston College, May 15, 1979.

3. I am indebted to Nancy Dughi, a former University of Maryland colleague, for capturing Wolfman Jack's dialogue. Both Nancy and Joseph Dughi were helpful to me in bringing together the features of the overseas military base.

4. Charles C. Moskos, *The American Enlisted Man: The Rank and File in Today's Military* (New York: Russell Sage, 1972).

5. Charlotte Wolf, *Garrison Community: A Study of an Overseas American Military Community* (Westport, Conn.: Greenwood, 1969).

6. Ibid., p. 68.

7. George McNeill, *The Labor Movement: The Problem of Today* (Boston: A. M. Bridgman, 1886), p. 230.

8. Denile Williams, "*Khaki Town*'s a Busy Place," *The Army Communicator* (Winter 1979): 59.

9. Department of the Army, *FM 11–50. Signal Battalion: Armored, Infantry (Mechanized) Division* (Washington D.C.: Headquarters, Department of the Army, February 1968), p. 1.

10. Paul M. Lee, *Why We Are Here*, orientation booklet issued to U.S. Army in Europe (Department of the Army, September 1977).

11. Ibid.

12. Department of the Army, *FM 11–50*, pp. 6–7.

13. Ibid.

14. Department of Defense, Office of the Assistant Secretary of Defense for Manpower, Reserve Affairs, and Logistics, *Uses of Women in the Military*, 2d ed. (Washington D.C.: Office of the Assistant Secretary of Defense, September 1978), p. 29.

15. Male and female trainees were integrated into common basic training units in 1976, according to the Office of the Director, Women's Army Corps (now defunct), "Addendum to ODWAC Notes" (February 10, 1978).

16. See Charles C. Moskos, "The Enlisted Ranks in the All-Volunteer Army," in John B. Keely, ed., *The All-Volunteer Force and American Society* (Charlottesville, Va.: University of Virginia Press, 1978), p. 47.

17. U.S. Department of Labor, *Employment Report to the President* (1978), Introduction.

18. James O'Connor, *The Fiscal Crisis of the State* (New York: St. Martin's Press, 1973), p. 161.

19. Moskos, *The American Enlisted Man*, p. 47.

20. Jessie Bernard, *The Future of Marriage* (New York: Penguin, 1972).

Chapter Four

HER ARMY: THE PROBLEM
OF FEMALE TOKENISM

He says we get greater respect. He obviously doesn't get the catcalls and obscene remarks that a woman in uniform gets when she walks down the street.

He says we get better treatment. He obviously doesn't live isolated from his co-workers, unable to visit their dayrooms or break their male inner circle.
— Woman Soldier, U.S. Army in Europe

WHEN WOMEN HOLD MEN'S JOBS
IN THE MILITARY: A REVIEW

Much of the extant research on what happens to women when they occupy male roles in the military has been supported by the Department of Defense, the U.S. Army Research Institute, the Naval Personnel Research and Development Center, the U.S. Air Force Equal Opportunity Offices, and the Assistant Secretary of Defense's Office for Manpower. Segal has held that much of the research on women has been done by uniformed personnel and civilians working on military contracts.[1] The problem with doing research for the military rather than asking questions from a broader theoretical framework is that the military defines what questions are relevant. As a result, much of the "hired hand" research reflects a narrow military-policy perspective within the tradition of "dust-bowl" empiricism.

Secondly, as Segal has noted, almost all of the research has been restricted to questionnaires administered to soldiers by military personnel on duty time. Few studies have involved independent observations in the form of field studies of actual gender-integrated situations. Much of the research on women occupying male roles in the military has been policy oriented, descriptive, controlled by the military, and primarily attitudinal.[2]

Male Attitudes about Women in "Khaki-Collar Jobs"

A relatively large number of studies have explored the attitudes of males toward women who are performing in formerly all-male roles. All of the research has been conducted since 1974, mostly under military contract or sponsorship. Durning found that men endorsed abstract and general nontraditional roles for women but opposed policies that would place women in combat.[3] Hicks' study, using a sample of nearly 2,500 respondents, concluded that enlisted males were more opposed than enlisted women to the assignment of women to jobs previously open to men only.[4] In a similar vein, Jordan found that male supervisors of women in nontraditional military occupations held the belief that women were less capable than men. However, supervisors in both traditional and nontraditional fields also felt that women learned job tasks and progressed in upgrade training as well as men.[5]

A few studies have found that males were more egalitarian than would be expected. Manley and associates reported that male and female managers possessed similar personal value systems and career objectives.[6] Gorman added that the attitudes of both men and women were highly favorable with regard to the role of women in the Marine Corps. However, the Corps has not expanded either the number of women or the number of specialties to the same degree as the other services.[7]

Savell and colleagues, in an Army Research Institute study, found that while men held more stereotyped attitudes about sex roles, the majority accepted women in less traditional roles such as radar technician, welder, and jet pilot.[8] However, these studies assessed attitudes in the abstract and did not differentiate between men who actually worked with women in nontraditional settings and men who worked with women in "pink-collar" military jobs. Moreover, there is little research that has focused on men and women in the same work settings. DeFleur and Gilman, in their study of Air Force cadets in the early phases of sex integration, which combined questionnaires with field observations, found that male cadets were more traditional in sex-role attitudes than were female cadets, both at the time of entrance of females and six months later.[9] More significantly, after six months of sex integration, male attitudes toward female cadets had become more unfavorable. Field observations supported the hypothesis that patterns of differential association existed. Males and females in the Air Force Academy tended to talk, associate, and choose best friends from the same-sex population.[10]

This brief review of the literature on military women leaves us with the hypothesis that females should expect to face difficulties when they enter newly integrated military occupations.[11] In this chapter, I will examine the experience that women faced when they integrated tele-communications work in the Signal Corps in Khaki Town. The primary issue addressed here is how these women came to articulate an identity in an enlisted culture dominated by men.

Earlier analyses of how individuals cope and find roles in highly skewed sex settings have been conducted in professional occupations outside the military. Rosabeth Kanter studied the situation faced by women entering male bastions in private industry and argued that women faced stresses due to tokenism.[12] The term *tokenism* arose first during white resistance to school desegregation in the South during the 1960s.[13] By accepting a few blacks, school boards could argue for a while that they were meeting government regulations. Kanter found that women managers faced an analogous situation. If women were included in a situation where they were dominated numerically, limits were set on possibilities. Kanter defined highly skewed groups as those with a female/male (minority/majority) ratio of less than 15:85. As tokens, females faced social isolation, a loss of individuality, mistaken identity, aloneness, and pressure to adopt stereotyped roles. They were less likely to do well because of their aloneness, which created mental and physical stress. Subprocesses of tokenism included encapsulations in stereotyped informal roles such as mother, seductress, pet, and iron maiden. Kanter hypothesized that changes in proportions of women would lead to changes in the behavior and treatment of those in token positions.[14]

Long Laws found that tokenism was present in any organization where a dominant group was under pressure to share power or other desirable commodities with a minority group. As in Kanter's research, Long Laws found that the token was an isolate who was operating as a marginal person on the turf of the dominant group. However, Long Laws' emphasis was on the partnership of the Token and the Sponsor in academic organizations; a member of the dominant group (Sponsor) voluntarily helped the Token.[15]

Spangler and her colleagues tested Kanter's hypothesis that minority achievements are diminished by the dynamics of highly skewed sex roles in another professional organization, the law school. The study of token women in law school supported Kanter's hypothesis. A tilted sex ratio created two contrasting strategies—underachievement and overachievement—as a response to being a female nearly alone in a male dominated institution.[16]

The concept of tokenism is important to an understanding of the behavior of females as well as males in an integrated setting. Lower-ranked females are in conflict with and are outnumbered by the men of

Khaki Town. However, tokenism in the military takes on somewhat different dimensions. All of the previous research has studied the strategies of token women in professional roles. In Kanter's study of managerial women, Long Laws' analysis of academic women, and the Spangler study of women in law schools, there was a clear incentive for women to weather the injuries of tokenism. But in the case of a low-status organization such as the enlisted military, participation was both emancipatory and oppressive. Even if the stresses of tokenism are disregarded, it is not clear that making it in the enlisted military is a real gain.

Another difference between this study and previous research is the marginality of the military as a quasi-occupation. Women are integrating roles that are considered to be dirty work by the larger society. Therefore, military women are double deviants; they face the problem of being a woman nearly alone in a male-dominated organization and also the problem of being a member of a disreputable group, the enlisted military. In order to understand how tokenism works in the military, it is necessary to explore the distinctive character of military service for soldiers of both sexes. It is necessary to also assess the limits of female participation in the Army. Currently, women have been included as temporary dirty workers rather than as a part of an affirmative action program. Thus, female tokenism in the Army has different attributes.

This chapter will explore the role traps to which Khaki Town's women were subject as a function of being women in a male-centered organization. Chapter Five will describe male enlisted culture and the response of males to token women. Finally, Chapter Six will specify the social context of the enlisted military. Together, this analysis specifies how tokenism works in the institutional structure of the enlisted military.

There are several important limitations to this enterprise. First, since there are no military units where more than 15 percent of the personnel are female, the effect of numerical differences cannot be directly compared. Because there are no units in which the proportions of men and women are relatively equal, the effect of such numerical equality cannot be studied to see how numbers affect change in the enlisted women's status and role response. Secondly, field data do not allow the test of statistical analysis of female tokenism in the military. Survey or experimental data seem to be useful tools for examining tokenism in different settings. Finally, the effects observed in Khaki Town are evanescent. Since 1978 the percentage of women in Khaki Town has increased from 5 percent to nearly 8 percent. Since the process of tokenism is continuously changing, it would be expected that individuals would be creating and emphasizing new forms of female enlisted culture.

Despite these limitations, it is valuable to examine how female tokenism worked in Khaki Town. How did it differ from that observed in previous studies of high-status organizations? How was it the same? The variety of problems and processes observed there are also important to a sociological understanding of the status contradictions of enlisted women, which is an undeveloped area of research.

From the end of World War II to the early 1970s, women constituted less than 1 percent of the total strength of the U.S. enlisted forces. Beginning in 1973, each service opened noncombat jobs to women. The total number of women in the Army grew from 37,994 in 1974 to 98,459 in 1979, with much of the expansion occurring in traditionally male areas such as the military police and telecommunications.

Figure 4.1 indicates that Army women continue to be heavily clustered in pink-collar specialties such as administrative, clerical, and medical fields. Traditional "khaki-collar" jobs such as telecommunications, electronics, and mechanical repair work have only small numbers of women. As Table 4.1 points out, the distribution of female assignments in the military services is only slowly changing to nontraditional fields. In 1979, over 50 percent of the women were in administrative and medical fields, while only about 10 percent were assigned to khaki-collar roles.

In 1972, in hearings before the House Subcommittee on the Increased Utilization of Women in the Military, the Assistant Secretary of Defense stated, "We are concerned that the Department of Defense and each of the military services are guilty of 'tokenism' in the recruitment and utilization of women in the Armed Forces."[17] While women have integrated previously all-male jobs within the military, the largest percentages continue to be in the traditionally female jobs. As Table 4.1 notes, less than 1 percent of women enlist in the air defense artillery, missile maintenance, and general engineering fields.

The Structure of Tokenism in Khaki Town

From 1975 to the spring of 1978, nearly 300 women had been assigned to field-intensive Signal Corps units in the electronic communication specialties. While I did not have access to official military data, my best estimate is that between 70 and 90 percent of the women initially assigned to those units had left their occupational area by the spring of 1978.[18] In order to successfully integrate previously all-male work domains, it is necessary for women to complete at least their initial term of service. If women do not complete their first term in a nontraditional skill, a cycle of failure in such jobs is perpetuated, which fuels male resentment.

The Army has encountered difficulties in both enlisting and keeping women in nontraditional skills. In electronic equipment repair, 76 percent of the 1973 female enlistees left the occupational group by the end of fiscal year 1976, as compared with 51 percent of the males. In administration, a

FIGURE 4.1. Distribution of Enlisted Women by DOD Occupation Group

(as of end, FY-1978)

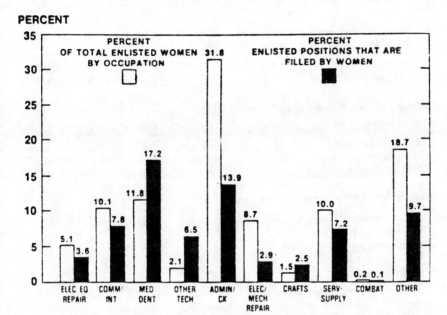

(DOD) Defense Department Occupational Codes

Electrical equipment repair; communications, military intelligence; medical and dental; other technicians; administrators, clerks; electrical, mechanical repair; crafts; service, supply; combat, and other

Source: Department of Defense. Compiled by the Office of the Assistant Secretary of Defense for Manpower, Reserve Affairs, and Logistics 1978.

traditionally female area, the trends were reversed: 70 percent of 1973 female enlistees had been retained as compared with 60 percent of the males. In the medical and dental field, 75 percent of the females were retained versus only 46 percent of the males.[19] The problems of females in nontraditional jobs in Khaki Town are broadly representative of an Army-wide problem.

When women hold males jobs, they find themselves subject to role

TABLE 4.1. Traditional versus Nontraditional Skills for Women
Enlistees, 1977–1979, All Services
(Percent of Women by Skill)

	1977	1978	1979
Traditionally Pink-Collar Jobs			
Administrative	27.7	26.5	24.5
Medical/dental	15.7	15.7	16.1
Mixed (less traditionally pink-collar jobs)			
Automatic data processing	1.0	1.5	1.4
Food service	8.0	6.3	5.3
Law enforcement	3.8	4.1	4.3
Military intelligence	1.1	1.4	1.3
Nontraditional or Khaki-Collar Jobs			
Air defense artillery (ADA)	0.0	0.2	0.5
Missile maintenance	0.0	0.1	0.1
General engineer	1.0	0.9	0.9
Transportation	6.0	6.2	6.1
Aviation maintenance	1.2	1.6	1.3
Mechanical maintenance	2.9	4.2	3.6

Source: Department of the Army, Office of the Secretary of the Army, unpublished statistics (November 30, 1979).

strain. Secord and Backman defined role strain as those situations in which persons experience difficulty in meeting role expectations.[20] Two sources of role strain are postulated. First, there is a perception on the part of males of an inherent and natural conflict between being female and participating in the military. Secondly, the presence of women in nontraditional jobs conflicts with enlisted male culture. Together, these perceptions result in stereotypes that are associated with interpersonal conflict and the failure of women to meet their goals of adjusting to khaki-collar employment.

Females were likely to be the "first" woman in their units, even though a number of token women had passed through khaki-collar jobs. While males were able to share folklore, lexicon, and secrets of how to cope successfully with Signal Corps work, women did not have access to a similar fund of culture. Because of the continual female turnover, there were few protégé networks and senior enlisted female mentors to orient the newcomer. In Khaki Town, there were no female chief master sergeants. In our sample, only 14 percent of the females had reached the lowest supervisory positions. For the Army as a whole, females constituted only 13 percent of the lowest noncommissioned officer ranks. For the senior ranks (E-7 to E-9), women constituted less than 0.5 percent of the positions for the Army as a whole.[21] If the higher attrition rates in nontraditional areas are considered, the percentage of women in non-commissioned officer ranks in these specialties is even lower.

Because women were retained in the administrative and medical areas at a higher rate, most female supervisors were located in the pink-collar areas. Only nine of the 21 female supervisors in Khaki Town were in traditionally male areas. However, this rate was substantially higher than would be expected from Army-wide statistics.

Because female enlisted culture was so undeveloped, each female experienced the first weeks in her unit as a stranger. Isolation was a characteristic pattern for Khaki Town females.

Isolation from Work Culture

The military male knows his own position and the exact position of everyone with whom he comes into contact. The uniform tells him where he fits into the whole scheme of things. When a woman wears the uniform, her position is marginal. Women were strangers to enlisted male culture and entered unfamiliar domains.

A female entering this situation is scrutinized as to her strength, emotional control, and motives for taking a man's job. A 40-year-old sergeant expressed the problem of entering each new job as a stranger:

> I have been in the Army now nearly six years and each time I move to another duty station I must prove myself all over again. I must prove that I have the stamina to pull my own weight. Each time they work on you to see whether you can take it, being a woman and all. They would not put all of that bull on a new guy. The common view is that no woman can possibly take it. The only reason why we joined was to get married or run around. We have to break traditional views on women's roles; cope with male supremacy. We have to fill too many roles at one time.

A 25-year-old staff sergeant found that men constantly test her when she first comes to a unit:

> If a woman is the first to come to a Company, she must work under the constant scrutiny of males. She must watch out. She must guard every conversation and be careful about who she talks to or runs with.

The typical woman soldier enters an all-male unit with no friendly person to meet and help her. On the contrary, being female tends to arouse ridicule and resentment. A voice-intercept operator expressed the dilemma facing the first women in men's jobs:

> We have to prove that we're not enlisted whores or lesbians. Some men prey upon us when we are new to a company for dates. If we go out with them, then we are whores to the other men. If we refuse, we are labeled lesbians.

Representative of the widespread feelings of women about having to confront assignments as strangers are the following comments of women soldiers:

> Women are regarded as novelties or freaks when they first come to a unit.
> Supervisors ignore us and hope we'll go away.
> Guys expect us to do physically more than we're capable of. They constantly test our capacity as soldiers.
> We have to put up with hostile stares by the dependent wives when we go to the commissary, PX, and the hospital. They don't know how to to take us.
> In the beginning of each new assignment, immature enlisted men won't return my salutes.
> We aren't accepted in the military community. Wives see us as threats and make comments.
> We want acceptance as individuals rather than as someone's wife, mother, or lover. They never see us as adults and capable soldiers.
> We are treated as sexual objects rather than as competent supervisees.
> There are continual complaints about our presence.
> Being token women, we have to prove ourselves.
> We are overly protected so we are never given the chance to prove ourselves.
> We are categorized. I'm an individual and don't approve of being categorized. They categorize us as "get overs" regardless of our rank and experience.
> We are mistrusted by the military community, especially by the married men's wives.
> The initial attitude of males is that we were sent here for their pleasure and abuse. We must always be content with that image, before we can get to work.

All respondents were asked, "Do women have to prove themselves in new military assignments, just because they are women?" Eighty-four percent of the females replied in the affirmative versus only one-third of the males. Eighty of the ninety-one women in the sample (88 percent) said they had personally seen negative male attitudes make it difficult for a woman to do her military job, and eighty-seven percent of the males (108 out of 141) agreed that they had personally seen women experience difficulties due to negative male attitudes.

Sexual Shakedowns in Khaki Town Units

There were frequent episodes of females being propositioned by both enlisted supervisors and junior enlisted men, as revealed in unstructured interviews with women. Sexual jokes, gestures, and leers occurred both on- and off-duty. Women soldiers were "sexualized" by Army newspapers, and newspapers and training manuals depicted women as sex objects. In the January 1976 issue of the *Army Times*, a female soldier was highlighted as a "cute grease monkey." Another article in *Army Times* was entitled "Wac of the Week: Fort Benning's Rhonda Catches Their Eyes" and featured a photo of a private first class soldier in a bikini.[22] A cartoon strip entitled "With Sgt. Mike" depicted a WAC questioning a supply sergeant: "You lost the requisition again? But this makes the fourth time you've had t'measure me for a flak jacket!"[23]

In order to make training manuals more appealing for males, females had yet another use. Army women in cheese-cake poses exhorted the trainees to use safety shoes, helmets, and general care in their jobs. An official Army publication, *PM*, used the shapely legs and bosoms of the cartoon characters, Connie and Bonnie, to inform maintenance men about equipment care and repair.[24] On the Armed Forces radio network, "Sandy" crooned to the boys in the barracks of Khaki Town: "This weekend, don't swim alone. Drive carefully and take care of your lovely bods!"

When the separate Women's Army Corps was deactivated, women were expected to adapt to male culture without a support structure. Kanter hypothesized that if the token could segregate conflicting expectations and had strong outside support groups with which to relax, stress-producing situations could be turned into opportunities for ego enhancement.[25] However, Army women, particularly in the overseas setting, had little insulation from the adverse features of tokenism: A letter to the Editor of the *Army Times* complained that the recent integration of women in khaki-collar jobs had exposed women to the full brunt of enlisted culture:

Collectively, Army women face difficulties unattended to these days and many of us are scattered as to be out of touch with one another as professional women . . . However, no supervisor can effectively deal with the subterranean features of institutional sexual bias that is inescapable in our Army, for both men and women.[26]

When women had a separate Corps or when they were concentrated in the clerical and medical fields, they had more opportunity to develop a support structure. In the nontraditional Khaki Town units, women were alone or nearly alone. Direct sexual shakedowns and comments could and did occur in any context, both on- and off-duty, according to the females. Over half of the women in the sample (47) told me of at least one instance of a sexual showdown during *on-duty* time. While women have been "harassed" as individuals in professional organizations such as the university, the corporation, or the law school, female soldiers, as a group, were targets for public and unguarded confrontations. For example, it is difficult to imagine the following incident, related by a radio operator, as an example of how shakedowns could occur openly and unexpectedly, occurring in a professional organization:

> I was leaving the mess hall one day and a guy said "hello" and I said "hi." Then he turned to me and said, "Boy do you have a cute ass. I'd like to put my wood to your three holes!"

Sexual harassment from immediate supervisors was very common in Khaki Town. A woman reported how she was confronted by her supervisor on the day she reached her unit:

> I brought my orders to Sergeant S_____. He looked at them and then he looked at me. "Sorry," he said, "no, we can't have an affair. I already have someone." I didn't know exactly how to react or who to talk to about the incident.

Females could feel the brunt of enlisted culture even after superficial acceptance by some males in the work group. A woman reported to me that she was visiting the hospital with a male from her unit whom she considered to be a friend. Yet, she was unexpectedly profaned in the following way:

> I thought Rick treated me like one of the guys and could be a friend of mine. I thought that he almost forgot that I was a woman. I really even felt like one of the guys.
> One of the guys in the unit was having surgery for a hernia and we visited him in the hospital. He was going to take a shower. I reminded him not to drink any of the water while he was showering because he was going in for surgery. Then Rick butted in, "That means you can't have any pussy, either!" I said, "Hey wait a minute . . ." but to no avail. I was interrupted by Rick: "Hey no problem man. There's no pussy to be had here." The other guy said, "I don't know about you, but to me, she's pussy. You're blind, man. Can't you see those tits?" I thought to myself, "You guys really have a lot of nerve."

A great number of women in Khaki Town units commented on day-to-day abuse at the hands of their male counterparts. A few representative comments from the women follow:

I was continually in the uncomfortable situation of being asked out for dates. I wore my wedding ring, but that didn't seemed to make a difference. When they asked me out, I told them that my husband expects me to be at home. They said, "That's no reason. What are you—some kind of dyke or something?"

This incident happened when I was in the States. Every time I went into the supply closet, Sgt. _____ followed me. First he tried to put his arm around me. I let him get away with it the first time. I thought maybe he's just a "touchie-feelie" type of person and I don't want to hurt his feelings if he's sincere. Well one day he grabbed me. I told him, "That isn't the reason why I'm in the Army. If you want a piece of ass, look elsewhere." Now if something like that happens, I get madder than shit. If I am at work and something like that happens to me, I get mean and nasty.

Another woman who fought back told me how she had become rougher and cruder in order to survive in the Army:

First, I have the biggest problem just being a woman around here. A girl can't be herself without harassment. Males make us feel weird. Many guys will make derogatory comments with sexual connotations to them. I learned that if I gross them out before they gross me out, I can one-up them. They really can't handle an aggressive female. If you get them, before they get you, they don't mess with you. No way. They kind of realize that, "If I don't mess with her too much, she won't come down on my shit." But the worst part of this job are the guys' stupid comments.

A private first class radio operator described her tactics for dealing with sexual abuse in a similar way:

I used to get shit on a lot. J_____ used to follow me around. They used to tease me about us making it together. Or they would tease me that I was a queer. I just used to slough it off. But it would kind of bother me. I would tell them to knock it off. No matter how many times I told them to knock it off, they wouldn't.

One day I decided not to let it ride. I teased them back. When they called me a queer, I told them, "It takes one to know one." It freaked them out.

I learned to hand it out in the same way they did. I got tired of being asked out all the time, since I'm happily married. They always said, "Do you want to go to the Disco, horse-back riding, or for a walk?" They wouldn't take no for an answer. I said, "No I don't want to go with you or no I won't have sex with you." It really irritated me.

Another radio operator described the problem she had with a supervisor who expressed affection for her in an inappropriate manner:

He fell in love with me. One day he told me to come with him to his office and he said, "I notice that we often make eye contact at work. Well, to make a long story short: My wife is on TDY [temporary duty] and I'm really in love with you. We could get married and be reassigned. I could see to it."

I was in shock. The only thing I could think of to say was, "Wow, that's real nice but I can't really fall in love with you." I didn't know what to say.

After that, he turned on me. He gave me the worst efficiency rating possible in my MOS (military occupational specialty). He wouldn't let me take off-duty courses at Maryland. Everything I did was wrong. He would write me up on everything. He used his rank against me. To this day, we don't get along.

A married corporal reported how her marriage was jeopardized by the male workers in the motor pool:

When I first got here, I didn't feel accepted. My NCO would sit and stare at me. I just tried to get along. In the mornings, I would wake up determined to change their attitudes. I would say cheerily, "Good morning." One guy once told me, "What's so good about it, bitch?"

Anyway, my husband came in one weekend to Khaki Town. You see we had been temporarily separated because his orders came later than mine. It was the longest time we had been separated since our marriage of three years. My husband came with me to work one day, because I wanted him to see how the guys were acting there. When we went home that night he told me, "You know your name is written in the head." I shrugged it off and didn't anything think of it. I had seen things written before in the woman's head. It was no biggy.

One day, a male friend I had made took me aside and said, "Lauri, who has it in for you in your unit?" I said, "What do you mean?" "There are some rather mean and nasty things written in the men's head."

I had him watch the door and I went into the head. It was a real shock. There were drawings of me having sex with different men. There were crude comments. I couldn't believe these guys were capable of doing this. I went right to my supervisor and told him I wasn't returning to work until the drawings were gone.

I felt there was something wrong when my husband and I were together. Things didn't click. He was moody but wouldn't say what was bothering him. Now things are O.K., but they weren't for a long time.

Another woman commented on how fear of sexual harassment isolates her from the co-workers in her platoon:

There's no chance to get away unless you lock yourself in your room. They're always after you. You can't tell them to fuck-off because they'll use it against you. You don't want to be a bitch all of the time. I don't like the abusive language, gestures, or insinuations from the men. Most women have to endure pressures from male soldiers.

One woman related the reality shock of discovering that sexualization of the soldier role in basic training involved sexual harassment:

My drill instructor was screwing three girls in our class and gave them preferential treatment. He propositioned me, but he turned me off. He really turned me off to the Army. I had planned to work hard, but learned you didn't have to be together to get somewhere in the Army. You just had to use your body. This made me set higher standards for myself. I am determined to stick it out for this term.

Many women reported incidents that were not direct sexual shakedowns but were inappropriate nonetheless. The following account is indicative of how women are placed in awkward situations at work, where there is an undefined sexual connotation present:

I don't know about J_____. He'll do weird things once in awhile. I'll go to the motor pool and he'll grab me around the waist and squeeze me so hard that it hurts. Then he'll let me go and walk away muttering, "Thanks I needed that." It's weird. I don't quite know how to react.

Another woman in a Signal Corps unit in Italy fought back when males in her office had *Playboy, Hustler,* and *Penthouse* nude pinups in their work areas:

What bothered me was the male's old double-standard. I purchased the *Playgirl* Men of the Year Calendar, and cut out the best four nudes and placed them on my wall in my office. I got some interesting reactions before I was forced to remove them. My supervisor commented that these pictures were obscene. What they really objected to was that a *female* had nude pictures of a male in her office! I have since been accused of sleeping around, of being loose, simply because I was bold enough to challenge the males.

Many of the female soldiers commented that they had difficulties establishing boundaries between their role as a soldier and their role as a woman. The problems of sexual shakedowns in Khaki Town were representative of a Defense Department with problems. In a Congressional investigation on sexual abuse by male soldiers, women told the House Armed Services Committee of numerous similar incidents:

Lori Lodinsky, a former Military Policewoman, now a civilian, said she was molested by an NCO in a squad car while driving at a high speed across the

Meade [Fort Meade] airstrip. But she said she did not report the incident to
her commanders because "the officers themselves talked about doing the
same thing. They had made comments to that effect."

Jacqueline Lose, another former Military Policewoman, told the subcommittee that one male soldier sat on her chest for 45 minutes and told his
two friends, who watched, that he was going to "give me what she
deserved." "He touched me and kissed me," Lose said, "but then let me go."
Lose told the panel that her platoon leader, a Lieutenant, slipped her a note to
call him. "He said I'd be in serious trouble if I reported it," she said. She
eventually was discharged because of "inability to cope."

. . . The sexual abuse problem is not limited to MP units. She told the panel
that her husband, a Signal NCO, tells stories of other NCOs who take
women troops into supply closets with plans for sexual encounters. "But in
the Army, you learn to deal with these things."[27]

Sexual shakedowns were not reported to higher command because of
the fear of male retaliation, especially from males of higher rank. A
mechanic who worked in the Khaki Town motor pool described the
continual uneasiness she felt working alone with a group of men:

At first they are very apprehensive, the way they are talking to you. You can
tell they are talking down to you. I always think to myself, "Here we go
again." Then there are others who want to be your friend. Do they want a
sexual encounter or do they want to help?

I don't think of myself as a military woman. I am a woman period no
matter what I do for a living. Being enlisted, I feel like an enlisted man
sometimes. I don't think my supervisors think of me as a woman really, but
only as a little girl. This puts a cramp on my social life.

The Heightened Visibility of Army Women

Women soldiers also experienced what Kanter called "heightened
visibility."[28] Women stand out in the military and are noticed more. They
are the subject of official military surveys and human relations seminars
and are given more attention and scrutiny than their male counterparts.
They are the subject of rumor, innuendo, and ridicule in the work setting.

In the Army, visibility is almost always a disadvantage. To go
unnoticed is to escape guard duty, charge of quarters details, or cleanup
details. Women do not have the ability to remain in low profile; their
gender attributes set them apart. If a woman is missing from a work detail,
it is noticed. If a woman is on sick call, everyone comments on it. If a
woman cannot perform her duties, it is remembered. The negative
consequences of visibility for soldiers of both sexes are illustrated in a
female corporal's account of her first general inspection in Khaki Town:

After a lot of mind games, I finally got the picture. You had to try to go unnoticed. We were having our first inspection since I arrived and I tried to hide from the first sergeant. He spotted me about five feet from my locker behind a cabinet. He yelled at the top of his lungs, "Why is this place so shitty? Corporal, why isn't all this shit cleaned up?" [He was talking about something in the wall locker.] I said, "Sir, I don't know." He yelled, "Excuses are like assholes. Everybody gots one, and they all stink!" "I'm going to ask you one more time." [pointing to me] Then he took his stick and pounded it into the palm of his hand and snarled, "One more time, corporal!" I replied, "It wasn't done sir, because I didn't do it!" He walked away and I knew exactly where I stood in the matter.

One of the perceptions that enlisted males in Khaki Town have is that females receive special privileges and rights. In particular, many feel that the supervisors let females "get over" because they are women. Some supervisors may even subject women to additional tasks to demonstrate that they do not allow women to escape unpleasant duties. One woman reported that, in her company, women were especially chosen to do cleanup work:

We worked twelve hours on and twelve hours off. We had to keep busy, wax the floor, empty the trash, and sweep the floor. The supervisor told us, "I want you girls to do some work for a change. Let's see some equal work for equal pay," he said. He always seemed to find more bullshit for us to do, even when there was nothing to do and the guys were loafing around. There are only so many times you can sweep the floor in a tiny area.

That women were subject to heightened visibility was found in the following accounts:

I myself am not a women's libber, but I have found some indications that women are always being watched. I want acceptance as an individual rather than as a woman in the military.

I was the first woman in this unit. The NCOIC [Noncommissioned Officer in Charge] caused scars that I am still not over. I had to deal with personal attacks on my motherhood and womanhood behind closed office doors. My NCO constantly threatened me. Things are better now, but none of his viciousness will ever be erased from my mind.

Being a woman is tough here. It gets pretty bad when your supervisor asks you, "Well, how do you want to be treated today? Are you on the rag or anything? What you need is a good lay!"

Enlisted men put a label on you. You are either loose, stuck up, gay, or fucked up. The book covers most complaints, but nothing is ever done.

The attitude, "Hey—she's a woman, let her do it," makes it a lot harder to cooperate with unit members.

Most male supervisor subject us to continual hassles because we are women and also watch our off-duty lives.

Mistaken Identity

Another dimension of tokenism found in Khaki Town was the phenomenon of "mistaken identity," or inaccurate attribution. The following examples were cases of mistaken identity found in Kanter's study of women in corporate life: (1) the fact that women are not expected to be doing what they are doing, (2) the surprise that occurs when women are found in "male roles" or realms, (3) the confusion about the difference between work roles and sexual roles.[29]

In one sense, the previously discussed sexual shakedowns were cases of mistaken identity. Males defined some of the soldiers in their units as sexual objects rather than as comrades-in-arms. In a similar fashion, the men's initial negative definition of new women in their unit was a case of mistaken identity. Women felt that they were competently trained, while males defined them as little girls or sex objects who could not do the job.

During the course of my fieldwork in Khaki Town, a case of mistaken identity was reported by the *Army Times*. Apparently, a widespread belief among male soldiers was that female soldiers would not have to remain in the Army if there was to be another war. Females were thought of as persons who would be removed along with dependent wives and children in case of attack. General Bernard W. Rogers, then Army Chief of Staff, had to affirm that women would endure the same hardships as men in case of war:

"Some people believe women soldiers will not be deployed in the event of hostilities," he said, "and therefore consider them 'part-time soldiers' who are here in peace and gone in war . . . The Army cannot operate effectively in this manner." Rogers said, "Women will deploy with their units and they will serve in the skills in which they have been trained."[30]

The surprise that occurs when a woman occupies what is perceived as a man's job was conveyed by an Air Force woman working as an air traffic controller. She recalled the first time she cleared a pilot to land:

His voice came back through the microphone very startled, and he said, "What was that!" Then my supervisor, a man, took over, and the pilot said, "I thought I heard a woman's voice." He still wouldn't believe it when he was told that it was a woman's voice.[31]

In Khaki Town, jobs entailing field duty tended to be automatically labeled as male. While women reported feelings of heightened visibility when it came to sexual harassment, the opposite pattern was found in assignments to khaki-collar jobs. All of the women in the sample had been trained in telecommunications specialties, yet 25 members of the group had been assigned out of their trained area to pink-collar jobs such as administration, drug counseling, food services, and mail service. Some of these transfers resulted from supervisors' views that the field was no place for a woman.

In February of 1978, Signal Corps units were being readied for brief field maneuvers. I observed that several women were not even informed that their units were being deployed. Others were left behind to work in the mail room. In other instances, women were not deployed with their electronic repair teams; instead they were sent to the main site to type or transmit telephone messages. Because all of these women had attended special schools for their occupational specialty, it can be assumed that they expected to perform work in their area of competence. However, supervisors appeared to "mistake" them for sex objects, clerks, typists, or domestics or chose not to see them at all. A female transferred to the clerical pool observed that a higher command was respnsible for women transfers out of khaki-collar jobs: "The Top believes that women should have 'women's' jobs. But since we have other MOSs [Military Occupational Specialities] we should be allowed to work in them."

An E-4 telecommunications specialist was one of three women chosen to attend a special military intelligence school and related the following story, which dramatizes the problem of mistaken identity:

I guess they were not used to having women in the school. The barracks where the women were staying was located a half mile from the rest of the base. One day I was walking to work and was stopped by a colonel in a jeep who yelled, "Hey corporal, get over here. What's the matter down there? Don't you know Army hair-cut regs?" I replied, "Yes sir, I do!" He started yelling again and I interrupted him. "But my hair-cut is regulation—for a woman!" He started to turn red and then it dawned on him, that he had mistaken me for a man.

A woman radio repairer described to me how women in her barracks once waited three hours for a general inspection: "The men get inspected first and they forgot about us!"

In another case, a Signal Corps woman was referred to a Veteran's Hospital in the United States for treatment. At the admissions desk, she had the following conversation with a male administrative clerk:

Woman Soldier: "I have been referred here from Fort _____."
Clerk: "But you are a female!"
Woman Soldier: "You must have heard of them before. They are in the Army you know!"
Clerk: "But *we've* never had one before."

The above incident reflects the awkward and serious problem of mistaken identity that females face in a predominantly male environment. Women must constantly articulate the soldier role in order not to be mistaken as a helpless female.

SOCIAL TYPES OF ENLISTED WOMEN IN KHAKI TOWN

The first duty station assignment is a critical period for women to learn how to articulate successfully the soldier and female identities. The term, *Army woman* is really a contradiction in status, according to enlisted male typifications. You are either a woman or you are in the Army, according to the stereotypes of many enlisted males. Because the structural conditions of tokenism made it difficult for women to retaliate against the male enlisted culture, it was necessary for many to develop role accommodations. In this section, the social types of military women in Khaki Town are studied. Klapp views social types as "charts to role-structures otherwise largely invisible and submerged."[32] A knowledge of the role accommodations of Army women is helpful in understanding the female response to tokenism in the Army. If the structure of tokenism were changed, due to increased female participation in traditional male roles, it is my argument that new social types would emerge.

Discarding the Soldier Role: Underachievement

In order to understand the social types of females that emerged in Khaki Town, it is necessary to study the structural conditions that have retarded the development of female enlisted culture. Moskos argued that the existence of a (male) enlisted culture is a virtual truism. That is to say, when men join the Army, they generate and maintain patterned accommodations to the military environment:

Moreover, the enlisted culture is to large degree a working-class culture in the elementary sense, that to begin with, most enlisted men come from working class origins. This configuration of social traits—young, working-class, unmarried males—would alone give the enlisted culture a distinctive character. . . . the enlisted culture remains as a vestige of male sanctity.[33]

But when women enter khaki-collar military jobs, they lack cultural guidelines as to how to adapt successfully to the more adverse features of military life such as field duty, encroachments on time, and assaults on identity. While males have well-developed support systems to insulate them from the worst features of military life, female isolates lack a support network. Worse yet, women arrive at the Signal Corps alone or nearly alone.

Bruckel's study of infantry teams in the Army confirmed the importance of the peer groups for reducing strain in difficult jobs. Group solutions to everyday problems were found because everyone was in the same boat.[34] However, women are not in the "same boat" as their male counterparts in the Army. Women, from the beginning, are not allowed on the men's boat! If Army women expect any help at all, they have to prove to the men that femininity can be overcome or that it is of slight value.

By simultaneously attempting to fulfill roles as soldiers and women, the women in khaki-collar jobs found that they were subject to the brunt of male discreditation. Women who entered pink-collar jobs did not threaten the enlisted male culture to the same degree. Pink-collar women in the military did not suffer many of the psychic and social costs because they were doing traditional women's work. More importantly, military nursing and clerical work are well-developed roles in the military. Military nurses were legitimized as early as 1860, as we learned in Chapter One. Women clerks have been included in the military as at least temporaries since World War I. However, for women who attempted to integrate the khaki-collar Signal Corps units, there was little history or tradition to back them up. As a result, female enlisted culture in such jobs was undeveloped. There was also the state of mental conflict that Robert Park termed "marginality":

Social maladjustment, whether slight or great, then becomes characteristic of modern man. One sees this social dislocation clearly and sharply in the case of those individuals, who fall between two major racial groups, but it is also apparent in the relations of minor groups such as social classes, religious sects, and communities. The individual who through migration, education, marriage, or some other influence leaves one social group or culture without making a satisfactory adjustment to another finds himself on the margin of each but a member of neither. He is a marginal man.[35]

Everett Stonequist's development of the concept focused on the stresses that create conflicting values for the person. Fate has it that the marginal personality is the outsider:

> The marginal man is a personality type that arises at a time and place where, out of the conflict of races and cultures, new societies, new peoples, and new cultures are coming into existence. The fate which condemns him to live, at the same time, in two worlds is the same which compels him to assume, in relation to the worlds in which he lives, the role of a cosmopolitan and a stranger.[36]

Female soldiers in formerly all-male jobs are caught in a cultural transition. They are initiated into two conflicting traditions, female socialization and traditional military culture. When women begin to occupy men's jobs, they threatened the jokes, language, and camaraderie of a male bastion. When they attempted to enter such spheres, males questioned their strength, emotional control, and motives.

Females in khaki-collar jobs faced a double bind. If they succeeded in their jobs, doubt was cast on their femininity. If they failed, their sex role was affirmed at the expense of their work role. At the unit level, this was translated by a Khaki Town radio operator as meaning, "If I don't like a certain group of guys because they're too pushy, I am labeled as a 'dyke.' If I date a lot, I'm a whore!" The dyke and whore stereotypes were broadly representative of two actual patterns of accommodation. Females resolved the status contradiction by either carving out an identity as a hyperfemale or as a super-soldier who denied her femininity. These accommodations also paralleled the underachievement and overachievement strategies of women law students in the Spangler study.[37]

Amplifying Femininity

Daddy's Little Girl

> I don't belong here. A male could do my job better.
> —20-year-old teletype operator, Khaki Town

One solution to the status contradiction of being a woman in a male job within the military is to allow the soldier role to wither away. By exaggerating "femaleness," token females may find willing male role partners. When women voluntarily withdraw their claims to martial roles, male harassment can be neutralized.

There are many rewards to "normalizing" relations with male enlisted culture. First, when females give up their claim to the soldier role, they are less threatening to male definitions of femininity. Secondly, since these women no longer compete for male jobs, jokes, as well as ridicule and harassment, are reduced. Those women who abandon the battle for sex integration in a retreat to femininity receive swift male rewards, including attention and assistance because the feminine role amplification involves few changes in values, attitudes, and definitions for males.

A frequent paternalistic gesture extended to women who abandon the soldier role is protection from male-oriented military duties such as field exercises and simulations. The male supervisors, the "Sergeant Daddy Warbucks" types, assign the helpless and the vulnerable to the mail room or other clerical duties when it is time for the unit to deploy to the field.

During field exercises in Khaki Town in the spring of 1978, I observed that male supervisors often failed to assign certain women to such duties as guarding the perimeter, assembling radio antennas, and changing tires on two-and-a-half ton trucks. Men assisted women and then reported to me that they were "forced" to "take up the slack" when women were assigned to field jobs. As a private first class woman put it, "The guys yell favoritism, at the same time, they are the ones who do all the favoring. They don't have to help us, but they offer. They're very quick to take over."

Why do men render paternalistic assistance to females? One woman sergeant observed:

> To me, men really felt outdone when a woman performs her duties better than he does. This is a very childish attitude. Men should grow up and accept the fact that some women are better able to do a specific job than some men. Women are often able to perform on the same level but aren't given the chance.

Other women argued similarly that males deliberately tried to instill doubts in women in order to allay their own fears that a woman could endure in a difficult job. A maintenance specialist made the following observation:

> To me, men really can't handle women in jobs like these. They try to instill an attitude in the females that they don't know what they're doing. Once this is done, they come in and offer help. Then they say women can't do the job and we have to cover the "slack."

A radio operator added:

> Men constantly think they have to look out for your welfare, to the extent that they interfere with your duties. Harassment by men and not being treated as an equal are my biggest gripes here. Men you work with are

overprotective even during off-duty time. It's hard to be an equal with lots of males, because of the WAC reputation.

A woman team supervisor described the patterns of male paternalism in the following way:

We are treated as children by male supervisors who think they have to watch out for us. Male supervisors do not task individual women to develop their greatest potential. Men ignore suggestions to change these behaviors. Sexist attitudes of older NCOs and "lifers" created divisiveness among women and limited awareness of military oppression. Women, as a result, are unwilling to discuss problems and present unified demands. Women in the military have a long way to go before they are regarded as equals rather than as novelties or servants for the services.

An example of the ambivalence of women soldiers toward their own oppression is epitomized in the following passage:

If they [women] are capable of doing a job, they should do it. Like tonight for example. We had to install a communications tower. The materials weigh a lot. One of the females asked a male for a little bit of help. He said, "Equal pay for equal work." Another woman told him, "Listen, I can't carry as much god-damn weight as you males." He said, "Like I said before ladies, "Equal pay for equal work."

I see his point and I see her point. Women should be prepared for incidents like this. She should be prepared for anything that is about to come to her in the course of her work. She should feel she has the capacities to perform any aspect of her work. It is the same with a guy. Let's say we had a 5'5" 90-pound guy out there. He shouldn't be assigned to that job if he can't do it. I don't know if a guy would have asked for help in a case like that. I think that because a female asked for help, remarks automatically were made. I don't think the man's comeback would have been given had it been a man requesting a hand.

I overheard the following incident in headquarters on an uncommonly humid day. Two women were mowing the lawn in front of headquarters on special detail:

A male colonel called and complained to the company commander. "Why do you have these women mowing the lawn in this weather?" The company commander replied that the lawn had to be mowed and these women had been assigned to the detail. Fifteen minutes later, two males from another unit appeared in the company commader's office and reported that they were sent to relieve the women.

Despite the trivial nature of this incident, it is examples like these that represent the paternalism that discourages women from performing physically demanding jobs. When women are not allowed to function "normally," both males and females consider them to be only "part-time soldiers." Resentments and claims that women "get over" ensue when males must assume extra duty because of the paternalism of supervisors. Such situations are the glue for the symbiotic relationship between paternalistic supervisors and females willing to relinquish the soldier role in order to exaggerate the female role.

The social type of "Daddy's Little Girl" creates divisiveness within the nascent female enlisted culture. For women still battling to be accepted as soldiers, Daddy's Little Girl undermines female gains. When females perceive the paternalistic role expectations of Daddy Warbucks and his Dutiful Daughter, they often blame the female. The following remarks are from "isolates" who resented male paternalism. From an electronic equipment private first class:

> I think that the problems of a woman in the military are often brought out by the woman. She can be treated the way she wants to. It depends on how she acts. Many women in the Army have a long way to go before they are regarded with respect.

From a woman assigned to clerical duties:

> First impressions of Army women are hard to change. Some women here are the problem. A few of them can be real bitches. The behavior of a few women can affect the treatment of us all.

From a radio operator:

> We have a problem here with lower class women who don't want to work. They give a bad name to those who get here and deal with their jobs. Some women are unwilling to do their MOS [military occupational specialty] and use sex to get a cushy job.

From a telecommunications specialist:

> Many of us [women] work together. But from time to time, an individual EW [enlisted woman] might use her role as a female to shy away from heavy, but not unreasonable work.

From a motor pool maintenance person:

> I think there are some women here who just want to find a man. At least they don't seem to want to do any work.

From an electrical repairer:

Military women think they are capable for the most part. It is mostly the men who see them as delicate. Most of the women would get a hernia before asking a man for help. However, there are some women who use femininity for all it's worth. If they don't know something or can't handle something, they should tell their supervisors. I blame the supervisors because they go along with this kind of action. But when a woman goes into a Signal Corps job, she should know what to expect. If she were to go into administration, she shouldn't expect much lifting. But if you are assigned to telecommunications, you know it, God damn it, that you will have to do something requiring some physical effort.

If you have the title, you should be able to do the job. If she tries to get over, she wastes the Army's money for her schooling and she still can't do the job. And there are a lot of other people who could have done that job, but will never get the opportunity. My personal feeling is that women need to know their limitations and be intelligent enough to know when they can't do an MOS [military occupational specialty]. If you can't lift a ton of weight, you shouldn't sign up for a job which requires that. There are also a lot of women who can lift a lot and there are guys who can't lift much. If I really can't do something, I'll admit it and not play little mind games. I am not a women's libber—far from it. But I do believe that women should get equal pay and do equal effort. They should not be allowed to do any less.

There is a difference between paternalism that is accepted by women and that which is rejected. Females commented on attempts by their supervisors to make them feel helpless. One female reported that while she was initially enthusiastic and confident about her ability to perform her maintenance job, males made attempts to undermine her confidence:

They made comments such as, "Hey Roy, look at the way Cathy screws in a bolt," or "Ah, you do it like a girl. Do it right."

Another woman recounted the following story about the "help" she received from male peers:

I was removing the tire from a two and a half ton truck and was having trouble with the lug nuts. I was making progress, but I needed a little oil on one of the lug nuts which had rusted tight. I went into the motor pool to get the oil and when I returned two of my male co-workers had entirely removed the wheel. They left without talking to me, but I overheard one guy say, "I say equal pay for equal work. Why don't they get women the fuck out of the Army."

The Dutiful Daughter role allows women honorably to remove

themselves psychologically and sometimes physically from work demands. The supervisor who forms the alliance with the Daughter creates resentment from isolates who are not included. The pet is excluded from aversive work loads, while other soldiers of both sexes must perform additional duties.

The Sexpot

A second form of hyperfemininity and underachievement is the Sexpot role. Some females tried to resolve the status contradiction by emphasizing their sexuality. Certain male supervisors, whom I will call Sergeant Seductos, were always looking for sexual partners among women troopers.

By forming a relationship with her supervisor, a female could find a shield from sexual harassment. Like Daddy's Little Girl, the Sex Object was removed from work demands. This role both contributed to the divisiveness among Khaki Town women and retarded the growth of female support systems.

The following remarks are reactions of other women to the Supervisor-Sex Object set. From an electrical repairer:

Some women are screwing their senior NCOs. This is disgusting and demoralizing.

From an intercept-voice operator:

Women are sometimes treated as sex objects. I really do lack confidence in some of them. I don't know what their problem is, but they do lower themselves.

From a teletype operator:

Some women should be knocked in the head. By offering sex in return for favors, they spoil it for the rest of us who try to do our jobs.

From a radio operator assigned to clerical tasks:

First impressions of Army women are bad. A few of them do join the Army to run around. But not all of us. Most of us are here to do a job.

From a woman who worked as a mechanic in the motor pool:

I think there are some women here who just want to find a man.

From a vehicle mechanic:

> I see most of the problems of women as self-inflicted. Many military women put themselves in the positions they complain about. I feel that women should do any job they are capable of. If they are not capable, they should be separated from the service. What I think is a real kicker is that some women don't give a shit about their Army job. They just want to get pregnant and get out.

In February of 1979, I received a letter from an enlisted woman in the Air Force that described her dismay about how an affair between a senior male officer and a junior female officer affected other women. Selected excerpts from the letter are representative of the divisive effect that such relationships can have on a work setting:

> I am a woman in the United States Air Force, stationed at _____ base. It is a career I selected by choice and I have been proud to wear the Air Force Blue. Through the years of active duty, it has given me a sense of patriotism, self worth, and loyalty to my country. Until recently, I have been impressed with the professionalism of both the officer and enlisted ranks I have been exposed to, especially those of my own sex. Those women who have a job to do should do it well, with high standards and moral values.
>   Over the past year and a half, I have been close witness to a set of very disgusting, demoralizing, and unprofessional set of extreme circumstances. It has taken the form of a very open and unguarded affair between _____ [a male officer] and _____ [female officer] . . . This type of activity is certainly conduct unbecoming of an officer and gives all women in the Air Force a very bad name, especially those of us who desire to make it on our own talents out of bed rather than in it with the boss . . . Weak leaders with no moral value or respect are a very poor example to younger members of the military.[38]

Mama

A third form of hyperfemininity that women can take is the Mother role. The Mother role is often played by an older enlisted woman. Junior enlisted men bring their problems to Mom, who mollifies them. Kanter has also observed that token females sometimes find themselves in a position in which they console groups of men in their work role.[39] Men seem to assume that some women, especially older women, are sympathetic, good listeners, and intuitive.

In the *Fort Devons Dispatch*, there was a feature on a woman who took on the Mother role: "They called me mother—not like swearing. I was just the oldest one, the most stable—I've been a mothering person ever since I can remember."[40] Mothers could also console junior enlisted women, as this account describes:

> She had just had a baby. It was her second child. The first had died. I felt something was wrong. I just couldn't put my finger on it . . . She had no one. I made arrangements with JAG [lawyer unit] to take care of her things. Therefore, one doesn't have to have experienced the same situation to understand that feeling. She thinks that's why she's good at helping people.[41]

The *Army Times* provides us with another twist on the mother theme. The feature story entitled, "Like Mother, Like Son," reported on the experiences of a male private and his mother who both enlisted in the Army. The Army assigned them to the same base so that they could be together:

> At Fort Sill, Oklahoma, the old saying "like father, like son" will have to be changed to "like mother like son" following Pvt. John Allen's recent graduation from basic training. Allen's mother, SP4 Jeanne Allen, joined the Army in August, 1974 and is assigned to the Training Command, Field Artillery Training Center. "John's glueing them back together," [the mother-son relationship] Jeanne said. "After all these years it's hard to believe I'll still be doing it" [the mothering role].[42]

In Khaki Town, there was a 40-year-old woman who reported that junior enlisted men frequently came to her with their problems and referred to her as "mom." However, she commented that she did not like to be treated as "mother" and preferred to maintain a more distant relationship with males. In this example, she was treated *as if* she were a motherly type. In *altercasting*, people are constrained to act in a particular way because of imputation.[43]

The phenomenon of altercasting may entail a key aspect of the formation of social types in Khaki Town. If women are imputed to be little girls, sex objects, or motherly types and action is directed toward them on these imputations rather than in the soldier role, women can be nudged out of conflicting roles. Women soldiers may or may not be taken in by the sexual advances and assistance given to them by their male peers and supervisors. However, the sergeant who acts in an intimate or fatherly manner defines the situation in a particular way that is difficult to block or divert, even for a woman who does prefer a more professional role.

Hewitt argues that the effect of altercasting may be especially severe in instances in which the victim is given a reason to doubt an existing self-concept.[44] The hyperfemininity accommodation may be the result of the limits placed on females by altercasting. Thus, women could retreat to such roles in order to escape the status contradiction of being a woman in a man's job, as well as to receive male rewards.

Amplifying the Soldier Role

Paralleling the overachievers found by Spangler and her colleagues in their study of token women in law school are the women of Khaki Town who fought it out in the sex-role arena.[45] Overachievers in Khaki Town were women who emphasized their soldier role.

Super-Soldier

One type of woman who did not submit to either male paternalism or sexual demands was the female Super-Soldier. The women who artic-ulated this identity tried to gain acceptance into the male enlisted culture by affecting masculine demeanor, lexicon, and what they perceived as the manner of "one of the guys." By attempting to acculturate themselves into the male enlisted culture, these women underplayed their femininity. This style minimized their potential as seductresses, daughters, or mothers. As may be appreciated from the examples in the preceding section, women who fought back and returned banter with the males were attempting to achieve acceptance as "one of the guys."

Physical attributes were deemed important by the woman who tried to play the Super-Soldier role. Participation in sports, preferably in a coeducational setting, was a common recreational activity among these women. Some Super-Soldier women were contemptuous of the hyper-feminine types such as the Mama or Daughter:

> Most women in this unit are not physically fit. They are soft. Many of them are "chubbettes." No fat women should be allowed to enter or stay in the Army. I see lots of them go crying to their supervisor that they can't do their job. I don't think that Army should put up with them. I would like personally to be in combat, but I think the Army should require us to have more training in the field.

Another attribute of Super-Soldier women was an exaggerated patriotism. Many felt the need for military regimentation and strict adherence to discipline:

> Some women are unwilling to do a job or stay in their MOS. But I don't want to sit behind a desk. I'm not afraid of getting dirty. I think they should make the requirements higher. They should tighten the discipline. Punishment should be leveled on those who break the rules.

From another woman articulating this role:

> When I arrived at this command, I was issued field gear and an M-16 [rifle].
> I think that I should have the training in order to use it.
> I find it hard to be strong enough. Sometimes I'm not that strong.
> I have never felt good about being here. The Army doesn't know how to
> approach people. There is always some man coming over when I am trying
> to work. I'm in the middle of a problem that is confusing and am trying to
> think it through. Then some damned sergeant comes over and says, "Why
> aren't you smiling?"
> One day a guy said to me, "Hey, what's the matter, why aren't you
> smiling?" "Smiling?" I said. "I am not smiling. I have work to do. I'm trying
> to get my thoughts straight and you're worried that I'm not smiling. Get the
> hell out of here. Leave me alone, you son-of-a-bitch!" These guys never
> understand that I have a job to do here. Sometimes, I am not really ready for
> fun and games, and I don't care for a lot of bull.

Another woman achieved parity with males by fighting back, according to
her description of the following incident:

> I got tired of all the little remarks and ass-patting one day. As Sergeant
> _____ passed me, he laid his hand on my tail. "You sure have a tight
> little ass," he said. I walked right up to him and pinched his ass as hard as I
> could. "Nice little ass," I said. He never bothered me again after that. So
> many guys can't handle it. The next day, I walked up to him and said,
> "How's that nice little ass?" He turned red and told me not to get near him!
> Now, every time I see Sgt. _____, he tells me to get away.

Another woman in tactical communications strongly identified with
her soldier role. Her pragmatic view of the military as an occupation of last
resort was typical of the Super-Soldier's careerism:

> To me, the military was a good opportunity to move to different places. To
> stay in a factory for 20 years bolting on a screw onto something else would
> drive me crazy. Fluctuations in this career are good. I devote my all to the
> military. I do the best I can to be a good soldier. I was raised to want a
> marriage and children, but could never manage it as a soldier. If I could find
> a man not fearful of me, I would also do the job of managing the home front.
> But as of now, I am a "lifer." I plan to make the Army a career for 20 years
> and maybe 30. I have been trained to do a job. I have progressed through bad
> times here, which have been quite a few. It is quite an achievement. When I
> thought about how many girls cried and couldn't even make it through Basic
> [basic training], I feel good about myself. I love America and I feel I am
> helping even if it is only in a small way.

The Super-Soldiers tended to adhere rigidly to military rules and regimentation. The women who chose this adaptation scored highly on job skills evaluations in Signal Corps jobs. Several of these women were considered to be the most knowledgeable soldiers in their specialty. To gain the respect of men in their units, these women acted like soldiers.

The following story was told to me by a woman who carried herself in a masculine manner and who epitomized many of the traits for this pattern of accommodation:

> I have always been kind of a serious person. When someone starts jumping at me, I'll react to it. Well after about a week after I was here, an inspector asked to see the whole company. "My name is Sergeant _____," he said. "You guys screwed up, and I'm going to nail your ass to the wall." He was real hard and mean. He came up from the ranks, Vietnam and all.
>
> My dad told me that you have to be able to dish it out as well as take it in the Army. I volunteered: "Sergeant," I said, "the reason why this fucking place is not cleaned up is because we just got back from the field." He told me to sit down and shut up. He proceeded to tell us that he would not put up with any more shit. You know, I'd work my ass off for that guy. He's tough but good. Once a lady officer told me to empty trash cans and he heard her ordering me around. I told her that I didn't have to empty no trash cans. I told her that she could "stick those trash cans up her ass." She told me, "I won't tolerate you talking that way. You are not acting like a lady!"
>
> I'm not going to act in any way that is not appropriate for the occasion. The next day, the sergeant called me the best man in his unit. He didn't particularly care for women in the Army, but told me that I wasn't like most women. I was almost like one of the guys. I think he liked me because when he gets on my case, I can give the shit right back!

Another woman reported that there were limits to the extent that she would play the "one-of-the-guys" role: "I don't have virgin ears. But some of these guys sit and curse all day. Most of the time I roll with it. But if they get really outrageous, I tell them to cool it."

Even if women carried off the Super-Soldier role perfectly, there was usually only superficial acceptance by males:

> A lot of men won't even bother learning the regulations about women. They are convinced that we won't be around for long and it would be waste of their time. In general, men receive respect as soon as they arrive in a unit. Women have to earn respect. Men have to earn disrespect.

One of the dangers that women faced when they chose a more masculine presentation of self was to be mistaken as a lesbian. One woman stated this fear in the following way:

I have to stick to myself pretty much here. I'd like to play softball for example, but playing softball means automatically that you are gay. I'm not gay, I just like sports, but no I can't do that here without a label.

The Lone Ranger of Women's Liberation

Another way in which women could adapt was through the Women's-Libber role. Only two women viewed themselves as fighters for the rights of women. Both of them belonged to an unofficial chapter of the National Organization for Women and attended meetings of that group at an Air Force base nearly 100 miles away.

One of the women had an occupational role in the telecommunications field but was hoping to transfer to the position of drug and alcohol counselor so that she could have more overall visibility on the base:

Prejudice against women in the Army is something I am trying to do something about. I brought a supervisor to the Human Relations Office for counseling after he harassed a woman from our unit. He received a formal reprimand from his superiors. Things are better now in that office. He has since been transferred from Khaki Town.

I feel that women can be taught how to protect themselves against unpleasant situations by teaching them where to find regulations and how to use them. There is something in the book to cover nearly every complaint. People have to be educated as to their rights. Some women are told by their supervisors that they must sleep with them or be kicked out of the Army. Others are told that they will receive bad evaluations if they don't cooperate. Some military women who are single mothers are told that they may lose custody of their child if they don't go along with their supervisors. Others are told they must have an abortion or be sent back to the States. This kind of situations can be stopped. Women can be taught the channels to use if supervisors give them a hard time. We must cope with male supremacy and break the traditional views of women's roles!

The other woman who identified herself as a "fighter" against sexism stated that she had the education to qualify for Officer's Candidate School but couldn't get an appointment. She indicated that she was frustrated with her chances of getting ahead in the military. She intended to leave after her first term but would continue to work for the rights of women:

I have been misled from the day I joined. I have seen so much sexual prejudice that the whole thought of the Army sickens me. What kind of problems do we face? Well, first women in general don't have any opportunities here. There are no senior NCO females to go to about problems. There is no one to fight with us and encourage us. Most supervisors believe that we are incapable. It is also hard for women to find a peer group which is intellectually and emotionally stimulating. Women can't seem to get it together as a group because there is a great deal of jealousy between them. Jealousy and vindictive gossip are problems. Women do not necessarily want praise. They just want to be equal and to be able to demonstrate that they can do the job. Yet we are singled out, watched, and continually must prove ourselves. Among other problems that we face are a lack of privacy, meaningless details, and a hypocritical application of military justice. I think that union representation to air legitimate grievances and lessen prejudicial harrassment is the only solution. Women lack cohesiveness and awareness of military oppression. They lack cohesiveness and as a result cannot present unified demands to the chain of command.

Many of Khaki Town's women soldiers were antagonistic toward those women formally associated with the women's liberation movement; they thought that women's liberation meant they would be sent to combat against their own choice. The women in my sample were also unable to grasp the structure of male domination in Khaki Town. There was a tendency to "personalize" many confrontations with males rather than to attribute the problems to being outnumbered. Interpersonal conflicts were viewed as "personality differences" rather than as a function of structure. If a woman was harassed in the mess hall or work setting, the male involved was thought to be weird, sick, crazy, or immature. Most of the women had highly stereotyped notions of women's issues, and many blamed themselves for their problems. The following quotations are from soldiers who disclaimed being "libbers." From a woman who stated that sexual harassment was her most significant problem in the Army:

> I can't agree with many ideas of women's libbers. I don't like the idea of going in combat, for example.

From a private who worked as a multi-channel radio equipment operator and who had earlier commented to me that sexual harassment was a personal concern:

> Although sexism is my most significant problem and it does get to me, I'm no women's libber. I have respect for women who try to make it here but I don't think she should have to do all Army jobs.

From a generator mechanic who stated that, "Women have to work harder here to prove themselves":

> I myself am not a women's libber. I appreciate a gentleman around to help you out at times. I'm not saying that I can't do things. I just need help at times.

From an electronic equipment repairer who commented that she would like to place her NCO in chains because of his sexist attitudes:

We need to get the NCO to understand new ideas and talk one to one as persons, not as soldiers. I also need to get my boyfriend to overcome his jealousy between the men I work with or male friends I have. We should be able to have friendships with the opposite sex without having either party get intimately involved. I can do it but I wish other people could learn to do it. I am not a libber and have many traditional attitudes toward job roles. For women, they must prove they can do some military jobs in case their performance is dangerous to the public.

From a telecommunications center worker who said that men tried to take advantage of her at work:

The only problem is the few men who think that women are good only for cooking and reproducing. The job has to be done no matter whether a man or a woman does it. I feel that women may do their job more thoroughly. Those few who haven't worked with women and seen this are just plain ignorant. A woman does not always have to work. It is easy to get married and let somebody else support you. Woman work because they want to. Not because they have to. And if a person does something because he wants to, rather than because he has to, he will usually do a better job. But I think that the women's movement is carried out too far! No woman can handle as many situations as men. Some women and some men have crazy ways of thinking!

ATTITUDES TOWARD EQUAL RIGHTS

An analysis of the questionnaire responses on women's issues revealed that only a third of the women strongly endorsed the Equal Rights Amendment while 44 percent were uncertain or opposed it; 54 percent of the sample (51 of 91) agreed that women should play principally support roles in society.

The structured questionnaire revealed that women were reluctant to endorse further dedifferentiation of female roles in the military. Only 25 of the women agreed or strongly agreed that they had the physical endurance to perform in combat. The same number endorsed a draft for women in the event of war.

The negative attitude of women on these issues is ironic and somewhat counterintuitive since many of these same women were victimized by the institutional sexism of the Army. At the same time, however, Khaki Town's women were aware of the higher command's lack of responsiveness to their problems. Only 30 percent (32) of the sample thought that the higher command was willing to investigate sex discrimination incidents. Only 25 of the women thought that supervisors in Khaki Town discouraged favoritism based on gender, and only about a fifth of the women thought that commanders were interested in the concerns of women. Despite this awareness, many women blamed themselves or other women for their problems.

WHICH WOMEN STAYED?

No attempt was made to estimate the number of women who fell into each social type: (1) Daddy's Little Girl, (2) the Sex-Pot, (3) Mama, (4) Super-Soldier, and (5) the Lone Ranger of Women's Liberation. Such an effort would have been hazardous because the categories were derived from fleeting unstructured interviews and impressions. Some women had characteristics that placed them into more than one type. There were also other types that I did not investigate fully; in addition, new types were emerging throughout the study. For example, women married to soldiers tended to have different patterns of adjustment. However, as we learned from the unstructured interviews, women married to male soldiers were not necessarily insulated from sexual harassment.

A better measure of overall military adjustment can be derived from the answers to the structured questionnaire. The questionnaire items on military identification and plans for a military career revealed that many women fit into the types that discarded the soldier role. Only 11 of the women (12.2 percent) planned to make the Army a career; another 11 planned to enlist for one additional three- or four-year period. Fifty-two percent of the sample were either not going to complete their initial term of service or were not considering another term of service. Another quarter of the sample (24.2 percent) were undecided as to their plans. The data broadly support the contention that many women were resolving the conflict between the khaki-collar role and femininity by leaving the service.[46] While we observed in Chapter Three that the males in the sample were of slightly higher rank than the females, only 25 percent (29 of 141) of the males were definitely leaving the military; 64 percent of the males had definite plans to make the Army their career. In order to compare men and women of similar career stages, we examined the sex differences for soldiers of only the middle-level enlisted ranks (E-3 to E-5). As is indicated in Table 4.2, there was a definite sex difference in military plans. Males in these ranks were far more likely than females to plan a military career. Given that the females had a higher aptitude and edu-

TABLE 4.2. Sex Differences in Military Plans for Ranks E-3–E-5 (private first class, corporal, sergeant)

	Male Soldiers (E-3–E-5)	Female Soldiers (E-3–E-5)
Leaving the military	29 (25.4%)	40 (50.6%)
Uncertain	25 (21.9%)	28 (35.4%)
Military career or at least one more term	60 (52.6%)	11 (13.9%)
Total	114 (100%)*	79 (100%)*

Notes: Kendall's Tau C = −.40 p < .0001; soldiers from the ranks of E-1 to E-2 and E-6 to E-9 were excluded from this analysis.

*Totals do not add up to 100% due to rounding error

Source: Women in the Military Questionnaire (Appendix B), Spring 1978 (compiled by the author).

cation level for these jobs, it is postulated that tokenism played a significant role in discouraging the women.

Because physical endurance was such an important theme throughout unstructured interviews, it was chosen as a variable for investigating the general question as to which women were more likely to identify themselves as persons with sufficient physical endurance to perform Signal Corps duties in the event of war.

Table 4.3 displays the effect of background variables on a subjective estimate of physical endurance. Age, mother's occupation, and race were statistically significant in their relationship to this variable. Younger women were more likely to view themselves as able to perform in combat than were older women. Forty-five percent of the 18- to 20-year-old women, but only 13 percent of the women between the ages of 24 and 29, saw themselves as battle ready. Women whose mothers never worked or were unemployed for various reasons were more likely to see themselves as able (32.4 percent) than were women whose mothers had blue-collar (18.2 percent) or white-collar (14.3 percent) jobs. Hispanic women (60 percent) and black women (32 percent) were more confident of their combat readiness than were white women.

While not statistically significant, percentage differences reveal that women of lower rank, whose fathers were employed in blue-collar jobs, were raised in the South or Midwest, were single, were of standard religious denominations, and came from large lower-class families were

TABLE 4.3. Kendall Tau and Chi Square Values for Background Characteristics and Military Adjustment Measures (percent of women agreeing or strongly agreeing that they had the physical endurance to perform combat)

	Number	Percentage
1. Age:		
18–20 years	29	44.8
21–24 years	33	24.2
24–29 years	21	12.5
Kendall Tau C = .24; p < .01		
2. Rank:		
E-1 to E-3 (privates)	30	36.7
E-4 (corporals)	40	27.5
E-5 (sergeant)	21	14.5
Kendall Tau C = n.s.		
3. Father's occupation:		
Professional, white-collar	16	12.5
Blue-collar	41	29.3
Not in labor force	34	32.4
Kendall Tau C = n.s.		
4. Mother's occupation:		
Professional, white-collar	14	14.3
Blue-collar	22	18.2
Not in labor force	55	34.5
Kendal Tau C = .17 p < .05		
5. Region of the United States:		
East	15	20.0
Midwest	17	35.3
South	31	38.7
West	20	20.0
Chi Square = n.s.		
6. Marital status:		
Never married	44	34.1
Married first time	22	18.2
Multiple marriages or divorced	25	24.0
Chi Square = n.s.		

7. Religious preference at age 16:

Standard Protestant	21	36.5
Catholic	13	39.7
No religious preference	16	22.2
Nondenominational groups	41	29.3

Chi Square = n.s

---

8. Race:

Caucasian	60	21.7
Black	24	32.0
Hispanic	6	60.0

Chi Square = n.s.

---

9. Number of brothers and sisters:

0–3	31	29.0
4–6	41	17.0
7 and above	19	36.8

Kendall's Tau = n.s.

---

10. Perception of social class at age 16:

Lower	14	42.8
Working	22	27.3
Middle or lower middle	55	13.2

Kendall's Tau = n.s.

---

11. Military occupational assignment:

Khaki-collar, Signal Corps	64	25
Pink-collar	25	32

Kendall's Tau = n.s.

---

12. Percentage of women physically able
by military plans:

Getting out	46	21
Unsure	22	36
Military career	22	50

Kendall Tau C = .37 p < .0001

---

13. Job Satisfaction

Negative	59	18.6
Positive	32	43.8

Kendall's Tau B = .24; p < .01.

Source: Women in the Military Questionnaire (Appendix B), Spring 1978 (compiled by the author).

most likely to succeed in Khaki Town military jobs. Ironically, women who had been assigned out of the most labor-intensive jobs reported the highest combat readiness. Perhaps the greater confidence of women in pink-collar jobs could be attributed to their relative insulation from male enlisted culture; the daily mortification rites over the issue of physical prowess were not directed at clerks or secretaries. As a result, the confidence of pink-collar soldiers may be inflated partially as a result of being tested less often over the issue of combat readiness.

Perception of physical endurance covaried with military plans and overall job satisfaction for women soldiers. Those who felt physically able to perform in combat had the highest identification with the military and were also the most willing to make the military a career.

Table 4.3 reveals that women of a lower social class background were most likely to see themselves as capable of performing combat. Younger women saw themselves generally as more physically capable than did older women. The age difference may reflect broad changes in socialization or differences in training. Background variables are not as illuminative as the unstructured field observations in explaining female adjustment. Unstructured interviews with these women confirmed the lack of anticipatory socialization for khaki-collar jobs.

Unstructured field observations also revealed that women were often arbitrarily released from strenuous assignments, such as performing guard duty along camp perimeters. When women were not allowed to perform tough jobs, self-fulfilling prophesies ensued. In my observation of mixed-sex work groups, I found immediate supervisors who did not even deploy women to some training exercises because of the nuisance of supplying extra latrine facilities and separate tents. If women are initially defined as weaker than men and then not given equal opportunities for training in khaki-collar jobs, they cannot possibly endure in such jobs.

SUMMARY

Unstructured and structured interviews confirmed the presence of role strains in U.S. Army Signal Corps units in Germany. A full test of tokenism would involve a comparative analysis of cases in which the sexes were more equally represented. It would also involve studying women who supervised males performing jobs formerly defined as "all female," as well as supervising males in "male" jobs. However, such a study would not be possible in Khaki Town or in the Army as a whole. In June of 1978, women constituted only 7 percent of E-5 positions, 1.9 percent of E-6 positions, and .09 percent of E-7 positions. There were only 17 women sergeant majors in the entire Army (.07 percent) and less than 10 percent of these women supervisors were in the khaki-collar sector. With so few female role models, it is not surprising that women occupying such jobs resolve gender-role conflicts by leaving the military.

A full study of tokenism in the enlisted military would also include the more socially representative Air Force and Navy. However, few jobs in the Air Force can be classified as being as difficult as the Army jobs studied in Khaki Town. In the Navy, women are not typically assigned to such jobs as boiler-tenders and boatswains, which would be comparable to the physically demanding labor of the Signal Corps.

It is precisely because women were sent to the dispirited Signal Corps that this is such an interesting case study of token women in the military. If the structure is rigged to be inimical to women, self-fulfilling prophesies based on gender-role strains will continue to exclude women from full participation in the military. For Signal Corps women, it may not be such a great advantage to adjust to garrison life under such adverse circumstances. Even for women who overachieved in the military by taking on roles such as the Super-Soldier, there were many social injuries and stresses. As the all-volunteer Army diverges further from social representativeness in the direction of a permanent underclass, women will most likely continue to fill temporary number requirements for the Defense Department. Women continue to be functional as temporary dirty workers to solve the Army's manpower shortages in the all-volunteer force. However, if the structure of tokenism in these settings is not changed, expansions in numbers may not result in any permanent gains for women to supervisory positions because of the structure of male domination.

Paralleling Kanter's theoretical study, Khaki Town women faced isolation from the work culture, sexual shakedowns, heightened visibility, and mistaken identity.[47] As a response to these stresses, they developed two broad patterns that parallel what Spangler and her colleagues called *underachievement* and *overachievement*.[48] The first three types were patterns of accommodation in which women resolved their status contradiction by underachieving: (1) Daddy's Little Girl, (2) the Sexpot, and (3) Mama. In contrast, the Super-Soldier and the Lone Ranger of Women's Liberation were amplifications of the work role. If the proportion of female soldiers was increased and the female enlisted culture strengthened, other social types could be expected to develop, but, like the whore-lesbian stereotype of women subscribed to by enlisted males, women currently either underachieve or overachieve in their soldier and female roles. Until the structure of male domination is altered, it is difficult for women to perform the female and work role at the same time. Male enlisted culture is both numerically and socially too powerful to allow women to interweave femininity and khaki-collar employment.

Long Laws found in her study of academic women that members of the dominant group voluntarily helped the token survive in the organization.[49] In the next chapter, the attitudes of the Army's dominant group will be assessed. We shall learn that few male soldiers are willing to sponsor the token woman soldier.

Because so many women have left the military, it is questionable whether military participation as tokens has been a real gain. In prior studies of women in professional organizations, tokens gained social status as lawyers, professors, or managers. In contrast, the women of Khaki Town did not even achieve medium-level managerial positions within the organization or the benefits of military retirement. However, these women did leave the military with educational benefits that could be cashed in *outside* the military. If it was advantageous for these women to weather the social injuries of tokenism, the rewards would accrue outside the Army. One difference between tokenism in a low-status organization such as the Army, compared with professional organizations, may be that payoffs occur *outside* the low-status organization. However, this hypothesis cannot be verified without a longitudinal study of what happens to token women in the Army after they leave the organization. In the next chapter, we shall learn more about how women have been "cooled out" of the Army.

NOTES

1. Mady Wechsler Segal, "Women in the Military: Research Progress and Prospects," in David R. Segal and John D. Blair, eds. "Young Women in the Military," *Youth and Society*, special issue (December 1978): 108.

2. Ibid.

3. Kathleen P. Durning, "Women at the Naval Academy: An Attitude Study," in Anne Hoiberg, ed., *Armed Forces and Society*, special issue (Summer 1978): 569–88.

4. Jack M. Hicks, "Women in the Army," in Hoiberg, *Armed Forces and Society*, special issue, pp. 647–58.

5. Marcelite C. Jordan, "Utilization of Women in Industrial Career Fields" (Proceedings of the Fifth Symposium on Psychology at the Air Force Academy, Colorado Springs, Colo., April 1976), pp. 91–94.

6. Roger Manley, Robert J. Lucas, and Eleyse T. Manley, "Men and Women Managers: A Comparative Study of Values and Career Objectives" (Paper presented at the 34th Annual Meeting, Academy of Management, Seattle, Wash., August 1974).

7. Steve Gorman, "The Marines Are Looking For a Few Good Women," unpublished manuscript (Washington, D.C.: Headquarters, United States Marine Corps, 1977).

8. Joel M. Savell, John C. Woelfel, and Barry Collins, "Attitudes Concerning Job Appropriateness for Women in the Army" (Alexandria, Va.: U.S. Army Research Institute for the Behavioral and Social Sciences, June 1976).

9. Lois B. DeFleur and David Gilman, "Cadet Beliefs, Attitudes, and Interactions During the Early Phases of Sex Integration," in Segal and Blair, eds., "Young Women in the Military," pp. 165–90.

10. Ibid.

11. This review only describes research conducted on male-female relations. For a more

complete review of military women covering such topics as military effectiveness, see Segal and Blair, and Hoiberg. M. C. Devilbliss has recently completed a series of studies of enlisted women available through the Secretariat of the Armed Forces and Society Organization at the University of Chicago.

12. Rosabeth Moss Kanter, *Men and Women of the Corporation* (New York: Basic Books, 1977), and "The Problems of Tokenism" (Paper presented to Wellesley College, Center for Research on Women in Higher Education and the Professions [now Center for Research on Women], 1974).

13. Charles F. Marden and Gladys Meyer, *Minorities in American Society* (New York: D. Van Nostrand, 1969), p. 271.

14. Kanter, *Men and Women of the Corporation*, pp. 248–49; Kanter, "The Problems of Tokenism," pp. 13–17.

15. Judith Long Laws, "The Psychology of Tokenism," *Sex Roles* 1 (1975): 51–69.

16. Eve Spangler, Marsha A. Gordon, and Ronald M. Pipkin, "Token Women: An Empirical Test of Kanter's Hypothesis," *American Journal of Sociology*, vol. 84, no. 1 (1978): 160–69.

17. Assistant Secretary of Defense for Manpower, Reserve Affairs, and Logistics, unpublished statement (July 1972).

18. Commanders and Khaki Town were unable to provide me with these data. It was my experience that commanders experienced "chronological confusion" because they truly did not know how many women were assigned to their units. The overseas military environment is marked by a rapid turnover of personnel. At any one time, it is not possible to know the exact numbers of women. Even at the Assistant Secretary of Defense level, I discovered errors in the estimation of numbers. In general, when commanders were asked about the history of women in their units, the were unlikely to be able to recollect numbers.

19. Department of Defense, Office of the Assistant Secretary of Defense for Manpower, Reserve Affairs, and Logistics, *Use of Women in the Military*, 2d ed. (Washington, D.C.: 1978) pp. 10–13.

20. Paul F. Secord and Carl W. Backman, *Social Psychology* (New York: McGraw-Hill, 1964), chap. 15.

21. Assistant Secretary of Defense for Manpower, Reserve Affairs, and Logistics, unpublished data, 1979.

22. Editors, "Wac of the Week: Fort Benning's Rhonda Catches Their Eyes," *Army Times*, February 6, 1974.

23. Letter to the editor, "Sexist Cartoons, Article Draw Fire," *Army Times*, March 8, 1976.

24. Since 1978, the Defense Department has been phasing out these characters from their training materials.

25. Kanter, *Men and Women of the Corporation*, p. 240.

26. Letter to the editor, "Army Women—Thrown to the Wolves?", *Army Times*, March 3, 1980.

27. Jay Finnegan, "Panel Told of Sex Incidents: Fort Meade Cases," *Army Times*, February 25, 1980.

28. Kanter, *Men and Women of the Corporation*, p. 210.

29. Kanter, "The Problems of Tokenism" pp. 18–21; this dimension of tokenism was a dominants' response described in Kanter's earlier work but not described as such in *Men and Women of the Corporation*.

30. Don Hirst, "Rogers' Message: Female Troops No Part-Timers," *Army Times*, March 20, 1978, p. 4.

31. *Air Force Times*, May 24, 1976.

32. Orrin Klapp, "Social Types: Process and Structure," *American Sociological Review* vol. 23, no. 6 (1958): 674–78.

33. Charles C. Moskos, *The American Enlisted Man: The Rank and File in Today's Military* (New York: Russell Sage Foundation, 1970), p. 64.

34. J. E. Bruckel, "Effect of Morale of Infantry Team Replacement System," *Sociometry* vol. 18 (1967): 129–42.

35. Robert E. Park, "Human Migration and the Marginal Man," *American Journal in Sociology* (May 1928): 881–82.

36. Everett Stonequist, *The Marginal Man: A Study in Personality and Culture Conflict* (New York: Rusell and Rusell, 1937) pp. xvii and xviii.

37. Spangler, Gordon, and Pipkin, "Token Women."

38. Personal letter, January 1979.

39. Kanter, *Men and Women of the Corporation*, pp. 233–34.

40. Honey Rand Knapp, "Call Her Soldier, Call Her Mom," *Fort Devons Dispatch*, January 1980, p. 5.

41. Ibid.

42. Editors, "Like Mother, Like Son," *Army Times*, May 24, 1976.

43. See John P. Hewitt, *Self and Society: A Symbolic Interactionist Social Psychology*, 2d ed. (Boston: Allyn and Bacon, 1979), p. 151.

44. Ibid.

45. Spangler, Gordon, and Pipkin, "Token Women," pp. 167–69.

46. During the early years of the volunteer military, women had a lower attrition rate than their male counterparts. However, recently these trends have been reversed. The *Wall Street Journal* reports that, as of August 1980, women soldiers failed to finish their initial term at a much higher rate than men. The fallout rate for women was expected to reach 46.7 percent. Much of this fallout can be attributed to sex-role strains because women enter the Army with higher educational levels and higher aptitude.

The official Defense Department explanation for this paradox was reported in hearings before the Military Personnel Subcommittee of the U.S. House of Representatives, "Women in the Military," (February 11, 1980), p. 110. According to Robert White, the Assistant Secretary of Defense, attrition in recent years is linked to lower female quality:

"While first-term male attrition rates have shown a downward trend, first-term attrition rates for females have increased and current projections indicate that they will continue to increase. Factors influencing these forecasts are: reduction in female entrance scores from 59 to 50 during fiscal year 1978 and from 50 to 31 during fiscal year 1979; [Males have been allowed to enlist with scores as low as 16 during the same period.]; increase in female losses from the trainee discharge program and physical disqualifications during the first six weeks of service; reduction in female entrance educational requirements in fiscal year 1980 by allowing at least 3,000 non–high school diploma graduates to enlist."

47. Kanter, *Men and Women of the Corporation*, pp. 248–49.

48. Long Laws, "The Psychology of Tokenism."

49. Ibid.

Chapter Five

MALE ENLISTED CULTURE AND
THE STRUCTURE OF TOKENISM

ANTIEFFEMINACY AND MILITARY MASCULINITY

In Chapter One, we noted that the military, historically and cross culturally, has been the province of males. Except in times of extreme external crisis, women have been proscribed from martial roles. In Chapter Two, it was argued that women have been included in the all-volunteer army as a reserve force of last resort. Both of these patterns circumscribe male attitudes toward women in today's Army.

The decline of traditional virility as a useful attribute has been observed in virtually every contemporary social institution. However, the enlisted male culture has been a relatively protected bastion of male sanctity.[1] The military is one of the last legitimate channels, other than football and hockey, for the full expression of preadolescent aggression, where males participate in organized violence both actively and vicariously.

The cult of manliness is emphasized in recruitment and training. Males are encouraged to join the Army to become a man. The Marine Corps wants only "a few good men." In basic training, males who do not perform well are labeled as "women." As Arkin and Dobrofsky found, sex-oriented rhymes functioned as cadence counts in basic training:

I don't know but I've been told. Eskimo pussy is mighty cold.

I got a gal in Kansas City. She's got gumdrops on her titties.[2]

Elkins studied the conversation of enlisted soldiers and found that it reflected a disdain for authority and a freedom from the social restraints that characterize civilian society. One group of expressions conveyed the image of strength and virility: "In the Army, as in other male societies, in the work gang, the college fraternity, the sporting and gambling worlds, these vulgar words for physiological functions and the sex act enjoy a greatly extended and exaggerated role."[3]

The swaggering and satorial masculinity reinforced by enlisted male culture is openly disdainful of women. Men who performed clerical duties were viewed as male WACs and "chickens." If men did not measure up to the image of the dogface who could close in on the enemy and make him say hello to his dead friends, they were thought of as "pussies."

Dixon argued that antieffeminacy pervades military organizations. He tried to account for misogyny with a psychosocial explanation:

1. Some men, for reasons rooted in their early family situation, have serious doubts about their sexual adequacy and/or physical strength and size.
2. Such men may deal with their feelings of inferiority by adopting a compensatory style of life in which they strive for reassurance in some suitably symbolic role.
3. The prevailing ethos of many military organizations provides this reassurance.
4. Hence, a percentage of men will seek acceptance by the armed forces simply because such acceptance is a warranty of their masculinity.[4]

SOCIAL TYPES OF ENLISTED MALES

As the research in Chapter Four indicated, the women of Khaki Town employed four general strategies of structuring their military women statuses. The male soldiers of Khaki Town created many of the normative expectations that circumscribed female adaptations. In this section, the social types of enlisted males in Khaki Town will be described in order to shed some light on the reasons for the patterned stereotypes they used to label the enlisted women.

Social-type analysis operates on the assumption that recognizable, nondeliberate, and dynamic links between personality and social structure can be drawn. Social types emerge as meaningful recipes for social action in particularized social settings. Klapp sees the study of social types as useful in mapping webs of social relations:

First, in connection with statuses, they permit a more exact specification of the behavior to be expected from a person than the formal statuses alone generally provide. Second, they are a source of new formal statuses. Third, social types serve, as do statuses, to place individuals in society and to control their behavior when formal statuses are not available. Fourth, they aid in an individual's self-concept by emphasizing those features of his behavior which the group finds significant.[5]

The Army's social types are recognizable in virtually every garrison community. In bases outside Khaki Town, there are structurally equivalent argot roles in the forms of Lifers, Short-Termers, Goons, Heads, Juicers, Brothers, Trained Killers, Turkeys, Students, Red-Necks, and poverty-stricken Married Men. Social types, as articulated in male enlisted culture, were numerous and heterogeneous. The question of how women soldiers find meaning in enlisted culture is inextricably linked to their relationships with their male counterparts.

Barracks Rats

Barracks Rats are a social type of single GIs whose major interests are "drugs, sex, and rock and roll!" According to a widely shared stereotype in the military community, Barracks Rats spend much of their off-duty time listening to high-powered stereos, drinking cheap wine, taking drugs, stealing, and fighting. They are seen as sensual oafs and are blamed for the decline of the Old Army by senior noncommissioned officers.

A reference is made to Barracks Rats as a discredited type in the October 1977 *Newsletter* of the Khaki Town Army Community Service:

> Barracks rats!!! How about Housing Rats? Everyone talks about the Single GI's who do nothing but lay around the barracks on their time off. When was the last time you got out of your house and went somewhere other than the Commissary or PX? I know what you are going to say—"What is there to do?" Now you are guilty of being a Housing Rat. In the *Khaki Town* Military community alone, there are over 30 Private Associations that provide recreational facilities.[6]

Goon Squad

The distinctive feature of the Goon Squad types is their deviance. "Goons" are administrative or judicial dischargees on their way out of the Army. Goon Squad members are no longer part of a unit. Instead, these soldiers are placed in special work details. When others are performing their jobs during a work day, Goons pick up paper, trash, and perform other menial tasks. At night, their behavior is particularly distinctive. They make animal cries similar to the sound of Gibraltar rock apes in the early morning hours. While not formally incarcerated, the Goons are confined to quarters, in contrast with other enlisted persons who received passes. Since Goon Squad members know that their receiving dishonorable discharges is inevitable, they devote themselves to antagonizing the command, acting out symbolic aggression against what they perceive as the Green Machine, which rejected them.

There is a population of Goon Squad types in virtually every garrison. Prime candidates for the Goon Squad are individuals who have been discharged against their will. To protect themselves against assults to their identity, they affect a reaction-formation in the form of a "fuck the Army" attitude. The ubiquity of this social type is partially determined by the large number of individuals who are discharged before they complete their first term of service. In 1977, 40 percent of all Army first-termers failed to complete their initial term.

Representative of the antisocial behavior displayed by Goons was the case of Mark E_____. Mark sewed bells, baubles, ribbons, and stars on his uniform and attempted to board a military aircraft, carrying a tray of mandarin oranges and "joints." Mark was immediately discharged administratively rather than being court-martialed.

Heads

The drug culture of the late 1960s is alive and well in the barracks of Khaki Town and other overseas garrisons. The drug counterculture has filtered down from the upper middle class to the working class setting of American enlisted culture. As Jay Finnegan, writer for the *Army Times* observed, "I would be hard put to find a better research site than the barracks for a study of the drug culture":

> Hard rock blasts from oversized speakers. Men debate the merits of Jamaican, Lebanese, Columbian, and Panamanian marijuana. They grumble about shortages of certain brands of exotic pot. Then they switch to a discussion of hallucinogens—"orange sunshine," "strawberry acid," "purple haze," "chocolate mescaline," "cosmos," and "microdots."[7]

Heads often decorate their living spaces with black lights, posters of Jimmie Hendrix, or psychedelic posters from the Vietnam protest era. German vendors outside the gates of Khaki Town's bases have discovered a lucrative market for drug paraphernalia. Turkish and other Middle Eastern *gastarbeiters* (guest workers) turn large profits from the sale of drugs to Heads.

In a report entitled "The Boys in the Barracks," written by Major Larry Ingraham as an in-house study of the "drug problem" in the U.S. Army in Europe, it was acknowledged that extensive drug networks existed in the barracks:

Drug use is no longer the province of an isolated, deviant fringe. It is so thoroughly embedded into the ongoing activities of the barracks that it is almost as difficult to find evenings when someone is not using marijuana as it is to find evenings when someone is not drinking beer.

In general, drug use is no big deal for soldiers. It is simply accepted as part of everyday life, like eating or sleeping.[8]

Bryant argues that there has been a long historical association between narcotics and the military establishment:

From ancient times until the present, military men, and especially those engaged in actual fighting, have turned to chemical substances to prepare them mentally for the ardors of battle and to sustain them in the monotony of garrison duty.

In previous wars, however, narcotic usage by military personnel did not pose a significant problem in terms of extent, although the number of veterans who were addicted was relatively high.

The Vietnamese War has produced a military drug problem of significant proporptions. Some observers have reported that as many as three-fourths of the GIs there smoked marijuana, and even some official reports have indicated that thirty-five percent of troops have used marijuana.[9]

My estimate is that one in six enlisted soldiers who lived in the barracks were heavy users of drugs. This excludes the occasional users of "hashish," who do not identify themselves as Heads, per se. Heads give off signals that they are drug-using types; they may wear their hair parted in the middle and may wear "granny-style" rimless glasses.

Lifers

Hair is an excellent boundary marker separating social types in the Army. Within the narrow boundaries of a military regulation haircut, subcultural differences can be expressed. While the military exerts total control over the maximum length of hair, individuals still find ways to express their subcultural memberships. In enlisted culture, the most distinctive boundary in the expression of hair style is between Lifers and Short-Termers. Lifers are most often noncommissioned officers who identify with traditional military culture and who anticipate that the Army will be a permanent home. Lifers identify with the organization and "signal" their intentions to remain in the Army through their reenlistment decisions. Lifers, in general, wear their hair shorter within the parameters of military hair regulations than do Short-Termers.

Social life for Lifers revolves around the Rod and Gun Club, the NCO

Club, and German *gasthauses*, where men exchange war stories and folklore about military life. For the most part, people who identify themselves as careerists are self-policed and thought by the higher command to be the "backbone of the enlisted force."

Juicers

A subgroup of Lifers are known by Heads and others as Juicers because of their heavy alcohol consumption. Every overseas base has a Class VI store, which sells alcohol, tax-free, to service personnel. It is possible to purchase a gallon of low-grade whiskey for under $4.00 in the Class VI store. Happy hours at NCO clubs are another source of cheap liquor. During happy hours, it is possible to buy bar drinks for twenty-five to fifty cents.

Bryant observes that drinking plays a prominent role in the military subculture:

> Military garrison duty is monotonous, often uncomfortable, sometimes unpleasant and frequently lonely. With nothing to do, nowhere to go, and often nobody (relatively speaking) with whom to do it, drinking becomes an institutionalized way of spending one's free time. "Fun" may have to be vicarious and conviviality may have to be contrived. Alcohol facilitates these processes. From the standpoint of the authorities, alcohol serves to help solve the problem of morale and boredom and helps prevent the buildup of potentially disruptive if not dangerous frustrations.[10]

The boundary between those who use drugs and those who use alcohol was a source of divisiveness in Khaki Town. Heads commented negatively on the Lifers' drinking, while Lifers criticized the drug usage of Heads. Finnegan summarized the demarcation between druggies and Juicers in this way:

> While dope-smoking soldiers look down on booze-swigging "lifers," they also drink a considerable amount of beer and cheap wine. But drugs are normally used in conjuction with other activities—playing cards, prowling through bars in search of women, or making a snack run.[11]

A third boundary between Lifers and Short-Termers is the choice of music. Music is a signal of group identity in the same way that hair and substance consumptions are. Lifers tend to prefer country music while Heads prefer "acid" or "punk rock." In barracks living areas, high-powered stereos, capable of making the hall light fixtures gyrate, were conspicuously displayed. At the day's end after reveille, one could simultaneously hear country western, blues, acid rock, soul, and "bubble gum" music. Music was as good an indicator as any of social types within the male enlisted culture. At the NCO Club, which was managed by senior noncommissioned officers, country music and soul music predominated. In the barracks, the type of music generally played symbolized the value system of the listener.

Other than the lifer- short-termer dichotomy, there was considerable overlap among social types. Blacks, while constituting over 40 percent of the enlisted force in Khaki Town, did not in general form a homogenous subculture. Blacks in Khaki Town were most likely to be included in groups such as the Goon Squad, Short-Termers, and Lifers. In a few Khaki Town units, however, some blacks formed a separate group.

Brothers

In some companies, blacks "packed their hair" and wore Afros off-duty symbolizing heightened racial consciousness. However, lifer-short-termer boundaries were much less penetrable than black-white lines. Unlike in civilian society, it was common to see blacks and whites form friendships both on- and off-duty. A black senior NCO was more likely, for example, to form friendship ties with other NCOs than he was to identify with other blacks. Junior enlisted blacks sometimes formed alliances with other blacks as Brothers but were more likely to be a part of other junior enlisted groups.

Other Social Types

Trained Killers

In virtually every military community, there is an individual known by his peers as a dangerous and irrational person. While the "trained killer" may or may not be a liar, it is clear that he is not a professional soldier. I met a Trained-Killer type in Khaki Town, who was the husband of one of my University of Maryland students. I was invited to dinner at my student's house. Despite the protestations of my student, "Killer" insisted on telling me war stories accompanied by a slide presentation. One slide, in particular, sickened me; it was a picture of "Killer" with two of his buddies posed before the bodies of three Viet Cong males. The "Killer" had apparently severed the head of one Viet Cong and was depicted scooping out the brains of the corpse with a spoon.

The Trained Killer is a social type who defines himself strictly in terms of his aggressiveness and combat readiness. He is the type of individual who sleeps with a bowie knife under his pillow, poised for enemy attack even in peacetime duty. Trained killers are not necessarily highly regarded by peers. In wartime, a Trained Killer may be the person whose poor judgment and recklessness causes unnecessary death and injury.

Turkeys

Another discredited social type in Khaki Town was the Turkey. The Turkey was a social type played by individuals who were illiterate, incompetent, or so poorly motivated that they could not perform a job. The military duties of the Turkey had to be covered by others in the unit. If they couldn't be administratively discharged, Turkeys were often shifted from unit to unit until their term of service was completed. An assiduous eye was kept on Turkeys by other men in the unit. In Khaki Town, a Turkey had electrocuted himself and several other members of his unit when he attempted to set up a radio generator in a trench. In another case, a Turkey tried to give his two and a half ton truck a jump with his radio generator. The difference in voltage gave the Turkey a tremendous shock and also ruined the truck's engine. Turkeys had to be watched continuously so that their "fuck-ups" did not endanger the equipment and lives of other men.

Students

Since 1949, the University of Maryland has taught university classes to overseas service personnel. Some commanders encourage their soldiers to take off-duty classes at night. In Khaki Town, there was a social type who identified more with the student role than with the soldier role. The Student was more likely to define himself in terms of his future professional role and was likely to be a Short-Termer with definite goals. Students deviated from enlisted culture in several ways. First, Students were less likely to spend off-duty time in the clubs, prostitution zone, or barracks. They were more likely than other soldiers to spend off-duty time traveling in Germany or studying in the library. Secondly, Students were more likely to be motivated to learn the German language. This skill also gave them advantages in forming relationships with German women.

Finally, Students were likely to bring their books to work. In garrison life, there are many periods when soldiers must put in time without having actual duties. Students tried to fill this time by doing homework assignments and extra reading. Sometimes this adaptation caused resentment from non-Students. In Khaki Town some commanders forbade Students to read on duty. They were ordered to "look busy" even if there was nothing to do. In other cases, commanders placed barriers limiting the student role. Some soldiers were not given permission to take courses. The excuse given in these instances was that education interfered with military duties. Another tactic designed to subvert the student role was to assign a soldier to the field during the middle of a semester. If a Student was considered by his peers to be a reliable team member in other ways, barriers against the student role could be easily circumvented. But if a Student was considered to be a shirker or a malcontent, formidable barriers were erected. In one poignant incident, two Student types taught one of their company members to read while performing charge-of-quarters duty. This act placed them in a position favorable toward fulfilling their own educational goals.

Red-Necks

The Red-Neck is a social type who listens to country music and participates in the rodeo and stock-car circuits of garrison bases in Europe. The Red-Neck signals his identity chiefly through clothing. When off-duty, the Red-Neck wears "shit-kicker" cowboy boots, a Stetson, and drives a pickup or van. The weekend for the Red-Neck may involve hunting wild boar, wrestling steers, working on a stock car, or participating in a demolition derby. Red-Necks are often Lifers or junior enlisted men who identify with the military as a career.

Married Enlisted Men

Over 50 percent of Khaki Town's enlisted males were married. Historically, the enlisted male culture has been thought of as a single man's occupation; however, in the volunteer era, many men enlisted in order to receive remunerative benefits for their families. Married service-men identified with many of the preceding social types but also had a distinctive character as a result of marital status. During the period of my research, married servicemen, particularly in lower enlisted ranks, faced an array of financial and psychological difficulties in an overseas setting. If lower-ranked personnel had to support their families without command sponsorship, they were likely to face poverty.

The Report on Junior Enlisted Personnel Stationed Overseas presented to the Armed Services Committee of the House of Representatives in 1978 revealed the following hardships:

1. Over 70 percent of junior enlisted personnel elect to take their families overseas at the present time.
2. The current overseas station housing allowance tends to discriminate against junior members. Some senior members received a housing allowance somewhat greater than their expenses and some junior members tend to receive less.
3. The high cost of auto insurance rates, together with the high cost of transportation, generally was found to be a considerable burden, especially on the most junior personnel.

In Khaki Town, there were many cases of hardships to families of junior enlisted personnel. The Armed Services Committee documented the following cases, which are generally representative of the severe problems confronting the married serviceman overseas:

An E-3, 21 years old with 20-year-old wife and one child spent $335 to bring his family to Germany. Initial cost of $440 for deposits on apartment and utilities. Pays $365 for a month rent and utilities for one-bedroom un-furnished apartment in poor condition even by local standards. Sold car owned one year at $495 loss. Thirteen-mile distance from home to job dictated purchase of car in Germany. Borrowed $1,850 from credit union for car and insurance—pays $115 a month repayment. Full coverage insurance costs him $1,788 per year. Necessities (food, clothes, laundry, etc.) run about $245 per month. Result: Member has an unfavorable information file for bad debts and bad checks.

An E-3 brought his wife and child to Germany at his own expense. After 6 months of living on the German economy, the member developed major financial difficulties. Consequently, the member had to send his family back to the United States at his own expense. He moved into the enlisted dormitory to complete the rest of his tour. Marital problems developed from this unfortunate situation which also led to disciplinary problems and several letters of reprimand.[12]

The preceding cases illustrate the plight of the junior enlisted man with a family. Cases such as these gave rise to articles and cartoons in German newspapers, which cast the once affluent GI in the role of a now impoverished soldier begging for handouts from the German population. It was striking to observe that the pockets of poverty in Khaki Town generally consisted of the badly maintained apartments rented by the American soldiers and the Eastern European guest workers. The personal and family difficulties of the impoverished married servicemen precluded their full involvement in the male enlisted culture.

When women integrated Signal Corps jobs, they added yet another dimension to the social types found in the male enlisted culture. Women formed alliances such as the Daddy Warbucks-Daughter and Sergeant Seducto-Sex Pot partnerships with extant types in the enlisted military. For example, women in the Daddy Warbucks role alliance found their partners in the Lifers or Juicers groups. The Sergeant Seducto could be a subtype within any number of existing types such as the Lifers, the Students, or even the married men.

FEMALE SOLDIERS AS THREATS
TO MILITARY MASCULINITY

Prior to the introduction of women into the military, enlisted culture had begun to change rapidly. The integration of blacks into the services and the Vietnam War brought many changes, as did the transition from the draft Army. In addition, the military itself, through changes in the technology of war, made traditional definitions of the soldier role obsolete. There has also been a general change in the basis of discipline as well as in the ethos of traditional military organization. Janowitz's study, *The Professional Soldier*, first described the slow and continuing transformation of authoritarian discipline in the military to a more civilianized management of soldiers.[13] In the new military, ascendant managerial, technological, and bureaucratic roles have replaced drunken conviviality, profane values, and heroics. As a result, the management of killing has been transformed. Physical strength has been replaced by strategy and tactics. However, the Marine's fight cry of "Kill! Kill! Hate! Hate! Murder! Murder! Mutilate!" is atavistic to the Air Force, which proclaims that "Peace is our Profession." Profane values and supermasculinity are valued more in the labor-intensive Army and Marines than in the technically oriented Air Force and Navy.

Even in the Army and Marines, women successfully occupying men's traditional roles create fears about the changing nature of the military. If a woman can do the job, the job can't be a way of affirming masculinity. More importantly, when women enter the traditionally male domains, enlisted men's freedom from social restraints, as well as the jokes, language, and camaraderies of a previously all-male domain, are threatened. It is for these reasons that the enlisted male culture resists the incorporation of women in traditional military roles. The next section explores male attitudes toward the inclusion of women in khaki-collar jobs in the Signal Corps. These women, as we shall learn, found few males willing to support their integration.

The Male View of Female Tokenism

They're shoving them down our throats from above.
— Anonymous Staff Sergeant, Khaki Town

There is a striking parallel between American enlisted men's attitudes toward the inclusion of women in formerly all-male domains and British male coal miners' attitudes toward women in underground mining jobs in the 1840s. In volume 1 of *Capital*, Karl Marx described official government surveys of the attitudes of male miners. Women were included in underground jobs chiefly to load coal and draw the wagons to the canals and railways. They were primarily the daughters and widows of working miners and ranged in age from 12 to 60 years. The findings reported by Marx showed that the typical male miner was opposed to the inclusion of the female proletariat:

I think it is degrading to the sex.

There is a peculiarity of dress. Yes. . . It is a man's dress, and I believe in some cases, it drowns all sense of decency.

I believe that women having children (and there are plenty on the banks they have) cannot do her duty to her children.[14]

In answer to the issue of women's economic need to work, males responded that they would prevent women from taking this type of employment, even if the women could not find employment elsewhere. The question of the moral character of female miners brought the following responses: "It is injurious to their morality"; "the degradation in this social bearing on the girls is deplorable in the extreme"; "When those girls become colliers' wives, the men suffer from the degradation, and it causes them to leave their home and drink."[15]

The male workers viewed the employment of women coal miners as both a sex role and an economic threat. Hartman's analysis of the opposition of male workers to women stresses the dual and contradictory character of their opposition:

That male workers viewed the employment of women as a threat to their jobs is not surprising, given an economic system when competition among workers was characteristic. That women were paid lower wages exacerbated the threat. But why their response was to attempt to exclude women rather than organize them is explained, not by capitalism, but by patriarchal relations between men and women: men wanted to assure that women would continue to perform the appropriate tasks at home.[16]

Engels believed that females' lower wages enabled them to be used as a "reserve army of labor." In *The Conditions of the Working Class in England*, he reports an incident that occurred in the 1830s in Glasgow:

The Committee put a price on the heads of all backlegs [strikebreakers] . . . and deliberately organized arson in factories. One factory to be set on fire had women backlegs on the premises who had taken the place of men at the spinning machines. . . hostility to the competition of young females, almost certainly less well trained and lower paid, was common enough.[17]

The Image of Women in Official Reports of the High Command

It is a mistake to blame the problems of women in Signal Corps jobs solely on the attitudes and behavior of enlisted males or sergeants. The official side bet of top command is that women will have problems adjusting to khaki-collar work.

The *Final Report* of the Army Administration Center in 1978 identified the following issues as possible limitations of women: size, strength, grip, arm and leg length, endurance, coordination, aggressiveness, toughness, mechanical ability, pregnancy, and self-image.[18] Much of this report was focused on sex differences based upon physiology and psychology. By postulating these differences *a priori*, the higher command did not visualize women as successfully fulfilling physically demanding jobs. Before women even occupy such jobs, there has been an initial definition of the situation that blames women for failure. Excerpts are culled from this Army report on the utilization of women:

The issue of pregnancy is perceived by the Army in the field as the greatest impediment to the full integration of women in the Army.

In many cases the women do not pull their share of extra duty, are exempted from field duty, draw pay and allowances without earning them, and are not required to maintain minimum dress standards. Morale of other soldiers is lowered by the real or perceived inequitable treatment.

Based on a literature search and review, there is compelling evidence to indicate that in leadership roles women will be significantly less effective than men in the near term.

The introduction of women into previously all male groups will alter the dynamics and affect the performance of that group [negatively].

The comment is frequently heard that women do not hold up well under stressful conditions. For this reason it has been argued that women should not be in stress potential jobs.[19]

When the Department of Army had actual data on sex-role tensions, they frequently took the stand that women were responsible for any problems that were created. The following passage from the *Final Report* reflects this "blaming the victim" position:

Sexual fraternization is an inevitable consequence of the widespread integration of women throughout the Army.... Cited as especially vulnerable to the problems of sex fraternization are mixed gender teams or small units with remote, isolated missions. Of grave concern are the speculative effects on combat potency. Widespread rape is also feared in stressful situations.

Women are distractive to men and as long as the ratio of men to women in the Army remains large, many male soldiers, if not the majority, will accept women as women, but not as soldiers.[20]

Women were sent to Khaki Town units with very little attempt from the higher command to provide a structure "conducive" to integration. The *Final Report* admits the hiatus in policies and programs for women:

Senior commanders, when faced with having female soldiers assigned to their organization, have not always imparted an objective and/or positive attitude down the chain of command. In some instances, this has taken the form of battalion and company commanders not assigning the female soldier to work in the MOS [military occupational specialty] for which she was trained. As a result, the soldier worked in one of the more traditional jobs for females, such as typist or clerk.[21]

High command provides little training in military leadership regarding the special problems of male-female interaction. In every level of management, supervisors are uncertain how to deal with the particular problems and prospects of women. The *Final Report* states that there is no effort to assist supervisors in "leading" women in formerly all-male domains:

Currently in the officer basic and advanced courses for the combat arms [specialty], no education program exists that acquaints these officers with the fact that they might have to supervise or lead female soldiers and that there are some basic differences between male and female soldiers that must be considered to assure effective leadership.

In advanced courses for combat arms, non-commissioned officers, the emphasis is on technical expertise at the platoon sergeant level, with the leadership aspects only addressing what is necessary to lead men to perform within the platoon.[22]

In addition to the failure to instruct supervisors, there is little effort to change the structure of military life in any way to accommodate women. Military "realities" are accepted as the way things must be:

Commanders faced with the assignment of women and no monies to renovate billets have generally given the women the authority to reside off post. ... This action frequently creates a morale problem because the men see it as a special consideration for women while they [men] have to continue living in overcrowded and unsanitary conditions. The men also perceive that the women are exempt from company duties and therefore getting over.

Numerous enlisted career fields are lacking noncommissioned officer "role models," in comparison with a large female content in the E-1 to E-4 categories.

The only day-care facilities at Army posts in the United States are those provided by non-appropriated fund activities or by wives' clubs. These facilities are limited in the hours they remain open, as well as the actual facilities provided.[23]

There is little attempt made to do something about the constraints of female tokenism. Male supervisors are correct in finding the command remiss in policy and practice. Public statements by military commanders or retired military leaders have also lent credence to the notion that sexism begins at the top.

At first, all the service academies and their superintendents were opposed to the admission of women.[24] General Berry of West Point threatened resignation from that institution if women were admitted.

Retired General Matthew B. Ridgeway, commander of forces during the Korean War, said that the growing reliance on women threatens the esprit de corps and effectiveness of our armed forces—a blow at discipline, without which no military unit is worth its keep.[25]

Many of the women of Khaki Town perceived all male soldiers to be pure and unashamed bigots. When women were harassed, they surmised that nearly all males were opposed to them. The types of men that are known most widely for sexism are the Daddy-Warbucks and Sergeant-Seducto types. An Army woman remembers the time she was accosted outside the mess hall but does not as easily recall the nonprejudiced men on the base. When I interviewed the males of Khaki Town, however, I found a variety of attitudes and behaviors of males vis-à-vis their female co-workers. A small but significant number of supervisors were what Merton called the unprejudiced nondiscriminator or All-Weather Liberal.[26] That is, these supervisors were neither prejudiced nor discriminatory in a military environment that was hostile to the integration of women. Although the consensus within male enlisted culture was that women did not belong, these men extended equity and sometimes goodwill to women. From a 27-year-old platoon sergeant:

I don't have problems with anybody that will work. Some of the women are my most intelligent and best soldiers. I don't find them any bother at all. On the contrary, they are often my best workers.

From a 23-year-old team chief:

Women are all right. Men are their biggest problem.

From a carrier supervisor:

Many male supervisors have these Victorian views of the female role. Instead of giving the women a chance to perform their duties to their full potential, they constantly give them other tasks to do which are both boring and demoralizing to their intelligence and professionalism.

From a platoon sergeant:

I'm just a small time sergeant in a big time Army and I try to treat females and males the same. All these things that males say about females "getting over" is the male supervisor's fault. Males are the creaters of it all.

These nondiscriminatory male supervisors were not social-action activists. Their creed and practice was pure and simple equity. They felt that women should be given a chance to function in the same way as male soldiers. From a sergeant major:

Some women can do the job just as well or better than the men. The largest problem seems to be the officers in the field who don't let the NCO put women in all duties as men. Women can't pull guard, work in relay sites, or anywhere by themselves. That's the only problem I see. I think that all supervisors will someday have to come to grips with this problem. Women are here to stay. They ought to be treated with the same respect as their male counterparts.

From a sergeant first class:

My observations of women in the field reveals that most women do their fair share of the work. I see men getting over as well as women. In my unit, I never allow MOS-transfers to clerical areas. When women are assigned to my unit, I use them. I have confronted the problem directly and have virtually eliminated any problem.

From a 33-year-old team chief:

Rome wasn't built in a day, now was it? Things will work out with women. Right now some people just can't adjust to women in the military. The time is not right for some. Women are OK by me. Some supervisors in this command do not have faith in any female as far as military duties and do not afford females a proper chance.

Nonprejudiced supervisors were an exception in an otherwise resistant male culture. While there was a consensus that females faced formidable barriers, most males blamed women themselves for the problems. Many of the males had "natural law" explanations for why women faced problems, but it should be emphasized that official Department of Army reports also saw physiological and psychological variables as reasons why women would fail. The enlisted male view was a less sophisticated version of the view of the higher command.

Natural Law: This is No Place for a Woman

A sergeant major from Raleigh, North Carolina, was one man who invoked natural law as an explanation for women's failure in khaki-collar jobs. In a conversation I had with the sergeant major, he told me that he thought the basic problem with women in the military was that men and women had an instinct to reproduce. When I asked him to tell me more about this "instinct," he responded in this way:

> You and I know women bleed and they have babies. Men don't. No matter how much self-discipline there is, the instinct to reproduce is well known.
>
> Males must protect their method of reproduction. A female protects hers by staying out of wars and raising her offspring. This is also a part of God's Plan.

Other male comments with a similar "natural law" imputation of women soldiers' motives and abilities were the following:

> I feel that the problem faced by Army women is because of the weaker sex in which they belong.

> Pussy is the most powerful force in the world. Show me a woman who won't. . . . Get them the fuck out of the Army!

> I think women are in jobs they shouldn't be in. I don't think it's their place to fight.

> Women aren't strong enough to construct a relay tower or to change the tires on a deuce and a half [two and a half ton truck].

> I lack confidence in women's ability to do this kind of work.

> Women apparently don't know what they're getting into here. They can't do the job no way.

> It's not a good idea to send them here. This is no place for a woman.

Blaming the Junior Enlisted Man

We should expect to find that predominant attitudes would even be more negative if the views of junior enlisted men were examined. In my sample, only 7.1 percent (10) of the males were privates or corporals (E-3 to E-4). Many of the supervisors blamed the younger enlisted men for problems:

I have to deal with poorly educated males who don't think that females can do the job.

Some men don't like the white girl-black man relationship. It seems to create an atmosphere of anxiety among my men.

Some of the more immature soldiers don't know how to deal with women. They make lewd jokes and comments. In general, they don't want women in the Army. These guys look at women as free lays.

Women are definitely treated as sex objects. The guys in my platoon lack confidence in their ability to do the job and think their role should be in the bedroom.

Women have an inability to talk with their peers on a buddy-to-buddy level. There is a lot of mutual mistrust in my unit.

Lots of guys feel that women don't do their share in the field. It is true that certain female soldiers come into the Army expecting too much on the side of soft work. Males don't like it when women goes on sick leave to avoid duty. It means more work to them.

Some females are given special privileges and rights because of their supervisor. I haven't seen this done for sexual favors, but wouldn't be surprised if that was the reason. When the other guys in the units see this, they are pissed. It just means more work for them.

The Military Manager and Women

The average rank of the 141 males in the Khaki Town sample was E-5, or staff sergeant. While some E-5s are primarily technicians, nearly all in the sample had at least some supervisory responsibility. The structural position of the first-line supervisor role is squeezed between the junior enlisted ranks and the officer corps. Roethlisberger's study of industrial foremen is useful in understanding the role of the male supervisor vis-à-vis women. Foremen, in Roethlisberger's view, were men in the middle, wedged between management and workers. Foremen were in a position where they had to enforce policy that they had no role in making.[27]

A common perception of first-line male supervisors in Khaki Town was that higher command created many of the problems that women faced because of its lack of understanding about what happened at the unit level. Could a colonel understand the problem of a phone call at 7:00 A.M. from a woman soldier who had no child care for her five-year-old for the upcoming field exercises? How could the policy of keeping military and parental responsibilities separated be enforced without antagonizing both junior enlisted women and men? Would males be willing to absorb the extra tasks necessary if the woman was left behind? If the sergeant drew the hard line this time, what would happen to the child? Many supervisors felt that policies toward women were either vague or unrealistic.

A 29-year-old staff sergeant from the South Bronx with two women under his immediate supervision expressed the view that the Department of the Army caused many of the problems with the integration of women by not informing supervisors about how women should be treated:

> How should women wear their hair while on duty? For blacks, packed hair is sometimes acceptable, but what is the rule about women? Should they be able to wear it in pigtails or what? The uniform is another matter. What should pregnant women wear to work?

Lack of clear guidance from the Department of the Army was viewed as contributing to female problems. A platoon sergeant from Florida commented that, "Women in the military is a must because that is the way official politics are." From a private first-class telecommunications clerk:

> I feel that women in the military brighten up the Army. I enjoy the Army women. It's something different but if there's going to be change the one making all the rules at the top should come down here and see how it's working.
> Women should not do things they are physically incapable of doing. If there's going to be a change it will have to be at the top, and the Department of the Army, they don't give a damn!

From a platoon sergeant from Mississippi:

> The Department of the Army didn't do their homework before they sent women to Khaki Town. Women married to fat cat politicians and Department of the Army fat cat generals bear down on us causing a lot of unneeded changes.

It was the view of several supervisors that the higher command arbitrarily transferred women out of their military occupational specialties. Representative of the opinion that women were pulled out of their khaki-collar jobs to type or file papers was this statement by a section chief from Maryland:

> Women are treated as little girls by the higher command in regard to duties that can be performed. Women tend to be pulled out of the assignment process at higher levels in degrees of "prettiness." The prettier the girl, the cushier her job, though her MOS may be telecommunications. Women work out of their MOS, but still get promoted. Sometimes you have women "putting out" for the officers and get promoted that way.

Another supervisor stated that women do not do their share of field duty and increase the work of men:

> I think they should go to the field. If they don't, it doubles the work load on my men. Lots of women get over because they are women. The chain of command is easier on women.
> Female MOS mismatch is experienced in this unit. Some women request their MOS and get stuck in clerical duties. They feel they are capable but they are not asked to do their job. Almost every unit in this command has a case of a female with a Signal MOS doing administrative duties in the lower unit and individual sections.

The origin of the contradiction in the higher command's treatment of women begins in basic training, according to the view of a young lieutenant. Lieutenant T_____ felt that communications training itself created problems for women:

> Washington says that there ought to be the same standards for men and women. Women couldn't meet many of these standards. In particular, physical training and cross-country road marches were areas in which the women failed. Women were superior to men in intelligence kinds of things such as "military stakes." The military stakes is equivalent to a College Bowl in the demonstration of military skills over a cross-country course. Basic training lasted eight weeks. The women of the Signal Corps would spend six additional days in administrative bivouac. In the combat arms, in contrast, trainees have four weeks of tactical bivouac. In the infantry, in particular, about half way through they have a "Go-Blue," which is the equivalent to the status passage of masculinity. They are all in their combat gear, camouflaged and all that. They all wade out into a marsh-like river and with smokers, machine gun assimilators, and with helicopters over them, they take the infantry oath. In contrast, communications training is like a high school classroom. The women then get assigned from an administrative unit to a tactical unit. Then they come to me and complain, "Hey they've put me in the war!" Most of the women think they are going to be assigned to the

Pentagon or some Headquarters building. It is a real disappointment when they get to a tactical unit such as in Khaki Town and find out they are in the real Army!

Beginning with basic training, the women of Khaki Town found the real Army to be opposed to them. I have argued that male attitudes descend from the top of the chain of command. Senior officers, removed from the day-to-day operation of units, are opposed to women in word and action. Worse yet, they do not prepare women for the kind of Army that they find in places like Khaki Town. The attitude of the male NCO is that women are a bother in His Army. The junior enlisted man sees women as competition for his job. Since women generally have higher educational levels and aptitudes than the male soldiers, the presence of women is particularly threatening. It is little wonder that women soldiers can find few comrades-in-arms. Many women soldiers decide to leave the service rather than to stay where they are not wanted. Like the male coal miners of the 1840s, military males feel that nontraditional roles for Army women are "deplorable in the extreme."

In the next chapter, we shall see the ways in which such service is deplorable to both sexes. This chapter will also suggest ways of improving the quality of enlisted life for both male and female soldiers.

NOTES

1. Charles C. Moskos, *The American Enlisted Man: The Rank and File in Today's Military* (New York: Russell Sage Foundation, 1970), p. 64.

2. William Arkin and Lyn Dobrofsky, "Military Socialization and Masculinity," in Joseph H. Pleck, ed., "Special Issue on Men's Roles," *Journal of Social Issues* (May 1977): 204–35.

3. Frederick Elkins, "The Soldier's Language," *American Journal of Sociology*, vol. 51, no. 5 (March 1945): 419.

4. Norman Dixon, *On the Psychology of Military Incompetence* (New York: Basic Books, 1976), p. 213.

5. Orrin Klapp, "Social Types: Process and Structure," *American Sociological Review*, vol. 23, no. 6 (1958): 674.

6. Khaki Town *Newsletter*, American Community Service (October 1977).

7. Jay Finnegan, "The Boys in the Barracks: Drugs—The Only Way to Make It," *Army Times*, June 11, 1979, p. 56.

8. Larry Ingraham (Maj.), as quoted in Finnegan, "Boys in the Barracks."

9. Clifton D. Bryant, "Olive-Drab Drunks and GI Junkies: Alcohol and Narcotic Addiction in the U.S. Military," in Clifton D. Bryant, *Deviant Behavior: Occupational and Organizational Bases* (Chicago: Rand-McNally College Publishing, 1974), chap. 6, p. 136.

10. Ibid., p. 131.

11. Finnegan, *Boys in the Barracks*.

12. "Junior Enlisted Personnel Stationed Overseas," report of the Military Compensation Subcommittee, Committee on Armed Services, House of Representatives, Ninety-Fifth Congress, Second Session (Washington, D.C.: U.S. Government Printing Office, December 19, 1978), pp. 4–6.

13. Morris Janowitz, *The Professional Soldier: A Social and Political Portrait* (New York: The Free Press, 1960); see also Morris Janowitz, in collaboration with Roger W. Little, *Sociology and the Military Establishment* (New York: Russell Sage Foundation, 1965), p. 31.

14. Karl Marx, *Capital: A Critical Analysis of Capitalist Production*, vol. 1, ed. Frederick Engels, 1867 (New York: Modern Library, 1978), p. 498.

15. Ibid.

16. Heidi Hartman, "Capitalism, Patriarchy, and Job Segregation by Sex," in Martha Blaxall and Barbara Reagon, eds., *Women and the Workplace* (Chicago: University of Chicago Press, 1978), pp. 166–67.

17. Frederick Engels, *The Conditions of the Working Class in England*, as quoted in Michele Barrett, *Women's Oppression Today: Problems in Marxist Feminist Analysis* (London: Verso, 1977), p. 161.

18. Department of the Army, *Final Report: Evaluation of Women in the Army* (Fort Benjamin Harrison, Ind.: United States Army Administration Center, 1978), pp. 1–5.

19. Ibid., pp. 1–29, 2–93, 2–94, and 2–125.

20. Ibid., p. 2–109.

21. Ibid.

22. Ibid., pp. 2–83, 2–125, and 2–97.

23. Ibid.

24. See Lt. General Sidney B. Berry's letter in the *Army Times* of November 12, 1975, which sets the record straight regarding his attitude toward female cadets at West Point.

25. Editors, Retired General Matthew B. Ridgeway quoted in "Women Warriors: A Shift to Barbarism," *Army Times*, February 26, 1979, p. 17.

26. Robert K. Merton, "Discrimination and the American Creed," in Robert K. Merton, *Sociological Ambivalence and Other Essays* (New York: The Free Press, 1976), pp. 193–95.

27. Fritz J. Roethlisberger, *Management and Morale* (Cambridge: Harvard University Press, 1943).

Chapter Six

FEMALE TOKENISM AND THE ENLISTED ARMY AS A VENAL INSTITUTION

When Descartes, the father of modern philosophy, decided to resign from the military, he wrote a letter that expressed his uneasiness about calling the military an ordinary profession:

> Although custom and example render the profession of arms the noblest of all, I, for my own part, who only regard it like a philosopher, value it at its proper worth, and indeed I find it difficult to give it a place among the honorable professions seeing that idleness and licentiousness are the two principal motives which now attract most men to it.[1]

The tension in military participation noted by Descartes is coextensive with the contradictory structure of today's volunteer military. If we assume that the military is necessary to a modern industrialized country, participation in the military could either confer expanded citizenship rights on the participants or it could be organized as a form of "dirty work" in a quasi occupation. I argue that, in the case of the U.S. volunteer forces, military participation takes the latter form. In order to understand female tokenism in this social context, it is necessary to contrast military service with participation in closely related organizations.

For its lower-ranked participants, the Army is a "special society" in which work is done under a rational plan in a symbiotic community cut off from civilian society. In its recruiting slogan, the Army says, "This is the Army. It's not just a job, it's an adventure!" As we have learned, the Army was more than an ordinary occupation for the women of Khaki Town. It was also a coercive social institution.

During the years of the volunteer force, recruitment has been directed at those looking for an occupation: "Get a Good Education!" "You Will

Make a Good Salary!" "In Today's Army, the Soldier is a Man Who's Living His Own Life!" "His Army" is a *venal institution*, which offers remuneration in exchange for absolute control over a soldier's time, energy, and identity. His Army is a work-oriented total institution that greedily extracts compliance from its enlisted members of both sexes.

Through the Uniform Code of Military Justice, commanders have a legitimate arsenal of social-control devices, ranging from nonjudicial harassment to the death penalty, which can be used to accomplish the Army's special mission of "taming the troops." It is the *venal* features of military life that give female tokenism in the military its distinctive character.

Other occupations also have venal features. Company towns, offshore oil rigs, and merchants ships have traditionally used coercive forms of discipline while at the same time retaining the remunerative basis of compliance. In this chapter, the general attributes of the venal institution will be drawn from a comparison of the Army with closely related organizational forms, and venal features of enlisted life in Khaki Town will be described. At the end of this enterprise, we will have begun to describe the features of a total institution with task-oriented goals.

This chapter is divided into four sections. The first section contrasts the compliance structure of civilian organizations with military participation at the enlisted level. This illuminates the contradictory structure of military domination. Next, features of enlisted military service are compared with participation in Goffman's *total institutions* and Coser's *greedy institutions*. It is argued that the *venal institution* is a social hybrid encompassing features of both total and greedy institutions but having a character of its own. The venal institution is here defined as an additional category of formal organization that further specifies Goffman's rough groupings of total institutions.[2] In the third section, the sources and dimensions of the venal institution are described. A comparison is made between the enlisted Army and Max Weber's notion of a pariah group. For Weber, pariah groups include those involved in such occupations as bath attendants, money lenders, and other outcasts who live endogamously in a symbiotic society and in a precarious situation before the law.[3] Finally, a general portrait of life in a venal institution is created through an examination of unstructured interviews with enlisted male and female soldiers of Khaki Town. This section considers the important factors of men's and women's social fate as lower-ranked participants in the Army.

ORGANIZATIONAL INVOLVEMENT: WHERE DOES MILITARY SERVICE FIT?

According to Etzioni's paradigm of organizational involvement, there are three forms of power used to ensure an individual's conformity to group goals: (1) coercion, (2) utilitarianism, and (3) normative control.[4]

Coercive organizations depend upon techniques of raw domination such as flogging and imprisonment in order to extract custodial control from powerless participants. Individuals, dominated by raw organizational power such as the whip and the chain, have no right to strike a bargain as to the use of their time and energy. Superiors direct the activity of lower-ranked participants through commands. There is a congruence between raw domination and the subsequent alienative involvement of participants.

In contrast, utilitarian organizations such as factories, offices, and businesses use appeals to individual self-interest in order to advance group goals. Organizations of this genre, which encompass most ordinary occupations, offer money in return for individual conformity.

A third form of control is the normative type, in which organizations such as monasteries, communes, or voluntary associations rely on a "calling" or moral involvement to meet group goals. The quid pro quod for individual involvement in moral groups is belief in the organization.

Table 6.1 depicts how different forms of organization intersect with individual involvement. According to Etzioni, the type of power employed molds the character of subsequent individual participation.[5]

Number I represents predominantly coercive organizations such as prisons or mental hospitals, which are able to secure only custodial control over inmates. The predominant form of individual involvement in response to raw domination is alienation, and the goal of such organizations is to keep participants on a "short leash." The major organizational task is to keep inmates from escaping.

Number II depicts task-oriented organizations such as businesses, factories, and most occupations in the capitalist state. Here, the individual trades conformity for money.

Number III includes the task-oriented organizations that demand a

TABLE 6.1. A Typology of Compliance Structures

	Individual Participation		
	Alienation	*Self-Gain*	*A Calling*
Raw coercion	I Prisons		
Money		II Factories	
Normative			III Monasteries

Source: Adapted from Amitai Etzioni, *A Comparative Analysis of Complex Organizations* (New York: Harper & Row, 1971).

commitment or calling from their members. While physical walls may separate participants from the world outside, symbolic boundaries are relied upon to insulate the participant from the dominant society.

MILITARY SERVICE: MIXED COMPLIANCE

Each of the organizations discussed thus far can include members who are involved at different levels. A prisoner may identify with his captors. A worker may feel a bond to his organization. A priest may enjoy the material benefits of his "calling." Table 6.1 describes only the predominant form of involvement.

Our task here is to determine where the enlisted military fits in Table 6.1. In the beginning, the first mass armies of the sixteenth and seventeenth centuries recruited their members from the poorest of the proletariat. European mass armies, as we learned in Chapter One, relied upon a large pool of the impoverished male proletariat. In the United States, citizen-soldiers have volunteered to serve their country in extreme crisis, but many others have also been conscripted against their will. More recently, peacetime advertisements have come to reflect a utilitarian thrust: "Army! Air Force! Navy! Marines! We don't ask for experience—we give it! You won't read it in a book. You'll live it! Pick a service! Pick a challenge! Set yourself apart! Army! Air Force! Navy! Marines! What a great place—it's a great place to start!"

In the volunteer Army, the military seems to be using remunerative appeals. At the same time, the military is more than an ordinary occupation. As the advertisements put it, the military *does* set its members apart—in extraordinary ways. It is helpful to understand the contradictory compliance structure of the Army by comparing it with other types of what I will call the *encroaching institutions*.

Not all participants experience the same structure of domination in the same way, yet the consequences of differences in compliance structure are far-reaching. These authority relationships illuminate adaptation of similarly situated individuals. Hence, the study of authority within encroaching institutions is an important methodological tool for understanding the struggle between the individual and the social structure.

THREE ENCROACHING INSTITUTIONS:
TOTAL, GREEDY, AND VENAL

Total Institutions

In Goffman's study of "Central Hospital," a mental institution of 7,000 inmates, he develops the character of what he calls "total institutions."

Total institutions are defined broadly as places of residence *and* work where a large number of like-situated individuals, cut off from wider society for an appreciable period of time, together lead an enclosed, formally administered round of life. Goffman notes that, regardless of purpose, the central features of total institutions include the following:

1. All features of life are conducted in the same place and under the same single authority.
2. Each phase of the member's daily activity is carried on in the immediate company of a large batch of others, all of whom are treated alike and are required to do the same thing together.
3. All phases of the day's activity are tightly scheduled, with one activity leading at a prearranged time into the next, the whole sequence of activities being imposed from above by a system of explicit formal rulings and a body of officials.
4. The various enforced activities are brought together into a single rational plan, purportedly designed to fulfill the official aims of the institution.[6]

Goffman lists five types of total institutions. First, there are institutions which are designed for the custodial care of the incapable, the blind, the aged, and the indigent. Secondly, there are places for the custody of people both incapable of caring for themselves and who are also a potential threat to the community: TB sanitaria, mental hospitals, and the leprosaria. Third, Goffman groups organizations which keep people who are potentially dangerous to the community such as the jails, P.O.W. camps, and concentration camps. Next, there are organizations with worklike tasks such as army barracks and work camps. Finally, there are establishments with a mission such as abbeys, monasteries, and cloisters (of other types.)[7]

Greedy Institutions

Coser has attempted to refine Goffman's typology further by making a distinction between establishments with a mission and the rest of the total institutions. He argues that there is a difference between organizations which ask for commitment and the others which ask that the individual only bide time. The greedy institution, in Coser's view, stems from the need for organizations in modern society to actively compete for an individual's time and energy:

Such competition for loyalty and commitment is a perennial problem because these are scarce resources. Not only do human beings possess only finite libidinal energies for cathecting social objects but their resources of time are similarly limited. As a consequence, various groups having a claim on individuals' energies and times compete with another in the effort to draw as much as they can, within normative limits, from the available pool of resources. The struggle over their allocation is as much a root fact of social root fact of social life as is the competition among users of social resources in economic affairs.[8]

While Coser discusses greedy institutions in conjunction with the roles of eunuchs, aliens, royal mistresses, domestic servants, and housewives, our attention is directed toward greedy formal organizations and collectives, especially those such as the Bolsheviks and Jesuits, which aim at changing the world. These organizations set themselves apart from civilian society and ensure that their participants devote total energies to the mission. Greedy institutions ask a great deal from their members. Each individual must have an undivided commitment to group goals that is attained through a "calling."

Many of Goffman's total institutions expect only that members serve time. In contrast, greedy institutions expect their members to be true believers, who devote all of their time and energy to the attainment of group objectives. While Goffman focuses on physical arrangements (locked doors, high walls, and barbed wire), Coser emphasizes symbolic boundaries (use of time and favorable social interaction). Greedy institutions are based upon the most effective form of social control, self-control. Compliance to group values occurs as a consequence of the time, frequency, and quality of social interaction. Compliance to group definitions is based upon loyalty rather than upon the locked doors and high walls used by total institutions.[9]

The Venal Institution

I have made a further distinction between those oganizations whose chief activity is work and the rest of the total institutions. These venal institutions, while sharing features of both greedy and total institutions, have a character of their own.

The term *venal institution* is particularly appropriate for the study of the volunteer enlisted military. The dictionary definition of the word venal is "ready to sell honor, mercenary." Venal also connotes autocracy. In his interesting but much neglected *Theory of Social Control*, Richard LaPierre defined the *venal organization* as one in which the employer has seduced his workers into accepting domination:

Organizations such as diplomatic, military, and similar agencies, whose services are for the most part unmeasurable, would seem to be especially inclined to become venal. In many instances a peacetime military force, when thrust into actual combat has turned out to be an army of non-fighters with no ability to resist its military opponent. In such cases what has happened is that during the period of peace each of the many members of the service has evolved his own little autocratic sphere of influence and has pampered his personal desires at the expense of the organizational needs, with the consequence that the military force has become an army of generals, servants to generals, and servants to servants, all fat and flabby and all engaged in the effort to extend the rights of their offices and avoid the obligations.[10]

Today's volunteer military "seduces" its soldiers with appeals to their self-interest, yet the goal is also to immerse the soldier in as much of the day-to-day activity of the garrison community as possible. For lower-ranked participants, the military is exorbitant in its demands on time and energy. Even when the soldier lives outside the actual physical plant of the garrison, there is always the threat of being interrupted from deep sleep by a telephone call or a knock on the door announcing a "black alert," a maneuver, or that the Russians are coming across the Czech border. The venal institution concentrates less on the corruption of the military than does LaPierre's venal organization. The venal institution combines the features of total and greedy institutions with the attributes of an ordinary occupation. Thus, the venal institution is a task-oriented total institution that also devours an individual's time and energy.

If the venal institution is combined with the greedy and the total institutions, a typology of encroaching institutions is constructed, which is coextensive with Etzioni's three forms of compliance. Total institutions use coercive power and obtain only alienative involvement. Total institutions, in the restrictive sense used here, are institutions designed for the care of the incapable, the dangerous, and the inept. (This corresponds to Goffman's first three types of total institutions.) Venal institutions are organizations that use predominately calculative appeals such as money; therefore, individual involvement in the venal institution is predominately for self-gain. Total institutions with a worklike task, such as army barracks and work camps, can be defined as venal (Goffman's fourth type). Greedy institutions, Goffman's fifth type of total institution, include organizations with a mission such as an abbey, monastery, or cloister. Table 6.2 compares and contrasts three types of encroaching institutions, total, venal, and greedy.

SOURCES OF VENALITY IN THE U.S. ARMY

This section will be concerned with the special attributes of the venal institution. In order to understand how the venal institution differs from

TABLE 6.2. Three Types of Encroaching Institutions

	Total	Venal	Greedy
Compliance structure	Coercive	Calculative	Normative
Individual involvement	Alienative	Self-gain	Moral
Legal rights	Minimum rights	Circumscribed rights	Ordinary rights
Group boundaries	Physical	Physical and symbolic	Symbolic and physical
Use of time	Serving time	Serving time and performing tasks (mixed)	Giving time
Purpose of institution	Custodial control	Work and wait	Mission, world transformation
Examples	Prison, P.O.W. camp	Army enlisted culture, company towns in nineteenth century	Communes, sects, revolutionary cells

Source: Compiled by the author.

the total and the greedy institutions, it is useful to examine its sources and features, as exhibited by the Army.

Historically, the structure of military compliance was based upon coercion, not remuneration. In the early U.S. Navy, flogging was a primary social control device. The reaction of commanders to the elimination of flogging was sheer panic: "If we abolish flogging there will be a mutiny on every ship."[11]

While self-control is the most effective form of group commitment, military commanders traditionally thought that military discipline required the enforcement of absolute obedience. The beginnings of coercive punishment in navies, for example, are found in the Laws of Oleron. The origins of this code date from Edward III and were in force through the reigns of Henry IV, Henry V, and Henry VI:

Anyone that should kill another on board should be tied to the dead body and thrown into the sea. Anyone that should kill another on land should be tied to the dead body and buried with it in the earth. Anyone lawfully convicted of drawing a knife or other weapon with the intent to strike another, or of striking another so as to draw blood, should lose his hand.

Anyone lawfully convicted of theft should have his head shaved and boiling pitch poured upon it and feathers or down should be strewn upon it for the distinguishing of the offender.[12]

Lord Macaulay, writing about the Victorian army, thought that soldiers must, "for the sake of public freedom, be placed under a despotic rule. They must be subject to a harsher penal code and to a more stringent code of procedure than are administered by ordinary tribunals."[13] From the beginning, acts not punished in civilian life became capital offenses if committed by soldiers.

The severity of discipline in the Roman army was described by Polybius, who wrote, "Methods were primarily based on terror." The Romans punished even slight neglects of duty with death. The most well-known punishment was "decimation," in which every tenth man was selected by lot to be clubbed to death by those remaining in the cohort.[14] Individual executions were summarily ordered for malingerers, shirkers, and deserters. When replacements were difficult to find, humiliating degradation ceremonies replaced death for minor offenses. Octavian, for example, punished his centurions who were guilty of minor offenses by ordering them to stand all day outside the praetorium, sometimes dressed in tunics and without belts and sometimes holding measuring poles or even a piece of turf.[15]

Raw domination has been a ubiquitous feature of organized armies throughout history. In the seventeenth century, the military blasphemer was gagged and his tongue was scraped. In 1644, blasphemers were ordered to be punished with a red-hot iron that was placed to the tongue.[16]

Alexander's early nineteenth century diary documented that the British Army continued to use physical punishments such as floggings and beatings to extract total obedience. The following incident occurred in 1801:

The poor fellow got two hundred and twenty-nine lashes, but they were uncommonly severe. I saw the drum-major strike a drummer to the ground for not using his strength sufficiently. At length, the surgeon was interfered, the poor fellow's back, was as black as the darkest mahogany, and dreadfully swelled. The cat [cat o' nines whip] being too thick, they did not cut, which made the punishment more severe. He was instantly taken down and carried to the hospital where he died in eight days afterwards, his back having mortified.[17]

In Dahomey, the commanders of the French Foreign Legion ordered the following punishment for a private accused of striking back at a sergeant:

He was stripped naked, his hands were pinioned behind his back, and his ankles were tied together. Then his ankles were lashed to his wrists, and he was thrown on the ground looking very much like a trussed fowl. The agony incidental to this constrained position must have been beyond human endurance after a time, but in this poor man's case, the punishment was intensified by the fact that in no long time after he was tied up, his body was literally covered with a swarm of black ants—and anyone who has been in tropical Africa knows what that means. [18]

In the all-volunteer Army, flogging and summary executions have long since passed. Janowitz argues that organizational control has shifted from reliance on physical punishment to manipulation. This slow transformation reflects the changing nature of military work. In the Civil War, for example, 93 percent of enlisted soldiers performed purely military jobs, such as infantry, cavalry, and artillery, but by World War I, only about a third of all enlisted soldiers performed such roles. The majority served in combat-support roles or in administrative/logistics jobs. During World War II, the percentage of purely military jobs increased slightly to 36 percent.

Janowitz sees basic changes in military jobs, which correspond to a "civilianized" military. It isn't as effective to use the whip on a medic, a clerk, or a telecommunications specialist in the twentieth century military: "There has been a change in the basis of authority and discipline in the military establishment, a shift from authoritarian domination to a greater reliance on manipulation, persuasion, and group consensus." [19]

However, the transformation to an ordinary occupation has been incomplete. The enlisted military is still more than an ordinary job partly because of the retarding influence of traditional military domination. Senator John Stennis, arguing against the unionization of the military, commented on its distinctive character:

The existence of a military union, regardless of the nature of its powers, is inconsistent with the military chain of command. Military organizations are not democratic and they cannot be . . . The existence of a union is incompatible with the discipline that is necessarily the backbone of the armed forces. [20]

Recruitment to the Venal Institution

Total institutions receive their candidates from a pool of persons whom the state feels are either in need of custodial control for their own benefit or for protection of the community. In contrast, greedy institutions recruit their members from persons with a "calling" or belief in the mission of the organization. There is some debate as to who joins the enlisted military and other venal institutions. Hughes has proposed the term *dirty workers* to apply to people who do the odious tasks mandated by society: "Is there a sufficient fund of personalities warped toward perverse punishment and cruelty or are persons willing to do any amount of dirty work mandated by the rest of us?"[21] If dirty work is so aversive, why do people join the venal institutions? Is there a large pool of persons who are authoritarian or, alternatively, are persons economically conscripted for dirty work?

The second dimension of venality, which partially explains its contradictory character, is economic conscription. As we learned in Chapter Four, persons join venal organizations such as the volunteer Army because they have few alternatives.

In England, military service was originally a condition required of the peasant population in return for the tenure of land. From the time of Edward III, it became customary to raise forces for profit for a restricted period of time or for a particular task:

> And thus a foreign war became a mere matter of business and hire, and armies to fight the French were raised by speculative contractors, very much as men are raised nowadays to make railways or take part in other works needful for the public at large. The engagement was purely pecuniary and commercial, and was entirely divested of any connection with conscience or patriotism.[22]

Van Doorn characterized the first rational military organization of the Netherlands' Maurice of Orange as a business venture. This sixteenth century army was characterized as a manufacture-organization "because the laborers and their tools—the soldiers and their weapons—constitute the composite elements."[23]

In the same sense, Van Doorn contended that Frederick the Great also viewed the military as a labor-intensive organization to be perfected. Soldiers were taught precise movements and drills in order to build the first military machine. In fact, there was a similarity between Frederick the Great and Frederick Winslow Taylor, who rationalized industrial work:

> The similarity is not fortuitous. Both were confronted with the problem of how a mass of badly trained, moderately motivated individuals, who were also cut off from their old social milieu, could be welded into goal-attainment organizations. Both had the proletariat as a recruiting pool, and in spite of all differences which can undoubtedly be pointed out, their mechanistic image of man was also a product of the circumstances in which they had to work.[24]

Rothenberg found that abject poverty was the principal motivation driving men to soldiering in the early mass armies of Western Europe:

Although most continental states had some form of conscription on the books, economic considerations precluded the enlistment of productive and tax-producing elements, so that in practice the soldiery was composed of the poor peasants, vagabonds, criminals, and foreigners. Even then it was difficult to find enough soldiers and as difficult to retain them.[25]

Recently, military sociologists have characterized individuals who are willing to relinquish control over their voices, hair, eyeballs, and bowels in military jobs as answering a calling. Moskos, for example, thought that traditional military socialization rested upon a calling:

Military service has traditionally had many features of the calling: extended tours abroad; fixed terms of enlistment; liability for twenty-four hour service; frequent moves of self and family; subjection to military discipline and law; and inability to resign, strike, or negotiate over working conditions. These are features of the military above and beyond the dangers inherent in maneuvers and combat operations.[26]

Moskos' description of the contemporary military is essentially correct. However, he believes that the military has shifted from a calling to an ordinary occupation. In contrast, the view offered here describes the transition as moving from a coercive total institution to that of a quasi occupation. A calling connotes voluntarism. It is difficult to fathom how the Roman Catholic Church could hold an annual draft of priests. This is because the concept of a calling is associated with self-control within a community of true believers. It is implausible that the legacy of large standing armies includes a communion of the enlisted ranks with the officer corps, except perhaps in holy wars such as the Crusades. If men were called to the enlisted ranks, why did commanders require the whip and the chain to extract obedience? Presumably, if soldiers were as self-controlled as communicants in normative organizations, the history of military discipline would have been less draconian.

Data from Khaki Town support the notion that the predominant attraction to today's military is driven by larger economic forces, such as high unemployment and the general economic downturn in the United States. The military need not improve the conditions of service life in order to recruit from the ancillary force of the unemployed and the dispossessed. For some participants, as we discovered in Chapter Three, the confluence of normative ideologies and the need for stable employment prompted them to see their local recruiters. It is also the case, however, that blacks, lower-class whites, and women hear the "call" more often than do other citizens. Fabanyic found a powerful correlation between unemployment and accession rates, which was also consistent with much of the history of the mass standing army: "Failure to recruit and the national corresponding decrease in the force structure continued until mid-1974, when the national economic downturn and resulting high unemployment appeared to resolve the recruiting."[27]

Is Military Justice Like Military Music?

When men and women wave good-bye to their families at the processing station, they also wave good-bye to many of their constitutional rights. The Uniform Code of Military Justice grants soldiers few due process guarantees and is emblematic of the ways in which the venal institution differs from the ordinary job. Former Senator Sam Ervin said of military justice:

> Imagine if you will a system of justice with the burden of proving innocence imposed on the defendant, secret informants, no right to trial, no right to see the evidence, no protection against punishment even when found innocent, no right to legally qualified counsel, no independent judicial review, and no clearly defined rules of what is and is not against the law.
>
> If military justice is to true justice what military music is to Bach—then the discharge system is nothing more than beating on an empty can.[28]

In the volunteer military years 1974 to 1977, an average of 80,000 soldiers a year were given undesirable or bad conduct discharges. The Fifth Amendment, for example, is more restricted in the military than in civilian society. In the U.S. Constitution, the Fifth Amendment states that "No person shall be held to answer for a capital or otherwise infamous crime unless on a presentment or indictment of a Grand Jury, *except* in cases arising in the land or naval force, or in the Militia when in actual service in time of war or public danger."[29]

The military justice system that has evolved since the U.S. Constitution was written has taken a particularly expansive view of what constitutes the "present danger." Moyer finds of particular interest the rhetoric of justice and discipline that has been the primary justification for the precarious legal situation of soldiers:

> Is a criminal justice system whose object is *discipline* characterized by features that distinguish it from a system whose object is "justice" or is the difference only semantic? If the difference is real, is the object of military justice discipline, and, if so, should it be?[30]

There are several ways in which military justice differs from ordinary justice. The civilian justice system is in place to prevent individuals from behaving in antisocial ways. In the military, the definitions of "antisocial" behavior are particularly broad. Secondly, constitutional rights have been held by the U.S. Supreme Court as either inapplicable or only partially applicable to soldiers. Finally, military justice is a separate jurisprudence designed to be an arm of the commander. Military justice is based partially on the "chilling effect" of the individual commander rather than on a rational code of law.

From a military point of view, Faw suggests that the objectives of a military justice system must be broader than those of a civilian system:

> If the object of civilian justice is to regulate a civilian society, in a free society this regulation is limited to the prevention of certain anti-social acts proscribed by law... The law accomplishes its purpose when people do nothing affirmatively to harm the society. The laws are negative in nature: "Thou shalt not. . ." It seeks only to prevent the individual from behaving in a certain specified anti-social manner.[31]

In contrast, the purpose of military justice is to maintain military authority, not to serve justice. The booklet *Naval Justice*, distributed by the Bureau of Naval Personnel, describes naval justice in this way: "Naval justice is the disciplinary and court-martial system of the Navy. Its purpose is the maintenance of naval discipline, without which the navy cannot function as an efficient fighting force."[32]

As a result, many of the rights held by ordinary citizens are denied in military courts. In contrast, the last twenty years have witnessed a revolution in the protection of the procedural rights of the criminally accused in the civilian courts. The Warren Court focused on the protection of the individual from the most egregious abuses of the police, such as the illegal search, the coerced confession, and the rigged lineup. For soldiers caught in the military justice apparatus, a group disproportionately composed of the poor and young, military discipline supplants due process guarantees. Military necessity is the principle that justifies the evisceration of the procedural rights of the criminally accused. Nowak believes that military law is not a true body of law at all but merely a principle upon which the military is granted control of the law. As Blackstone stated:

> Martial law, which is built upon no settled principles, but is entirely arbitrary in its decision is... in truth and reality no law, but something indulged rather than allowed as law. The necessity of order and discipline in an army is the only thing which can give it countenance, and therefore it ought not to be permitted in time of peace, when the king's courts are open for all persons to receive justice according to the laws of the land.[33]

The Venal Institution as a Pariah Group

Max Weber was interested in disreputably employed groups that have historically been in a precarious legal situation. During the Middle Ages, certain occupations such as hangman, miller, bath attendant, and money-lender formed despised occupational castes. Other groups that Weber studied were the Bengalese wandering craftsmen, the Indian subcastes, and the Jews in Diaspora. Weber defines pariah groups as:

> . . . communities who have acquired specific vocational traditions of a craft or other nature, who practice a belief peculiar to their community, and now live in Diaspora, in a very precarious situation strictly segregated from all intercourse with outsiders which is not unavoidable, but tolerated because they are economically indispensable, and often even privileged groups: the Jews are the most sublime historical example.[34]

There are interesting parallels between the status of enlisted soldiers in the volunteer Army and pariah groups. Military bases are physically set off from civilian society. As with total institutions, barriers to social intercourse with the outside are built into the physical plant—most military bases have armed guards and high fences to separate the insider from the outsider. The military also uses symbolic devices, such as uniforms, ranks, and post-exchange privileges, to separate its members from the outside. Soldiers are not individuals in an inherited community like the pariahs studied by Weber, but they are segregated from civilian society with both physical and symbolic barriers. Both the pariah group and the enlisted military are segregated from civil communities, and both groups are expert at despised occupational skills. Both are scattered in a diaspora. The military, like the pariah, lives in a precarious legal situation with civilian society.

In the next section, I will demonstrate the ways in which soldiers perceived the "venal character" of enlisted life in Khaki Town. Chapter Seven will suggest ways to improve the status of the men and women there.

VENALITY IN KHAKI TOWN

As noted in Chapter Three, unstructured interviews with soldiers of both sexes took place between January and June of 1978 in Khaki Town. As a portion of the overall research question of whether the men or the Army were responsible for the woman soldiers' problems as women in the

Army, participants were asked the following questions: (1) What are the best and worst aspects of your military job?, and (2) What problems do people like you have in your job? These initial questions piqued in-depth responses on the extraoccupational demands of Khaki Town life. In general, lower-ranked participants of both sexes felt that the military was excessive in its demands on their time. Respondents also frequently commented on the difficulties in establishing and maintaining an identity in Khaki Town.

Encroachments on Time

One of the most demoralizing features of service in Khaki Town was the way in which time was seized from the individual soldier. There was a basic incompatibility between the work-payment structure and the military's exorbitant demands on time and energy. Coser argued that when groups compete for the loyalty of individuals, the arena for conflict is over the use of time.[35] In greedy institutions, the individual believes strongly in the mission, whether it be the collectivization of the world or preparations for the Second Coming. In venal institutions, there is a greater struggle over time than in organizations where a large number of individuals are "called." When the men and women I interviewed joined the Army, they viewed it as an occupation that would give them more money, training, education, and travel. But the command structure views the military as "more than a job." Individuals expressed their struggle with the command structure over the use of time in the following accounts: From a woman supervisor in telecommunications:

> I don't fit into the military mold very well I guess. I would like regular hours such as 8 to 4:30 so I could have an outside life. The military doesn't meet my expectations. It is a waste of time.

From a male platoon sergeant:

> There are too many Mickey Mouse details. I don't like the 60- to 80-hour workweek during field exercises and inspections. We are always on call. There is no off-duty time. I guess we're like the fire department being always on call. Except in times of war, we should punch a time clock like everybody else.

From a male radio repairer:

> The Army is a complete waste of my time. I know it's necessary but it's sheer boredom. If I had a job that used my talents, I would stay. There's also a lot of

waiting around. Once I get out of here, I'll never wait around in a line again. I can't stand the lines.

From a private first class woman mechanic:

There are too many demands on my time. There are too many number one priorities that have to be done now. "Why, I ask?" I hear, "Because I said so."

From a 22-year-old female corporal:

To me the worst part of the Army is the undue demands on my time. They don't care for me as an individual personality. They use me with the same consideration they give to a deuce-and-a-half (two and a half ton truck).
    I don't feel we should have to work more than eight-hour days. I think the military should treat us as persons and not as instruments.

In Khaki Town barracks, as was noted in Chapter Three, there was little privacy and a permeable boundary between on- and off-duty time. The woman soldier who commented above on how military persons were treated as instruments mentioned one male encroachment on off-duty time, as well:

They should know that we don't like to be watched all of the time. They think they have to know what is going on with all aspects of our lives. I cannot understand why military persons have to be so tough and calloused.

A 20-year-old woman from Baton Rouge, Louisiana, saw barracks conditions as a significant problem in her life:

The most significant problem in the military for me is to be treated as a human being. There are just too many room inspections. You live in that room after all. You would like to call it home. But no, you can't. And by the way, try the mess hall. You won't like it. It is lonely for me here, but yet there is not the time or the place to be alone.

A male radio equipment operator from Connecticut expressed similar ideas:

There is too much boredom around here. Living in the barracks and being so close to your work at all times is not natural. When I finish work, I need to get away from this environment. We are in the military at all times. I'd like to get away from the barracks, so I couldn't constantly be forced to do childish and unnecessary duties.

The scheduling of time was a problem related to the organization of the barracks, according to a female corporal in telecommunications:

If it isn't unscheduled shakedowns, it is inspections, early morning alerts, or field exercises. These problems are exacerbated by the behavior of women in the barracks. There is a strong bias toward straight-day [Monday-Friday] workers which goes unacknowledged by headquarters. It is difficult for the shift-workers here to get any sleep because of the constant military harassment and the stereos. We lack privacy, which inhibits the development of male-female relationships. We are constantly subject to such impositions on our time as human relations seminars, meaningless cleaning details, and a hypocritical applications of Article 15s [nonjudicial punishment]. We should be allowed to have unrestricted visiting privileges. All personnel should have the option of living in the barracks or off-post. We should be paid separate rations and BAQ [housing subsidy]. We should be treated like adults on and off the job.

The preceding accounts reflect the contradictory structure of the enlisted military as an occupation. On one hand, volunteer army advertisements emphasize the benefits of military service, but military participation is also a coercive institution that extracts time forcibly on a day-to-day basis. These encroachments take the form of unannounced inspections, "search and seizure" missions, shakedowns for the recovery of stolen property, compulsory urinalyses, and forced assignments to undesirable overseas garrisons.

Perhaps the most odious feature of the venal institution is the control over the lower participant's time. In basic training, the recruit is "bird-dogged" on a 24-hour basis. Later in garrison life, "bird-dogging" is replaced with the "hurry up and wait" features of enlisted life. Many soldiers felt they were on tenterhooks. There were periods of appalling dullness, but at very short notice, a soldier could be awakened from her bunk to pull emergency duty. There was always the threat of an unannounced military maneuver or cleanup detail. The uneasiness and strain of this aspect of Army life was a source of much dissatisfaction.

Difficulties Maintaining Family Life

Single soldiers in the barracks weren't the only enlisted groups subject to the loss of control over use of time. Married soldiers found it difficult to sustain family life in overseas garrisons such as Khaki Town. Khaki Town wives had a saying to the effect that, "You don't marry a man. You marry the Army." According to McCubbin and Marsden's analysis of military family life, the family is officially subordinated to the military in the following ways:

1. The primary mission of the military is the defense of the United States; family concerns of service are always subordinate to this mission.
2. The military profession is far more than a job; it is a way of life for both service members and his or her family. Thus, the concerns of dependents (spouse and children) are clearly secondary to the professional requirements of their sponsor (the soldier); the family is expected to accept willingly the stresses of family life, which include extended family separations and frequent relocations.
3. The traditional and supportive but subordinate role of the military wife, which has been strictly and comprehensively defined by the system, must be maintained.
4. The tradition of the military to "care for its own" means that programs and benefits for family members are a reflection of the military's interest in them but these benefits should not be considered rights.[36]

The difficulties of military family life in Khaki Town and other overseas garrisons were due not only to official subordination of the family; the decline of the dollar in relation to the deutsche mark also represented a severe problem for the junior enlisted soldier. The lowest-ranked soldiers did not receive military sponsorship for their families. They faced a choice of a two-year separation or economic hardship if they brought their families to Germany. For military families who decided to be together in Germany, there were enormous expenses to be absorbed, including air tickets, lodging, and automobile expenses. When the military family arrived, they had to make their way outside garrison walls in an unfamiliar culture in which they did not have the money to live comfortably. Soldiers in Khaki Town and other garrisons lived in shabby dwellings in the poor neighborhoods of German cities and villages. These families often competed with Turkish, Italian, and Yugoslavian guest workers (*gastarbeiters*) for substandard housing. Many junior enlisted men chose not to establish an overseas household under these conditions. As a result, many were geographically and sometimes emotionally separated from their family network.

Interviews with Khaki Town soldiers confirmed that married soldiers experienced greater family stresses in the overseas setting. From a 24-year-old male radio operator:

I don't like being stationed outside the United States for such a long time without my family. Lower ranked EMs [enlisted men] should be able to have their families with them. The Army should assume the cost.

From a male generator mechanic:

I want my kids with me. They're not command-sponsored so they're over in the States with my folks.

From a female private first class radio operator:

> I was married only a week when I received orders to Germany. My husband got sent to Hood [Fort Hood]. We were happy together, but after the separation and all, I don't know if our marriage will work out or not.

From a male sergeant:

> There are many hidden costs if you are command-sponsored. My wife can't find work over here. We buy little things such as clotheslines over and over again because they can't be found after a move. One or two clotheslines would serve a lifetime if we were allowed to stay in one place. I've had to purchase a car and telephone for alerts. Military housing is disgraceful. Ours is falling apart. There has been a front door off its hinges for three months here! Civilians think we got it made in the shade. Because we move so often, we can never settle down. It is difficult to know where to purchase a house. Civilians don't know what shit we have to put up with here. Take medical care. One of my buddies brought his little two-year-old girl into emergency at the dispensary. A corpsman [enlisted military medical technician] took a look at her and prescribed aspirins. The child had meningitis. She is now permanently deaf. You tell me how the Army can compensate for that sort of thing. It's a real shame the way we're treated.

The following examples of problems faced by military families were drawn from the Report of the Military Compensation Subcommittee of the U.S. House of Representatives during hearings in 1978. They are broadly representative of the problems of sustaining family life in Khaki Town:

> An E-4, [corporal] 20 years old, with 19-year-old wife and infant son, paid $420 to transport family to Germany. Deposits ran $180 on apartment. Rent and utilities cost $212.50 for a small one-bedroom apartment 2 miles from base. Apartment is 80-year-old house with leaking plumbing, falling plaster, and in need of extensive repairs. Short notice PCS [soldier received little notice in the Permanent Change of Service where he was stationed] caused quick sale of car in United States [he owned it 2 months] at $350 loss. Bought car overseas for $400 but required $200 in repairs. Insurance [liability only] cost $400 a year. Necessities ran about $195 per month. Borrowed $1,000 for family transport, deposits, car, etc. Works at NCO [noncommissioned officer] club nights to survive. Is considering sending family home each month when the bills come in.

> An E-3 [private first class] with 2 years service, married and one child, had a part-time job in the United States. Between them, they earned approximately $250 extra a month to supplement the military pay. In order to save money, his family did not join him while he attended a 4-month technical school. The savings had been earmarked to finance their anticipated move to his

base of assignment from technical school. After the move [within the United States], it took them 6 months to return to a fairly stable financial situation. However, he was subsequently assigned overseas, which created a financial crisis. They had to sell nearly all of their belongings as they could not afford to store or ship them at their own expense.

A E-3 [private first class] with 2 years service, a pregnant wife, and a child, was an excellent worker with outstanding career potential. He was notified of selection for an assignment to Germany. At the same time, his wife developed complications with her pregnancy. The couple had no one to whom they could turn. As his reporting date drew closer he realized that he would be unable to raise enough money to bring his family with him overseas. He didn't want to leave his family at this critical time, but he had little choice. He soon developed a lax attitude toward his job and the Air Force. Subsequently, he applied for and received a Humanitarian Discharge.[37]

The above cases illustrate the difficulties that lower-ranked participants had in maintaining minimal family life in West Germany. Even if families were sponsored by the command, they were subject to constant interferences, including frequent moves, interruptions on short notice, and the venal features of military autocracy. Ebbert, in a service guide for Naval wives, described the command view of family life:

A Navy member who does not pay his bills may be embarrassed by letters from his creditors to his commanding officer. While the Navy considers the man's personal finances his own affair, it can not help but take some action when such letters are received . . . For one thing, it is concerned for the reputation of all Naval personnel and if one of them is becoming a bad financial risk that doesn't help the others any. For another, it knows that a financially harassed soldier will have trouble keeping his mind on his work.[38]

Assaults on Identity in the Venal Institution

The Stars and Stripes bookstore in Khaki Town sold a book entitled *Command Voice*, which instructed soldiers on how to develop a voice suitable for both giving and receiving commands. The military asks for total control over an individual's voice and hair. Even demeanor is regulated by military rules. As a result, both males and females in Khaki Town experienced depersonalization. The following comments are drawn from interviews about the nature of the Army job in Khaki Town. An E-7 section chief from Mississippi commented:

Life is planned for you. Decisions are made for you by the Department of the

Army who don't know what the real Army is really like. People become robots in the Army. We are programmed or told what to do. We are told when to be sick, even when to use the latrine. In green uniforms, we even look the same.

From a male radio and carrier supervisor from South Carolina:

Some days I feel I can't go on. The Army forces one to give up any individuality. You lose all control over your life, both on- and off-duty. I wish I could send time back four years, so I never would have had the experience of being in the Army.

From a 24-year-old female (E-4):

It's hard to be a person in this environment, let alone a woman. We don't have a human existence in this environment. There is a lack of respect for us as humans. Please let me out of here. I say that every day to myself.

From a 24-year-old female radio operator:

I hate uniforms. I hate to be moved around so much. When I start becoming secure and confident, there is always some interruption. There are endless hassles and interferences with my off-duty life.

From an 18-year-old female private:

The lack of privacy and the general living conditions turn me off to the Army. I don't like Germany much either, but the lack of privacy and harassment are the biggest problem to me.

From a 23-year-old man (E-5):

I wouldn't reenlist again because the military has continually attempted to take away my rights as a human being. It is impossible to change these conditions, so I'm going back to the *World* [argot term for the end of service and the return to the United States].

From a senior enlisted man from Alabama:

There is no privacy. Higher-ups have no respect for others. This sets a bad example for the rest. The senior personnel officers and NCOs don't give a damn about our health and welfare because they don't live in these overcrowded billets. They think we're too dumb to know the difference.

From a 30-year-old male production control specialist:

> They don't allow us to function properly as persons. They seem to want to tear us down rather than build us up. I feel that people should know the truth about living conditions in the barracks and in the Army. When you do your book on us, give it to the Brass good!

The fact that both males and females live in a venal institution provides a social context for understanding the character of female tokenism in the army. Over and above tokenism, female soldiers forfeit civil and human liberties. In addition to the social injuries suffered by women soldiers, the forfeiture of time, family life, and identity is a cost of enlisted military participation for both men and women.

With the volunteer Army, the penal aspects of military servitude have passed. But like Weber's pariah groups, soldiers are scattered in diaspora and live in a precarious legal and economic situation. They are situated in places like Khaki Town, where they are separated physically and symbolically from civilian society. They are tolerated by civilian society in the same way that pariahs have been. People don't join the venal institution as the result of a calling; instead, soldiers of both sexes find service to be comparatively more advantageous than their other options. However, the economic gains must be offset by the macro attacks on time, family, and self, and as we have seen, soldiers with families may end up economically worse off than they had been previously.

The overseas garrison is the prototype of venality. Its dual and contradictory compliance structure of autocracy and pecuniary controls is coalesced into an uneasy amalgam of total and greedy institutional features. The prison guard, or the lower-ranked policeman, is also situated in a command structure with coercive aspects. However, no utilitarian organization exercises such extreme and pervasive control over time, family, and identity as does the venal institution.

As long as there is an available reserve of economically and socially disadvantaged recruits, the volunteer military is likely to retain much of its venal character. Weber was right when he stated that military domination was the father of all domination. The bedrock of traditional discipline has remained, despite advertisements for the volunteer Army:

> Now that the All-Volunteer Army is a reality, the job of retaining good people is more important than ever before . . . That job is the bringing about of a change in attitude toward reenlisting forever . . . All we ask is that if you have found a challenging job and satisfaction in the Army, let it be known. We all know that today's Army is better trained, better equipped, and better

paid than ever before. But we sometimes foreget that the Army is only as good as its people. We're doing our best to bring in the best people. We should all be doing our best to keep them.[39]

The focus of this chapter has been on the contradiction between the calculative and coercive features of enlisted service. The *Oxford English Dictionary* defines service as "the assistance or benefit afforded by an animal or thing." It has been argued that the enlisted military is a quasi occupation with features of systematic servility. Reminiscent of the company towns of nineteenth century Massachusetts, lower-ranked soldiers live in rows and rows of one- and two-story barracks, painted in classic military dun. One by one, as the old paint peels, each is restored to total institutional green. Overseas military life in Khaki Town is far from the exotic occupation pictured in military recruitment advertising.

In the next chapter, I will suggest ways to improve military service for the enlisted soldiers. If the situation for both males and females is not changed, it is no great gain for women to be assigned to khaki-collar jobs in a venal institution.

NOTES

1. Descartes, as quoted in James Anson Farrer, *Military Manners and Customs* (New York: Henry Holt, 1885), p. 254.
2. Erving Goffman, *Asylums: Essays on the Social Situation of Mental Patients and Other Inmates* (New York: Anchor, 1961), pp. 4–5.
3. See Christian Sigrist, "The Problem of Pariahs," in Otto Stammer, *Max Weber and Sociology Today* (New York: Harper & Row, 1971), p. 240.
4. Amitai Etzioni, *A Comparative Analysis of Complex Organizations* (New York: Harper & Row, 1971).
5. Ibid.
6. Goffman, *Asylums*, pp. 5–6.
7. Lewis A. Coser, *Greedy Institutions: Patterns of Undivided Commitment* (New York: The Free Press, 1974).
8. Ibid., p. 1.
9. Ibid.
10. Richard T. LaPierre, *A Theory of Social Control* (New York: McGraw-Hill, 1954), pp. 398–99.
11. U.S. Naval Institute, *Naval Custom and Tradition* (Annapolis: U.S. Naval Institute, 1975).
12. Ibid.
13. Lord Macaulay, as quoted in Farrer, *Military Manners*, p. 220.
14. G. R. Watson, *The Roman Soldier* (Ithaca, N.Y.: Cornell University Press, 1969), p. 21.
15. Ibid., pp. 117–25.
16. U.S. Naval Institute, *Naval Custom.*
17. Alexander, Alexander in T.H. McGuffie, *Rank and File: The Common Soldier at Peace and War, 1642–1914* (New York: St. Martin's Press, 1975).

18. Ibid.

19. Morris Janowitz, in collaboration with Roger W. Little, *Sociology and the Military Establishment* (New York: Russell Sage Foundation, 1965), chap. 2.

20. Senator John Stennis, Hearings on "The Unionization of the Armed Forces," Committeee on Armed Services, United States Senate, Ninety-Fifth Congress, First Session (S 274 and S 997, July 1977), p. 6.

21. Everett C. Hughes, "Good People and Dirty Work," in Howard Becker, ed., *The Other Side: Perspectives on Deviance* (New York: The Free Press, 1964), pp. 23–36; this essay also appears in Everett C. Hughes, *The Sociological Eye* (Chicago: Aldine-Atherton Press, 1971), p. 496.

22. Farrer, *Military Manners*, p. 261.

23. Jacques Van Doorn, *The Soldier and Social Change: Comparative Studies in the History and Sociology of the Military* (Beverly Hills: Sage Publications, 1975), p. 10.

24. Ibid., pp. 11–12.

25. Gunther E. Rothenberg, *The Art of Warfare in the Age of Napoleon* (Bloomington, Ind.: Indiana University Press, 1978), p. 1.

26. Charles C. Moskos, "The Emergent Military: Calling, Profession, or Occupation?", in Franklin D. Margiotta, ed., *The Changing World of the American Military* (Boulder, Colo.: Westview, 1978), p. 200.

27. Thomas A. Fabanyic, "Manpower, Military Intervention, and the All-Volunteer Force," in Ellen P. Stern, ed., *The Limits of Military Intervention* (Beverly Hills: Sage Publications, 1977), p. 283.

28. Senator Sam Ervin, as quoted in E. Lawrence Gibson, *Get Off My Ship* (New York: Avon, 1978), p. 292.

29. Homer E. Moyer, ed., *Justice and the Military* (Washington, D.C.: A Project of the Public Law Education Institute, 1972), p. 5.

30. Ibid., p. 3–112.

31. General Duane L. Faw, Address before Navy JAG Conference (October 16, 1969), in Moyer, *Justice and the Military*, p. 3–113.

32. *Naval Justice*, NAVPERS 16199 (published and distributed by Standards and Curriculum Division, Training Bureau of Naval Personnel, October 1945), as quoted in Moyer, *Justice and the Military*, p. 1–150.

33. Blackstone, as quoted in John E. Nowak et al., *Handbook on Constitutional Law* (St. Paul, Minn.: West Publishing, 1978), p. 198.

34. Sigrist, "Problem of Pariahs," p. 240.

35. Coser, *Greedy Institutions*, pp. 6–7.

36. Hamilton I. McCubbin and Martha A. Marsden, "The Military Family and the Changing Military Profession," in Franklin P. Margiotta, *The Changing World of the American Military* (Boulder, Colo.: Westview, 1978), pp. 209–10.

37. "Junior Enlisted Personnel Stationed Overseas," report of the Military Compensation Subcommittee, Committee on Armed Services, House of Representatives, Ninety-Fifth Congress, Second Session (Washington, D.C.: U.S. Government Printing Office, December 19, 1978), pp. 4–6.

38. Jean Ebbert, *A Guide for the Sailor's Wife* (Annapolis: Naval Institute Press, 1976), p. 39.

39. *Army Times*, Advertising Supplement, June 14, 1978.

Chapter Seven

REFORMING HIS AND HER ARMY

WHAT IS TO BE DONE ABOUT HER ARMY?

The theory of Her Army hypothesized that many of the stresses experienced by women soldiers assigned to previously all-male domains were due to male resistance. The results of the unstructured interviews and questionnaires presented in Chapter Four confirmed that women had a variety of role strains in traditionally male military jobs in the U.S. Army Signal Corps. Khaki Town women faced isolation from the work culture, sexual shakedowns, and feelings of heightened visibility and mistaken identity.

As a response to these forces, the women of Khaki Town developed two broad patterns of underachievement and overachievement. Under-achieving females discarded the soldier role as the following social types: (1) Daddy's Little Girl, (2) the Sexpot, and (3) Mama. In contrast, overachieving types included the Super-Soldier and the Lone Ranger of Women's Liberation. When women held traditionally male jobs in an androcentric institution, they faced powerful pressures from their male counterparts. As a response to these pressures, many women decided to resign from their jobs and leave the U.S. Army.

Chapter Five described the males' response to female tokenism. It was discovered that many of the problems of female tokenism could be linked to institutional patterns and to the higher command.

Batch-Processing of Female Soldiers

The theory of female tokenism presented in Chapter Four argues that the structure of male domination can be changed if the proportion of women is significantly increased. Women are grossly underrepresented in all of the services. In khaki-collar work, they are alone or nearly alone. In the crafts area for all services, women fill only 2 percent of the positions. In electronic equipment repair and communications, women constitute only 5 percent of the positions, which was the actual proportion of women studied in Khaki Town's Signal Corps. The obvious policy solution is to add more women to the services, especially in the khaki-collar jobs.

Kanter argues that, if only a few women are included in an organization, it is difficult for them to generate a support network. However, if the sex ratio approaches 65:35 (male:female), the dynamics of the situation change. Men will still be the majority, but women become a "minority."[1] When a token group becomes a minority group, there is the potential for the development of a female enlisted culture. Minorities are less likely to be isolated from their work culture. They are also less likely to be targets of sexual shakedowns because there is a base from which to fight back. If the proportion of women is increased, they will then also become less visible. They are less likely to be mistaken by males as being out of place. The transition from token to minority is the first step toward full participation of women in the military.

Increased Numbers of Women and Military Effectiveness

Chapter Two described eight functions that women fulfill in the current volunteer military: (1) the Defense Department uses women to cultivate its image as a social welfare institution; (2) women soldiers serve as a reserve army; (3) women recruits are brighter and easier to train than the males; (4) an increase in female military participation contributes to a more socially representative military; (5) military women present fewer social-control problems; (6) female military labor is cheaper and helps to lower "manpower costs"; (7) women serve a useful role in replenishing the military's legitimacy fund; and (8) women serve as a reservoir of marriage partners for enlisted males. Dual-career military couples contribute to stability within the military.

If increased numbers of women were added to the military, the use of women as "flak catchers" would decline. More importantly, increased female participation would contribute to military readiness. In 1975 the Army found that units operating between the front lines and rear boundaries could include up to 50 percent women.[2] If a greater proportion of females were included, the military could benefit because women are a highly skilled and able group of soldiers.

In 1977 the impact of the presence of women was assessed in a 30-day REFORGER exercise in West Germany. REFORGER was an extended combat simulation scenario. It was found that up to 35 percent women could be deployed to support and combat-support units without impeding military readiness.[3]

Legal Barriers

One reason the services have not included women in more jobs is the presence of statutory regulations in the U.S. Code, sections 6015 and 8549, which restrict women from combat units in the Air Force and Navy. While there are no statutory restrictions on the use of women in the Army and Marines, commanders have interpreted the U.S. Code as restricting women to noncombat units. The problem with these laws, according to Navy Commander Gormley, is that they restrict the mobility of women in the services.[4] Because women are not allowed in combat jobs, they are viewed as temporary workers who will be left behind once the fighting begins. If the U.S. Code restrictions were repealed, Gormley believes that "the rug would be pulled out from under all regulations and policies prohibiting combat roles for women."[5]

The debate as to whether women should be included in combat has been particularly contentious within the women's movement, Congress, and among women soldiers themselves. However, there is little basis for the false dichotomy between combat and noncombat roles. If there is to be a major war, women will suffer casualties either as civilians or as noncombatants in the military.

In Khaki Town, for example, women are already in combat-support units. In a tank war or a limited nuclear war, Signal Corps women would suffer numerous casualties because of the shifting combat front. Women already serve as truck drivers, helicopter pilots, field communications specialists, and in other tactical roles. There is no apparent reason to exclude them from operating Redeye Missiles or heavy artillery. Many combat jobs are performed further from the front than are current support roles. The changing nature of warfare, which is based on technology rather than on brute force, does not justify the exclusion of women. If formal restrictions were removed, women would become full participants in the military and would not be subject to the criticism of male soldiers that they are "part-timers" or "temporaries." Since 1972, women have been assigned to the underground launch crews of the Titan Missiles. The removal of legal barriers would allow women to "man" other jobs currently defined as "combat."

Anticipatory Socialization for Khaki-Collar Jobs

When women were assigned to nontraditional jobs in Khaki Town, they experienced what Hughes called "reality shock." From a classroom environment in communications school, women were sent to tactical communications units in West Germany. It is not surprising that many women found the real Army to be both a disappointment and a shock. Particular attention should be given to a program of "organizational skills" for women entering previously male jobs. Women should be given additional instruction on how to cope with male harassment, as well as a "breaking in" period prior to their first assignment to tactical units. This could include discussions of and with women who have successfully adapted to khaki-collar jobs.

If the military is to increase the number of women in labor-intensive jobs, it should change its patterns of recruitment. In Khaki Town, there was a disjuncture between many women's previous socialization and the kind of work they had to do in telecommunications. A greater effort should be made to match female interests and abilities to military jobs. It is also reasonable to extend greater screening to male soldiers. Sex should not be the criterion used for selection for military jobs because there are considerable intrasex differences. As we discovered in Chapter Five, Super-Soldiers overachieved in their jobs. Some men, as well as some women, prefer labor-intensive jobs to clerical jobs. Therefore, it is reasonable to devote more attention to matching soldiers of both sexes according to their aptitudes, interests, and achievements.

In Khaki Town, a major source of enlisted tension for both sexes was the tendency of commanders to assign women out of their specialty area; 25 women in my sample were arbitrarily removed from their area of expertise, and a serious morale problem was created. Women felt they were not being properly utilized, while males felt that women were getting the softer jobs. It is important that soldiers of both sexes be selected carefully and then be allowed to do their jobs.

Coaching

Kanter suggests that "coaches" can assist individuals through difficult status passages by providing inside information and assistance. When women initially enter newly integrated settings, artificial sponsorship can be created for token women through connections with top management.[6] Tokenism in the U.S. Army is more difficult because there are few sponsor-token alliances. Instead, the Daddy Warbucks-Dutiful Daughter and Sgt. Seducto-Sexpot alliances created divisiveness within the female enlisted culture.

Two forms of sponsor-token relationships could be created. At the first-line supervisory level, promotion points could be awarded to NCOs who have a track record of assisting women. Points could be assigned on the basis of how many women reenlisted in their specialties within a platoon. Coaching at the mid-management level could involve positive reinforcement for assistance to females. Currently, there are few rewards for the NCO for the integration of women into his unit. Middle-level managers are caught between the conflicting pressures of junior enlisted men and the higher command. The coach system could well be the basis for a sponsor-token alliance that would help women weather the injuries of tokenism.

Kanter suggests the ingenious technique of promoting artificial sponsorship of women within the higher command.[7] If women have a tie to higher officers, they have channels for grievances as well as access to power. For the higher command, this system would give officers a greater sensitivity to problems at the unit level. As for the middle-level supervisor, promotion points could also be linked to the success of women under a higher official command.

A third coach that is essential for the full development of female enlisted culture is the female mentor. More female officers must be included in all of the services. Enlisted women currently have an extremely low probability of having another woman as a supervisor. Less than 0.5 percent of senior noncommissioned officer positions are filled by women. Military women need role models with greater organizational power so that they can see, on a day-to-day basis, the evidence that women can get ahead in the military. Currently, the vast majority of women officers are in pink-collar areas, such as nursing and administration. Before sufficient numbers of women can advance through the ranks, it is necessary to offer interim support in the form of coaches.

Action from the Top Down

If something is to be done about the problem of tokenism in the military, any action program must begin at the top. Ultimate responsibility for the problems of military women should be placed at the highest levels of the military command rather than at the noncommissioned officer level. The attitude of the higher command is the single most important factor in determining the implementation of reform.

A final suggestion is to integrate women into work settings that have high morale. In Khaki Town, women were sent into a setting already marked with an ethos of dispiritation. The presence of women became just one more encroachment on the lives of enlisted men who were already demoralized by the gross assiduities of venality. This suggestion leads us to the question of what is to be done about His Army. Her Army includes both female tokenism and also the problems of Army life in general. There can be no significant gain for military women or men if reform stops with women's issues. There must be a fundamental change in the quality of enlisted life. The venal character of the military must be transformed.

REFORMING HIS ARMY

In Chapter 6, I argued that the army is a venal institution that encroaches upon the enlisted member's time, family, and identity. Because the Army rests on a bedrock of traditional notions of discipline, the venal aspects of military service are more difficult to change than is female tokenism. With the volunteer Army, the military has become a revolving door to many, as we learned in Chapter Two. If morale could be improved within the military, soldiers of both sexes would stay in the Army long enough to become more experienced in their jobs and to reap the fruits of their training.

Why Not Return to the Draft?

Chapter one discussed how women have historically served as temporary military workers in periods of external crisis. In peacetime, women have been routinely proscribed from performing martial roles. This exclusion has had negative consequences on the economic, political, and legal status of women. Temporary participation in the military did not result in permanent citizenship rights because evanescent sex-role definitions were restored when women were demobilized.

Chapter Two developed an internal crisis explanation for the expansion of women in the volunteer military. The argument was that females served latent functions and provided the margin of success for the volunteer Army. If women are to receive permanent citizenship rights through military service, their numbers must be expanded in the volunteer force. If the male-only draft were reinstated, women's recent gains would be reversed. In fact, it is possible that such a draft would result in the exclusion of women from the peacetime military. In addition, the use of conscription is contrary to the rationalization of the military. If the draft were reinstituted, there would be no organizational incentive for improvements in the quality of enlisted life. The draft would be a step toward further venality and away from the occupational model.

Legal Status

The precarious legal situation of Khaki Town soldiers was a key feature of venality. It is essential to begin to civilianize the military justice system. The current restrictions on the constitutional rights of soldiers, in the long run, destroy the efficiency and dignity of individuals by depriving them of ordinary protections of life and liberty. Military counsel should be retained to assist military personnel. But the expensive and officious structure of the military courts must be eviscerated. The extension of constitutional rights would contribute to the further transformation of the military from a structure of domination to that of an ordinary occupation. Morgan rebutted the claim that there would be no discipline without the present system of military justice:

> Regarding those who tell me that—we won't have an army, if we have civilian trials, that we won't be able to have discipline. I just want to call to your attention in the early history of the Navy [flogging was standard procedure], and the reaction to eliminating it was that "if we abolish flogging there will be mutiny on every ship." It took years-decades to abolish flogging. And they abolished flogging and there is not a mutiny on every ship.[8]

Organizational Development

Structural reform of His Army should not stop at the extension of due process procedures to soldiers. It is also necessary to begin to examine long-range ways of improving the accountability of the organization to its members. It is necessary to improve the pay, housing, and family life for enlisted members. Bruyn has divided the general attributes of organizations into two broad subtypes: *command systems* and *democratic systems*. All large organizations are a mixture of both systems, but they tend to emphasize one or the other. Military organization emphasizes the command system; the organization makes and enforces rigid time and identity demands. This creates feelings of inferiority and alienation. The more democratic the system of decision making, the more likely it is that a greater number of soldiers will use their talents and their intelligence in mutual governance.[9] If the military is to lose its venal character, it must converge further with ordinary occupations.

In summary, the problems that both males and females face in His Army could be lessened by the extension of ordinary citizenship rights. Features of military life such as 24-hour duty, harassment, and extended tours abroad can be changed without destroying organizational discipline. Currently, because of the precarious legal status of soldiers in the venal institution, they have little insulation from the military command that desires total control over its members' hair, voices, and toilet habits. The structure of military domination is premised on the assumption that a large pool of persons, both males and females, can be either directly or indirectly conscripted. The master-servant role set has long been obsolete in industry. Military service for the enlisted soldier has become dangerously close to Hughes' notion of "Good People and Dirty Work."[10] Good people do not enter the military because they view the task as odious, but they mandate military domination. For the more than 2 million enlisted soldiers of both sexes, dirty work is done because they cannot hold their own in the industrial sector.

As we have seen, there is a real question as to whether military service is really the vanguard of new sex roles or only the retrenchment of patriarchal society. Without a change in the structure of enlisted life, there will be few gains for anyone in the adjustment of women to military life. The economic advantages of temporary work in the military, when they exist at all, are offset by the daily mortification of life in a venal institution.

If women are to receive expanded citizenship rights through their military participation, both His and Her Army must be transformed. Larger numbers of women must be sponsored and coached so that they can pass through the structure to supervisory positions. The growth of female role models and the official encouragement of a female enlisted culture are necessary to shield women from the stresses of tokenism in the short run, but all of these changes are premised on the assumption that His Army can be reformed.

NOTES

1. Rosabeth Moss Kanter, *Men and Women of the Corporation* (New York: Basic Books, 1977), pp. 208–42.

2. Department of the Army, *Women Content in the Army-REFORGER 77* (REFWAC-77) (prepared by the U.S. Army Research Institute: Alexandria, Va., 1978).

3. Ibid.

4. Patricia Gormley, "Legal Bars, Sexism Hurts Servicewomen's Progress," *Army Times*, May 12, 1980.

5. Ibid.

6. Anselm Strauss, as quoted in Kanter, *Men and Women of the Corporation*, pp. 279–80.

7. Kanter, *Men and Women of the Corporation*, pp. 279–80.

8. Charles Morgan, as quoted in Homer E. Moyer, ed., *Justice and the Military* (Washington, D.C.: A Project of the Public Law Education Institute, 1972), pp. 150–1.

9. Severyn Bruyn, "A Theory of Organizational Development: The Relation of Social Structure to the Moral Individual," unpublished manuscript, Social Economy Program, Boston College, Department of Sociology (May 1979).

10. Everett C. Hughes, "Good People and Dirty Work," in Howard Becker, ed., *The Other Side: Perspectives on Deviance* (New York: Free Press, 1964), pp. 23–36; This essay also appears in the collected essays of Everett C. Hughes, *The Sociological Eye* (Chicago: Aldine-Atherton Press, 1971).

APPENDIXES

APPENDIX A
RESEARCHING FEMALE ENLISTED LIFE
AMONG THE U.S. FORCES IN WEST GERMANY

The data for this study of female enlisted life was drawn from my experiences as a lecturer with the University of Maryland's European Division. The conceptual and analytical framework grew out of an ethnographic study of the overseas garrison community that I called Khaki Town. Sociologists have long demonstrated interest in the military context but have rarely used field research. In this Appendix, I will describe the chronology of my research roles and try to suggest ways to further the study of the military community.

EVOLUTION OF THE STUDY

Legitimate Entrance

From January of 1975 to October of 1978, I was formally associated with the American military community in Europe as a sociology lecturer with the University of Maryland, which maintains a European Division headquartered in Heidelberg, West Germany, and teaches courses to military personnel. Because I was associated with the University servicemen's educational program, I received a military identification card that entitled me to routine access to U.S. military bases and their facilities.

Education is a major activity in the peacetime U.S. military. Since the mid-1970s, a two-year associate of arts degree has had considerable value to NCOs for purposes of promotion. A Defense Department campaign has been directed toward improving the educational level of the troops in the volunteer forces.

In many of the bases, a junior enlisted soldier could choose business courses with the City Colleges of Chicago, law enforcement training with Central Texas College, or certification in fire fighting from El Paso Community College. Embry-Riddle Aeronautical University offered an airframe and power plant program, while Ball State University offered a program in management. Since 1949, the University of Maryland's European Division has offered programs of study in the liberal arts, business administration, and law enforcement.

The majority of my Maryland students were young junior enlisted men. Many were attending classes for the two-year associate degree, while a significant minority were completing courses for the bachelor's degree. Significant numbers of enlisted women, Department of Defense civilians, teenage dependents of military personnel, and foreign national workers in the American military community also attended these classes.

The motivation and previous preparation of my students was uneven, depending upon such variables as the branch of service, type of unit, whether they were male or female, years of military service, and whether they were pursuing a bachelor's degree or attending school for points to be used toward promotion.

In general, the abilities of students at Air Force and Navy bases were more similar to those of civilian college students than were those of the Army students. However, the Army bases with a high percentage of civilians, military intelligence gatherers, and women had students who compared favorably with the Navy and Air Force students.

Females tended to be better prepared than their male counterparts regardless of the service and unit, reflecting the higher enlistment standards and higher prior educational background of female recruits.

Career personnel tended to be more serious students than did short-term personnel. However, there were notable exceptions to this generalization, and those expecting to attend a university after their term of service were among the most highly motivated students. If career personnel were taking courses to escape unpleasant duty or to gain promotion points, their interest and preparation tended to be lower.

Classes were held between 6:30 and 9:30 in the evenings, usually twice a week, in military dependent school facilities or in makeshift classrooms in buildings such as mess halls or barracks. The course content was similar to University of Maryland courses at the home campus, and there were no unusual strictures on academic freedom. My expectations as to student performance fluctuated upward or downward, depending on the group. In general, the motivation and ability of these students compared favorably with those in my previous and subsequent teaching experiences at a community college, state university, and a private college of excellent reputation. The major difference between military and civilian students seemed to be in the extreme tails of the distribution. My best military students were often more mature and resourceful than their civilian counterparts, while the worst military students did not reach the threshold level of the poorest civilian students.

Observer as Participant

Much of my initial data were collected informally in my role as a university lecturer. My close association with students in a variety of military settings gave me a greater understanding of the social world(s) of the enlisted soldier. My University of Maryland teacher role legitimized my presence on a day-to-day basis, while my role as a sociology teacher allowed me to gracefully inquire about the jargon, values, and types present in each military community in which I taught. Altogether, I was able to collect unstructured observations at 25 different U.S. garrison communities in Germany, Italy, Spain, and Turkey. One initial advantage I had was exposure to many different male-female settings across the gamut of U.S. military units overseas, due to the frequency with which I was transferred from base to base.

There were four academic terms each year, as well as a summer term blocked into eight-week segments. The faculty for each military base was composed of full-time lecturers hired in the United States, local military and civilian instructors, and part-timers hired on a term-to-term basis, depending upon the needs of the education center. Full-time lecturers enjoyed higher pay and more military benefits than the other instructors but were more susceptible to frequent moves, often on a short-term basis. As a full-time lecturer, I was transferred to 25 different education centers on bases in four countries during four years. In areas with large concentrations of American forces, I taught at two and sometimes three different bases, during a single eight-week period.

I was initially favorable to frequent moves for two reasons. First, I was interested in sampling as many military settings as possible before deciding on a research setting. Secondly, I was interested in traveling as much as possible in Europe during my school vacations. Frequent moves allowed me to sample both intraservice and interservice differences in a relatively short period of time. I was also able to differentiate between the idiosyncratic features of any one particular base and the general features of enlisted military life.

In the beginning, learning the ropes of teaching in a military setting was an incredible effort. I taught 13 different sociology specialties, ranging from the sociology of the family to military sociology. Much of my initial data and observations were collected in conjunction with my teaching. During my short stays at many bases, students were helpful as key informants about the worlds of nonstudents. In some cases, I collaborated

242 / WOMEN IN KHAKI

with students, researching topics such as the "Role of the Military Police," "War-Peace Attitudes of High School Dependents," "The Problem of Alcoholism among Warrant Officers," and "Status Dilemmas of Military Wives." In my sociology of sex roles course, I supervised several mini-research projects on such topics as the "Problem of Dual-Career Military Couples in the Air Force," "Discrimination against Women at _____ Base," and "Enlisted Male Attitudes toward Women on Ships." These studies provided many insights that later became the basis of my work in Khaki Town.

In short, I could assume the role of a normal participant in the military community without arousing fears that I represented military authority. This was not to say that my life as a lecturer was free from interpersonal tensions, which was certainly not the case. Each class responded to me with reservations in the beginning. In a few cases I never felt at ease with some of my students, but in general, the lecturer role was comfortable. In many cases, I developed friendships with individual students in my classes. Positive course evaluations revealed that most students enjoyed working with me.

Transition to Observer as Participant

During the very early months of my teaching, I felt extreme discomfort in both my role as a lecturer and an observer. Prior to teaching with Maryland, I had had little contact of any kind with soldiers or the military. I never served in the military nor had any friends or colleagues who had served. Military culture, in many ways, was more foreign to me than the European cultures in which the bases were located. My field notes during my early teaching days revealed the loneliness and cultural shock that I was experiencing.

Part of my initial "military culture shock" was due to the location of my first assignment. This base was a field training area near the Czechoslovakian border in Bavaria, in the south of Germany. The ethos of this base was decidedly more military and in marked contrast to Heidelberg, where the headquarters of the University of Maryland is located. It was located in the midst of dense forest lands, nearly 100 kilometers from the nearest German city and was physically cut off from German life with barbed wire fences. The base was primarily a training area for tanks, heavy artillery, and missiles. During World War II, General Rommel's troops constructed a tower on the base, from which the General reputedly inspected his key tank battalions. The weather during the winter months was dismal with long periods of drizzle or snow. During the first two months I was there, there was not a single day when it was not either raining, snowing, or overcast.

My diary from the end of January of 1975 indicates the intense anxiety and deep depression that I experienced at this base. My first entry in the last week of January describes a conversation that I had on the train, the Bundes-Bahn, en route from Heidelberg to the base:

> I boarded a train to Heidelberg and changed trains at Weiden for G_____.
> I waited at the Weiden train station and met Dan, a 31-year-old staff sergeant
> from Tennessee. I asked Dan where he was headed, and he told me that he
> was going back to the same old hell hole of G_____.

> *Dan:* Yeah, I stayed at the BA [Bavarian American Hotel in Nuremberg] for
> the weekend. Had a damn good weekend. Went to the Wall [prostitution
> section located inside the old city wall] and had some Big Macs. [There is a
> McDonald's restaurant in Nuremberg.]
> *MR:* Why do you call G_____ a hell hole? Why is it so bad?
> *Dan:* Do you wanna know how bad that place is? I'll tell ya. My older brother
> was stationed in G_____ during the late 60s. To get out of there, he asked
> for orders to Nam! Let me tell you one thing, buddy. If you can do anything
> to get out of going to G_____, do it now!

In the first weeks, my sociological imagination was disabled by my personal distaste for G_____. I lived in military barracks that were built as temporary housing for the German Army in the late 1930s. As a civilian, I was charged $2 a day for a room that was painted an undistinguished yellow and was devoid of any decor except the banner of an infantry unit. The room was furnished with a standard army cot, reading table, and lamp. I shared the shower room and toilet facilities with 20 junior officers who were on temporary duty (TDY) there. The walls shook incessantly in rhythm with heavy artillery rounds that were exploded in the nearby training fields. I slept fitfully and occupied myself with class preparation. Since I did not have a car during my first term of teaching, I spent all of my "off-duty" time in the garrison. I played basketball in the base gym, drank in the enlisted men's club, and shared meals in the mess hall with the soldiers.

My first "classroom" was an abandoned mess hall located in the "tent city" area of the garrison. The building, painted in institutional green, was heated by a single Atlantic type wood-burning stove. The building was in obvious disrepair, and the walls seemed in danger of collapsing as they shook during the most intensive bombings on the practice range.

My students were transported to class in the back of two and a half ton trucks. Each student arrived in class with an M-14 rifle, which was cleared in a special container outside the classroom. They appeared more ready to meet the Russians than they were to meet the requirements of an introductory sociology course:

There were 35 students who were presumably prepared to study introductory sociology. However, none of the students carried the assigned text that was for sale in the base's Stars and Stripes bookstore. Few had notebooks or writing equipment. There was much horseplay and a few loud hoots of laughter before the class began. A few of the students had been up the previous night on field maneuvers. Most were wet and cold. One student dumped lighter fluid in the wood stove and caused the flames to scorch the wall. Another student threatened to really get the fire going by throwing a grenade into the stove.

When I was ready to begin class, I made the ordinary introduction but was drowned out by loud laughter from the back of the room. After several such starts were interrupted by shouts or hoots, I sat down, hoping that this would signal that class was ready to begin. As soon as I sat down, a gray-haired sergeant leaped to his feet and in a stern command voice yelled, "At Ease!" The classroom quieted down, and I began my introduction again: "Sociology is the study of people in groups and can be relevant to your everyday lives. For example, what was the military trying to do in basic training? [This reference was greeted with loud laughter and more hooting.] From the back of the room I heard, "Hey! this guy's a real horse's ass... ass... ass" [the words reverberated off the walls of the hall]. The walls then shook so violently from the force of a heavy shell that I became concerned for my safety. After several more minutes of bombardment from the nearby target areas, I started once more. This time I retreated, "Well, there's not much to do the first day of class, so I'll excuse you early. You should pick up the McKee text at the Stars and Stripes bookstore and begin reading Chapter One."

This comment was met with loud cheers, laughter, and cries of "Right on!", "Far fucking out!" Still others responded by thumping the long benches that served as makeshift desks. Several black soldiers seated in the back of the room remained seated with folded arms. Class was dismissed, and I made a hurried exit to the main gate.

My students, as I found out the second day of class, had been assigned to this base on temporary duty from their home base in Fort Hood, Texas, in conjunction with Brigade 75 field exercises. During my next classes, I gradually developed minimum order in the classroom and gained a greater understanding of the sociology of this particular group of students. A student particularly helpful to me was a first sergeant from my home state of Minnesota. Sergeant F. was respected by both junior enlisted men and NCOs and let me know the "inside track" on the reasons why people signed up for introductory sociology. Since the class was held during on-duty time, students could catch up on their sleep and escape unpleasant field duties for a few hours if they signed up for class. An unobtrusive indicator of this motivation and commitment was that only a few students regularly took notes during class discussions and lectures. Others, such as

Herman M., lounged in the back of the classroom, slept, or held "bull sessions" in the kitchen that adjoined the hall. One day Herman came to class so drunk that he fell out of his chair. I was in the middle of a lecture on social norms and observed lightly that Herman's classroom behavior would be considered deviant in some circles. Most students remained in their seats until class was dismissed. But Herman gathered his M-14 from under his chair, slammed out of the classroom, and in a short while fired an M-14 round into the air. That was the last I saw of Herman in Introductory Sociology.

Only 10 of 35 students completed the introductory course successfully, despite my efforts to adjust my teaching methods to the preparation and interests of the class. I gave the midterm examination and found that the mean grade was 42. During the next class session, I gave the same exam again and found the average grade to be 38!

By the close of the class, I was disillusioned with the teaching assignment. However, in other respects, the G_____ experience had spurred my understanding of the most aversive features of garrison life. At one point in the semester, I gave the students an assignment to write 20 statements about themselves (Twenty Statements Test) for a class discussion of the social bases of personality. Extracts from the protocols were revealing of the social origins and problems of the group. From my only A student, who was nicknamed Space Shot by his peers:

> I am a child of my heavenly father. Before I came to this earth I lived with my heavenly father as a personage of the spirit. Since coming to this earth, I have been many things at many places in many times and more importantly I am now one of his. I will not try to convert you even though I'm really into conversion. I am what I am what I am.
>
> I used to think of myself as somewhat of a free-spirited radical, anxious for evolutionary rather than revolutionary change. I now fall 180 degrees from that old view. Actually I am a very structured, organized person and when you really get into it may not be so ready for the fast changes that have occurred as of late.

Sergeant F. identified with me and helped me to maintain classroom order. His "Who Am I" reflected his desire to please me by using sociological concepts:

> I am a part of a family structure (son, brother, husband, etc.).
> I am a member of a secondary group (U.S. Army).
> I am a member of a primary group (platoon, Company C).
> I am a member of the human race.
> I am a member of an ascribed status (21 years old, Caucasian, and male).
> I am a member of an achieved status (Specialist Six).

I'm upwardly mobile, headed for the economic middle class.
I'm short termer in the military now (planning to retire).
I'm a college student.
I'm a good soldier and a hard worker.
I'm planning to get a Ph.D. in modern sociology.

Several of the self-identity tests were useful to me in identifying social types of enlisted men, such as the Student and the Head, which were later investigated in Khaki Town. The following two accounts illustrate how students used university courses to temporarily escape the ennui of military life at G_____. These students seized the moment to learn as much as they could, while others viewed classes as a socioemotive or recreational outlet. From a company clerk, Roland, who identified with the Student role and the Head subculture:

I'd like to see the problem of boredom with the United States Forces stationed in Europe discussed more. I'm a person with special desires and needs which set me apart from most people [in the military]. I am a person who feels that education is the most important single act one can do.
I am a drug user.
I am a hippie. Prior to military service I was a long hair.
I am a person who has been institutionalized since a very early age to believe in our society. (My father is a sergeant major in the Army in Iran.)
I am single but plan to get married in several years.
I have no set or permanent home. (Since my father is in the service, we have moved very frequently.)
I am a wanderer.
I believe in greater freedoms in the armed forces (longer hair, beards, abolishing saluting, etc.).

Anthony, another company clerk permanently stationed at G_____, wrote the following account:

I am a black man looking for hope and knowledge, that I can't find in the streets or in the Army. I am a young person who has strived all his life to be ahead of the next guy. I am a person who no matter what he was told or how he was hassled. I am a mix-upped person who needs answers. I am a friend to all unless you do me wrong. I am a person with a lot of growing up to do and a lot of defenses to destroy. I am a person who will refuse to give in or quit. I am determined to know.

From Vernon, an infantry soldier:

I am a man. I am willing to be open minded as possible. I am not a lover of society. I am just trying to function in this society. I am aware of class structure. I am a lover of the truth. I am just trying to finish college so that I can help other people that have not had a good start in life.

From Oather, an electronic repairman:

> I am in the Army. I am from a lower-class family. I am an amateur hypnotist. I am completing a college education to fulfill my personal, social, and emotional goals. I am emotional unstable at times in my own mind. I am undecided about staying in the Army. I am me.

More representative of social types in the base's enlisted culture are the following protocols, which reflect the more traditional images of the foot-slogging "grunt." From Dale, a truck driver:

> I am a U.S. soldier. I goof off a lot. I live to live freely. I am now a truck driver. I was a farmer. I like doing crazy ass things like getting high and crashing motorcyles. I don't like being a grunt in the Army much. I do like Germany. I like to chase their women. I am a male. I am 5'11" tall. 175 lbs. lean and mean.

From Charlie, an infantry soldier:

> I came to Germany a month ago. . . I like the duty. I don't talk very much. I like to play football. I don't like waiting in line. I like to have sex all the time. I like kids very much. I took sociology before in Alaska. I didn't like the cold weather there. I am a pretty nice guy, really. . .

From Reynolds, a first sergeant supervisor:

> I am a soldier in the Army. I tend to be old-fashioned. I am very hard headed and set in my ways. I fly off the handle too easily. I am very moody. I am too critical. I talk, when I should listen. I am an instructor. I find it hard writing about who I am.

From Pedro, a combat engineer:

> I am a peaceful person not willing to provoke other people. But I will not tolerate people thinking that they are better than me. I am a person who enjoys small pleasures such as being with a girl or just simply getting "high". I am a very crazy person with a crazy way of looking at different things.

A few of the "Who Am I" protocols reflected a heightened racial consciousness, but black soldiers were just as likely to identify with other roles such as Student or "grunt." From Richard, a truck driver:

I am a person of the Black American race. I am somebody. I am realistic. I fight for what I believe. I am a watcher. A thinker . . . a doer. I am a person who does not appeal to many.

From Parker, an infantry soldier:

I am Black! I am somebody! I am a man! I am a man trying to make it in life! I am me! I am a brother. I am the future, America. I am of the River that flows! I'm of the earth that turn! I'm the fire that burn! I'm of the sea that is wide! I'm of the mountain that's high! I'm what I'm not and that's you!

The "Who Am I" protocols were representative of the insights that I gained about enlisted life. While in one sense I failed as an instructor for many of these soldiers, it was paradoxical that I gained deeply from them. Middle-class students typically mask their emotions and are adroit in conveying the impression that they are deeply involved in the educational enterprise. But my soldier-students had not perfected an impression-management strategy.

The large number of students who did not take an interest in the materials that I taught did not extend this dislike to me personally. An incident from my March 1975 diary reflects that they could be loyal:

I received a call after midterm from the Heidelberg Office asking me if it would be okay for the German Area Supervisor to sit in on my class since it was my first term. I said that it would be okay, but I worried about the reaction of the class and the evaluator. Would there be horseplay which would cast doubt on my ability to maintain minimum classroom standards of discipline?

My doubts were allayed by the behavior of the class on the day that the supervisor visited. Unlike all previous sessions, the students were orderly and appeared to be actively taking notes during the lecture and discussion. Students who previously came to class without notebooks or pencils borrowed materials from their neighbors. Some even participated in the lively discussion on the future of the family. After the supervisor left, I asked the class why things seemed so good today. An infantryman spoke first, "We all know what it's like being inspected and all and we don't think you're such a bad teacher, really." Other students added that they always knew what to do when inspection-time came!

My next assignments were considerably less aversive than this first one. But the G_____ experience had rapidly acclimated me to the features of male enlisted culture that were less apparent in my later assignments.

In subsequent assignments, students played an increasingly important role in alerting me to features of the social world(s) of military women. At the same time, my increased reservoir of direct observational experience helped me to learn about the perspectives of various subcultures within the military community. By the summer of 1977, I was convinced that an important area of study was male-female relations in a military environment. Particular ideas about conducting a research project on women were germinated in my sociology of sex-roles courses, which were the classes that had the highest percentage of women enrolled in them. My students identified many of the problems that were later to be fully researched in Khaki Town.

Transition to Full-Time Field Worker

Later assignments gave me a diverse sampling of settings in which I was able to meet military women. Apart from classes, I jotted down notes on incidents in which I observed male-female interactions occurring in work settings, the mess hall, and other garrison activities. Daily interaction with a variety of military personnel allowed me to get closer to the meaning of overseas garrison life.

In Munich, several students helped me to develop a structured questionnaire that was to serve as a pretest for my research in Khaki Town. A network of 20 students and friends administered questionnaires to a sample of 200 men and women at 5 southern German bases. There were numerous problems with this effort. First, when I sought formal permission for the study, I was told that it would take six months to a year for formal clearance. Secondly, I had no financial sponsorship for the project. I had the questionnaires printed by a German publisher in Munich at my own expense. Several students and I assembled the questionnaire ourselves. Most importantly, I learned that the fixed-choice scales did not yield the kind of meaningful responses for which I was hoping. A number of respondents felt that the items forced them into meaningless categories. I still knew too little about the social world(s) of soldiers to know what to ask in a structured format. Military personnel are subject to a variety of structured tests, beginning at basic training. Many soldiers who responded commented that I failed to ask key questions, such as the number of years of service, military occupational specialty, and number of children.

In the fall of 1977, I continued to plan for a study of military women with the help of my students at an Air Force base and an Army base in Frankfurt. In October, several Army women helped me develop a new questionnaire that had a more flexible format. The semistructured instrument was administered by students to 25 women soldiers in the Frankfurt area. In addition, I continued to become more involved in collecting unstructured observations of women *in situ* at several bases. I began making plans to choose a research setting.

ROLE OF CONSULTANT

In December of 1977, the Social Actions Officer of Khaki Town called the Director of the Women's Studies Program at the University of Maryland and asked her about the possibility of offering special seminars in management skills to military women in Khaki Town. The Director, in turn, appointed me as a consultant to the project, which later was entitled "Organizational Skills Training for Khaki Town Personnel."

In my early work as consultant, I designed materials on the history of military women, found information on how women were used in the Army, and surveyed studies of women in nontraditional roles. I drew up a list of questions for discussion, which was based partially on my early questionnaires and field observations. The staff of the University of Maryland Women's Studies Program developed assertiveness-training materials, time-budgeting suggestions, and other management-oriented materials to be used in conjunction with my training module on military women. I received permission from Khaki Town's Social Actions Office to interview enlisted soldiers and to conduct a research phase, along with the organizational skills training.

Therefore, studying the men and women of Khaki Town was a fortuitous circumstance. My entrée was facilitated by three factors. First, I was associated with the military community as a University of Maryland instructor and was presumed to be sympathetic to the problems of military women. Secondly, I was able to strike an exchange bargain with a low-level official in the organization; permission was granted at the base level rather than at the higher command headquarters. In return for access to Khaki Town and the cooperation of the command, I would assist management in understanding male-female tensions. Thirdly, it was my experience that the Army is more open to outside investigators than are the Air Force or Navy, which prefer not to launder their "dirty linen" openly. The Navy and Air Force converge with civilian corporations in that they have more sophisticated controls against outside researchers and critics.

My willingness to share my expertise in the area of sex roles with management represented an attractive bargain to the captain in charge of Social Action. While the Army had successfully implemented a program of race relations, it did not have a similar program for ameliorating sex-role strains.

According to the Social Actions Program officers, Khaki Town had a severe morale problem, due to sex-role tensions. Initial problems that had been identified by Equal Opportunity Officers and the Social Actions staff included the following:

Male and female soldiers each had the view that the other was receiving preferential treatment from the chain of command regarding time off, promotions, and assignments.

Military managers increasingly faced difficulties in coping with rumors and cases of favoritism based on sex.

A common complaint of military males was that women did not pull their full share of field duty or that they didn't go the field at all (for training exercises). Another common view was that women "got over" because they were women, because of sexual relationships with their supervisors, and because of the paternalism of the higher command.

Women complained that some male supervisors treated them as sexual objects rather than as soldiers. Some complained that they had supervisors who demanded sex as part of the job.

Males defined the problems identified by women differently; they defined the situation as females unable to perform or "getting over" in other ways.

Organizational Skills Sessions
(Field Notes—January 12, 1978)

Beginning in the third week of January 1978, I conducted formal human relations seminars for predominantly noncommissioned officer males at four bases in the Khaki Town military community. It was decided that both males and females from Khaki Town units in which women worked should participate in these sessions. I taught all of the sessions with the male soldiers. The female-soldier sessions were conducted by women facilitators from the University of Maryland's Women's Studies Program. It was thought that same-sex settings would be more conducive to a candid discussion of the problems.

Table A.1 presents the topics discussed by instructors for both the male and female sessions.

General information units reflected on the problems of sex discrimination, male and female socialization, the problems of women in the military, and training in assertiveness for both groups. Each session was conducted with 20 to 30 participants and lasted from 6 to 8 hours, depending on the group's enthusiasm and the pace of instruction.

Each training session had at least two hours of free-for-all discussion of male and female soldiers' perceptions of each other. In the males' sessions, there was often very lively and impassioned conversation. I tried to play the role of "sympathetic listener" during these discussions and at no time attempted to return to curriculum materials.

Participants

Male participants were soldiers who either supervised or worked in mixed-sex settings. We did not know the exact number of Signal Corps

TABLE A.1. Outline of Training Sessions at Khaki Town Bases

Training Session Schedule

Unit I.   What Constitutes Sex Discrimination?
    A. Introduction
    B. Specific examples of discrimination
    C. Legal ramifications

Unit II.   Sex Roles in Transition: A Sociological Perspective
    A. Myth versus reality in the status of women
    B. Research on sex differences
        1. Well-founded differences
        2. Unfounded beliefs
        3. Ambiguities in sex-role research
    C. Process of sex-role socialization
        1. Differential socialization for boys/girls
        2. Masculine versus feminine identity problems
    D. The female occupational ghetto
        1. Vicarious versus direct achievement roles
        2. Role choices
        3. Problems of women in the marketplace
    E. What do women want?
        1. An introduction to the women's movement
        2. Crisis and sex-role change
        3. Implications for social policy

Unit III. Women in the Military
    A. Introduction
        1. Potential use of women
        2. The organizational climate and women
        3. The military as an occupational choice for women

Unit IV.   An Introduction to Assertiveness Training
    A. What is assertiveness training?
    B. How can assertiveness training contribute to more positive organizational climate?

Unit V.   Myth versus Reality about Military Women
    A. Utilization/performance
    B. Demand/supply variables
    C. Special problems of military women
    D. The future of women in the military

Source: Organizational Skills Training, USAREUR (U.S. Army in Europe), January 1978.

males who were *not* included in the sessions. The Social Actions staff attempted to include as many males from sex-integrated settings as possible, but circumstances such as field duty, maneuvers, temporary duty, and other duties precluded an indeterminate number from participating. My estimate is that about 60 percent of the total number of male Signal Corps soldiers participated in the study.

The female sessions included about 90 percent of the women enlisted in 15 companies. The only women not included in the study were those on temporary duty, sick leave, or vacation. The males in the sample were either the women's supervisors or co-workers.

Research Phase

At the beginning of the formal sessions, a semistructured questionnaire was administered to each participant by myself and other University of Maryland instructors. (This questionnaire is reprinted in Appendix B.) The questionnaire was used to compile baseline data on background characteristics and the scales used in the study. These data provided an overall context for the interpretation of the unstructured data.

Follow-Up Interviews

After the formal sessions, I was able to conduct unstructured interviews with 90 percent of the respondents in a variety of settings over a 6-month period. The bulk of the data reported in this work was derived from these unstructured interviews, which lasted an average of 45 minutes each. In addition, I conducted group discussions with participants at my convenience in my role as the Social Actions consultant. Women began discussions with complaints about their supervisors, work settings, or assignments. I was able to investigate some of these complaints by directly observing work settings or by asking males about the women's concerns. One general technique I used was to take anonymous complaints from unstructured interviews with women and present them in the following way:

Sgt. _____, some women in Khaki Town have told me that they weren't given the chance to perform their MOS [military occupational specialty]. Is there any truth to these rumors? Have you heard anything about this? Why do you suppose these women feel that way?

Lively discussion often ensued, which led to the definition of other problems and perspectives. While weekly human relations seminars were held only from January to March of 1978, the unstructured interviews extended into the month of June. Living in the Khaki Town vicinity enabled me to collect much of my data in natural settings at my leisure by participating in informal activities, such as pickup basketball games, guest-house (*gasthaus*) bull sessions, and other activities with both males and females. Because I openly revealed my identity as someone interested in the problems of soldiers, I received invitations to GI parties, intramural sports events, and other social activities.

I think that the women were willing to talk to me for several reasons. First, informal information had filtered to them that I was doing a book on military women, and they were interested in presenting their point of view. Second, my sociology courses were well received and the Khaki Town grapevine said that I was a "nice guy" and a person to be trusted. Third, students in my University of Maryland classes were helpful in introducing me to nonstudents. I was know as "the guy from the University of Maryland" interested in the problems of women. When I approached participants and asked to conduct follow-ups, I had few outright refusals. Ironically, I had greater difficulty interviewing males than females, since males were somewhat more hesitant to consent to unstructured interviews after the formal sessions. However, both groups were interested in talking to me about their own problems.

An advantage that I had with both male and female respondents was that there was no involvement of military commanders with the formal sessions. I was given complete freedom to conduct both the formal and research phases without observers from the command. In most human relations and management training programs, participants felt constrained because of the presence of higher-ranked persons in the discussion. For instance, in race relations sessions run by the military, it was common for persons to defer to those higher in rank. In my sessions, I set the stage by emphasizing that I was not formally associated with the military. In military communities, there are relatively few opportunities to discuss concerns outside the chain of command; even chaplains and physicians are addressed as superior officers. My role was different; I was a sympathetic outsider who knew "what was happening" in Khaki Town and not a lackey of the commander. My previous fieldwork and teaching gave me the confidence to carry out my role successfully, and willingness of the respondents to consent to follow-up interviews was an unobtrusive indicator of my success as a social-actions specialist and researcher.

At the beginning of each sesssion, I proceeded cautiously. I successfully conveyed the belief that my respondents were free to express their views without fear of command retaliation. There was a small number of women (four) who thought that there was little purpose in the organizational skills sessions, and 15 of the male participants stated that the seminars and interviews were a waste of time. However, most participants seemed to enjoy the classes and interviews.

I began unstructured interviews during the last week in January and completed fieldwork by the end of June. I taped over 50 hours of interviews with women but recorded subsequent interviews by hand because of my time constraints. With males it was often more useful to ask questions in a nonchalant way over lunch or in some other informal setting. After each interview, I recorded observations and notes as quickly and thoroughly as possible. Moskos, in his study of the enlisted men in Vietnam, used a similar strategy. In general, Moskos found that studying enlisted life in the military was far easier than most outsiders assume.[1] I found participant-observation work with the military far easier than my earlier work with nondenominational religious groups and the American Indian movement. When I studied the Moonies (World Unification Movement) in Maryland, I found it extremely difficult to gain both access and minimal trust. My access to the American Indian movement was ultimately unsuccessful.

Compared with my earlier studies, researching the military was much more comfortable. Of course, my University of Maryland teaching job gave me a more natural access to the enlisted military than I had with the other groups. I was also a much more experienced field-worker by the beginning of my military research. In any case, I found my respondents to be cooperative and helpful. The Social Actions staff of Khaki Town provided facilities for me, and a great number of my University of Maryland students helped to make the study possible.

The study was guided by a multiple-methods approach. Structured and unstructured interviews were conducted with respondents. While the structured questionnaires and interviews provided baseline data on background characteristics, the unstructured interviews and observations provided in-depth insights into the subjective world views of the respondents. It was not the goal of this study to develop precise statistical profiles of the soldiers of Khaki Town. The size and selection of the sample did not warrant this; rather, the goal was to appraise in detail the problems of males and females in newly integrated occupational fields. While statistical generalizations cannot be extended meaningfully to women in other branches of the service or even to other units within the Army, this study is broadly representative of the social forces affecting the utilization of women in other military branches.

Because the study was exploratory and ethnographic, few hypotheses were initiated at the onset of the study. Hypotheses and theory emerged together with the gradual accretion of my research experience in Khaki Town.

Difficulties

I was fortunate to receive full cooperation from officials in Khaki Town. In early attempts to gain formal access to research settings, I had been "cooled out" by the commanders. Some commands openly forbade me to conduct research on "their" bases. Several Air Force base commanders summarily refused my request to conduct research on military women. An Air Force Equal Opportunity Officer responded to a request to study women on his base in this way: "We prefer to launder our own linen. I sent a girl over to the women's barracks, and she reports that military women don't have any problems."

A problem of many "in-house studies" is the reluctance of subordinates to pass "bad news" up the hierarchy. Sending bad news about women's problems up the chain of command could have deleterious effects for the sender. In general, subordinates are blamed for any problems they report. The response of the higher command is often, "Why haven't you taken care of it? It's your problem. I know you can handle it."

Another form of resistance was the strategy of tentatively approving of my study plan with the condition that the study be postponed until higher commanders at the Defense Department level formally approved the request. In general, these stalls were tantamount to "cooling me out." After I returned to the United States in October of 1978, I attempted to extend my study to men and women in the Air Force. At a stateside Air Force base, I presented a research plan to two junior Social Actions officers. They feigned enthusiasm for my plan and agreed that research on women in the Air Force would be beneficial. However, they asked for copies of my research instrument and that I wait until they contacted me. When I called (nearly six months later) to ask about the status of the project, I was informed that my plan had been turned down because the base was preparing for "Women's Week" and key personnel were tied up with details.

Despite these difficulties, my research in Khaki Town was conducted without direct military interference. I was allowed complete access to the research setting in exchange for suggesting ways in which the military could improve the quality of life for military women. I was never asked to disclose personal information about the respondents or even copies of my research findings. I was asked only to advise Khaki Town's Human Relations Office on how to institute a program to improve the quality of life for Army women. My policy suggestions included many of those discussed in this book, such as instituting a network of female mentors.

A NOTE ON THE POVERTY OF MILITARY SOCIOLOGY

There have been relatively few studies of enlisted life conducted outside the contract-research system of the Defense Department. Much of the in-house research done on enlisted soldiers consists of large-scale questionnaire studies that have not contributed much to an understanding of the social setting of enlisted life. Wolf's study of Air Force enlisted life in Turkey and Charles Moskos' study of infantry soldiers in Vietnam, Korea, and West Germany are notable exceptions to the general lack of in-depth studies of enlisted life. Both studies were conducted without Defense Department grants. Moskos' affiliation with the military was as a journalist, while Wolf was a spouse of a Defense Department civilian employee.[2] Like Moskos and Wolf, I was a researcher allowed access to military bases but was outside of the military research and development apparatus. My study was guided by Max Weber's method of *verstehen*, which focuses on empathetic understanding of the individual's social matrix rather than an applied military-policy perspective. While this study used ethnographic materials, it also depended upon unpublished Defense Department statistics, historical documents, and journalistic accounts of enlisted women. Hopefully, these disparate materials successfully captured a causally adequate level of understanding of the enlisted woman's social networks.

The study undertaken here is not just a study of enlisted women in Khaki Town during the late 1970s; it is a study that assesses the social problems of today's volunteer Army. While Khaki Town, West Germany, is only one garrison community in one branch of the service, findings from Khaki Town can have value in understanding the more general problems of the enlisted woman, as well as the situations faced by many women newly employed in traditionally male work settings. As Everett C. Hughes believes:

> ... One of my basic assumptions is that if one clearly sees something happen once, it is almost certain to have happened again and again. The burden of proof is on those who claim a thing once seen is an exception; if they look hard, they may find it everywhere, although with some interesting differences in every case ...[3]

NOTES

1. Charles C. Moskos, *The American Enlisted Man: The Rank and File in Today's Military* (New York: Russell Sage, 1970), p. 185.

2. Charlotte Wolf, *Garrison Community: A Study of Overseas American Military Community* (Westport, Conn.: Greewood, 1969).

3. Everett C. Hughes, *The Sociological Eye* (Chicago: Aldine-Atherton Press, 1971), p. IX (preface).

APPENDIX B
WOMEN IN THE MILITARY QUESTIONNAIRE

Directions: We are interested in understanding your candid reactions to important social issues in the military. It is important to answer each question carefully.

Before beginning the survey:

1. Please read all directions carefully.
2. Please read all of the words in each question.
3. If any question does not apply to you or is inappropriate please write "does not apply" next to the question number.
4. Always respond with the answer closest to your true feelings. It is important for you to be as honest as possible.
5. The questionnaire will take approximately 45 minutes to complete. Please answer all the questions that apply to you.

Thank you for your participation in this study. The validity of this study depends upon your help. Results of this survey will be utilized by social policy persons who want an accurate picture of military social groups.

Please do not write your name on the questionnaire. We respect the confidentiality of your responses. We will take care to insure that no individual's responses are identified.

Michael L. Rustad
Sociology Lecturer
University of Maryland
APO 09102

QUESTIONNAIRE

PART I: BACKGROUND INFORMATION ABOUT YOU
AND YOUR PARENTS

1. Age _____ (years)
2. What is your sex? _____
3. Where did you spend most of your childhood years?
   _____
4. What is your current occupation? _____
5. If you are in the military, what is your rank? _____
6. What is your occupational specialty? _____
   Please describe briefly your job duties:
   _____
7. If you are in the military, what were the most important reasons for
   your entry? _____
8. As of today, what are your plans for your military career?
   _____
9. (For all respondents) What is your attitude toward your job?
   _____
10. What are the best things about your job? _____
    _____
11. What are the worst things about your job? _____
    _____
12. Father's Present Occupation _____
13. Mother's Present Occupation _____
14. Spouse's Present Occupation _____
15. How many brothers and sisters do you have? (Please fill in the
    number).

    _____ Older Brothers   _____ Older Sisters
    _____ Younger Brothers   _____ Younger Sisters
    _____ Others in household when you were growing up
    Please describe: _____
    _____
    _____

16. Race _____   17. Religious preference at 16 _____
18. Present Religious Preference_____
19. Present Political Preference _____
20. Highest Education Level _____
21. What is the highest educational level that you hope to attain?
    _____

22. Do you have long-range plans for a career? _____ Yes _____ No
_____ Undecided
Please describe your plans for the future. _____
_____

23. What is your current marital status? (Please circle one.)

    1. Never married
    2. Married, first time
    3. Married, more than once
    4. Divorced or separated
    5. Widowed

24. Total annual income before taxes _____
25. During most of your childhood, your family's social class was
_____

26. When you were growing up, who was usually more dominant, your
father or your mother?

    1. My father was much more dominant.
    2. My father was somewhat more dominant.
    3. Both had equal influence.
    4. My mother was somewhat more dominant.
    5. My mother was much more dominant.
    6. I grew up with one parent only.

27. Which parent did you feel closer to? Why? _____
_____

Please circle one:
28. How would you describe your father's relationship with you?

    1. Very warm and supportive
    2. Warm
    3. Alternately warm and cool
    4. Cool
    5. Rejecting
    6. Didn't know my father

29. How would you describe your mother's relationship with you?

    1. Very warm and supportive
    2. Warm
    3. Alternately warm and cool

4. Cool
5. Rejecting
6. Didn't know my mother

30. How would you describe your parents' marriage?

1. Very unhappy
2. Unhappy
3. Not too happy
4. Just about average
5. A little happier than average
6. Very happy
7. Extremely happy

31. How would you describe your marriage? (if applicable)

1. Very unhappy
2. Unhappy
3. Not too unhappy
4. Just about average
5. A little happier than average
6. Very happy
7. Extremely happy

32. My current social class is probably _____

33. When you were in high school, were you generally:

0. Did not attend high school
1. An "A" student
2. A "B" student
3. A "C" student
4. A "D" student
5. Did not complete

34. At what periods in your life was your mother employed FULL-TIME with wages for one year or more? _____
_____

35. How much would you say your mother liked being a homemaker during your childhood years? (Please answer even if your mother was employed during your childhood.)

1. Disliked homemaking a great deal
2. Disliked homemaking somewhat
3. Liked homemaking somewhat
4. Liked homemaking a great deal

36. What was the happiness level of your home when you were growing up?

1. Happy, most of the time
2. About even, happy/unhappy
3. Neither happy nor unhappy
4. Unhappy most of the time

IF YOU ARE IN THE MILITARY, please answer the next four questions. If not, skip to Part II.

1. Who encouraged you most to join the military? _____
   _____

2. What were your parents' attitude toward your enlistment in the military? _____
   _____

3. What are the most important things that you look for in a job? _____
   _____
   _____

4. What jobs did you do before you entered the military? _____
   _____
   _____
   _____
   _____

PART II: FEELINGS ABOUT SELF

Directions: Below is a list of statements dealing with your general feelings about yourself. Use the following code in responding to these questions:

1. Strongly Agree   2. Agree   3. Uncertain   4. Disagree
                  5. Strongly Disagree

	Circle the number:				
	(Agree)			(Disagree)	
1. I take a positive attitude toward myself.	1	2	3	4	5
2. At times, I think I am no good at all.	1	2	3	4	5
3. I often feel bored with everything.	1	2	3	4	5
4. On the whole, I am satisfied with myself.	1	2	3	4	5
5. I often feel guilty for having done something wrong.	1	2	3	4	5
6. I am able to do things as well as most people.	1	2	3	4	5
7. I feel that I have a number of good qualities.	1	2	3	4	5
8. I feel I do not have much to be proud of.	1	2	3	4	5
9. I feel that I am a person of worth, at least on an equal plane with others.	1	2	3	4	5
10. I wish I could have more respect for myself.	1	2	3	4	5
11. I certainly feel useless at times.	1	2	3	4	5
12. I feel alone in the world.	1	2	3	4	5
13. What happens to me is my own doing.	1	2	3	4	5
14. I generally have confidence that when I make plans I will be able to carry them out.	1	2	3	4	5
15. I frequently have religious experiences.	1	2	3	4	5
16. I am often bored with my job.	1	2	3	4	5

17. I feel that I am a part of the military
community.   1   2   3   4   5

18. I strongly identify with the military as
a career.   1   2   3   4   5

19. I often do things on the spur of the
moment.   1   2   3   4   5

20. I enjoy friendships with military
personnel outside the work context.   1   2   3   4   5

21. I usually let myself go and enjoy myself
at parties with a large percentage of
military personnel.   1   2   3   4   5

22. I don't find it hard to keep my mind on a
task or job.   1   2   3   4   5

23. Sometimes I feel like smashing things.   1   2   3   4   5

24. In my case, getting what I want has little
or nothing to do with luck.   1   2   3   4   5

25. A woman has a right to have an abortion
at will, since her body is her own.   1   2   3   4   5

26. Most people are downright dishonest.   1   2   3   4   5

27. My parents were always afraid of me
getting into some kind of trouble.   1   2   3   4   5

28. I often feel that the whole world is
against me.   1   2   3   4   5

29. People are not responsible to God, but
to themselves and other people first and
foremost.   1   2   3   4   5

30. No matter what I did, my parents seldom
praised me.   1   2   3   4   5

Circle the number:

(Agree)   (Disagree)

31. In spite of what some people say, the lot
(situation) of the average military person
is getting worse, not better.   1   2   3   4   5

32. I find it rather easy to lead a group.   1   2   3   4   5

33. I have the physical endurance and
strength to perform combat duty.   1   2   3   4   5

34. I enjoy organizing or directing the
activities of a group.   1   2   3   4   5

IF YOU ARE IN THE MILITARY, please answer the next questions. If not, skip to Part III.

Directions: In this section, we are interested in your perceptions of the organizational climate. Please use the same code as in the preceding section to answer the questions:

1. Strongly Agree   2. Agree   3. Uncertain   4. Disagree
5. Strongly Disagree

Circle the number:

(Agree)   (Disagree)

1. It is extremely important for me to have a
job which provides a cheerful, clean
work environment.   1   2   3   4   5

2. I require a job which gives me contact
with a lot of people during the day.   1   2   3   4   5

3. My job involves excitement, competition,
and new situations.   1   2   3   4   5

4. My job helps others or in some ways
makes the world a little better place.   1   2   3   4   5

5. My job gives me a feeling of really doing
   something important.   1   2   3   4   5

6. My job gives me more personal than
   financial rewards.   1   2   3   4   5

7. I would accept a job which involved
   physical risk, if it were exciting and
   important.   1   2   3   4   5

8. I enjoy jobs with a set routine with few
   changes.   1   2   3   4   5

9. I have a basic respect for the military.   1   2   3   4   5

10. I have sufficient opportunity to advance
    to supervisory positions in my job.   1   2   3   4   5

11. My job allows me to use my imagination,
    creativity, and own ideas.   1   2   3   4   5

12. My job involves little close supervision. 1   2   3   4   5

13. Military policies toward women are too
    protective.   1   2   3   4   5

14. A woman should have exactly the same
    job opportunities as men.   1   2   3   4   5

15. Women have to prove themselves in new
    military assignments, just because they
    are women.   1   2   3   4   5

16. I have personally seen negative male
    attitudes make it difficult for a woman to
    do a military job.   1   2   3   4   5

17. It is sometimes necessary to resort to
    force in order to advance an ideal one
    strongly believes in.   1   2   3   4   5

Circle the number:
(Agree)   (Disagree)

18. Thermonuclear warfare is likely; warfare in some form is inevitable so long as there is man.   1   2   3   4   5

19. Those who supervise me are usually responsive to my ideas and suggestions.   1   2   3   4   5

20. This command has a real interest in the welfare and morale of military women.   1   2   3   4   5

21. I am encouraged to give my best effort by other people in my work group.   1   2   3   4   5

22. I have confidence and trust in the members of my work group.   1   2   3   4   5

23. All in all, I am satisfied with my job.   1   2   3   4   5

24. All in all, I am satisfied with this command's treatment of military women.   1   2   3   4   5

25. All in all, I am satisfied with the progress I have made in the military up to now.   1   2   3   4   5

26. I am satisfied with my chances of getting ahead in the military in the future.   1   2   3   4   5

27. My assigned job gives me pride and feelings of self-worth.   1   2   3   4   5

28. This command has ensured that I have had equal opportunity for education.   1   2   3   4   5

29. In my chain of command there is a willingness to talk about sex discrimination issues.   1   2   3   4   5

30. People in this command discourage
favoritism based on the sex of the
individual.   1   2   3   4   5

31. I like living in Europe.   1   2   3   4   5

32. I enjoy the cultural aspects of traveling in
Europe.   1   2   3   4   5

33. I feel that the workload and time factors
are adequately considered in planning
our work-group assignments.   1   2   3   4   5

34. Women should be allowed to work at
any military job that they are capable of
performing.   1   2   3   4   5

35. Women are an oppressed group in
America.   1   2   3   4   5

36. Women have less ability to make
decisions than men.   1   2   3   4   5

37. My supervisor cares about the worker's
problems.   1   2   3   4   5

38. I think that most women in the military
have contemporary sex-role attitudes.   1   2   3   4   5

39. Most men in the military have
traditional conceptions about the role of
women.   1   2   3   4   5

40. If the Equal Rights Amendment (ERA)
were put to a popular vote, I would vote
for it.   1   2   3   4   5

PART III: SOCIETAL ATTITUDES, CONTINUED (for all respondents)

Directions: Use the following code in response to the questions in this section:

1. Strongly Agree   2. Agree   3. Uncertain   4. Disagree
5. Strongly Disagree

Circle the number:
(Agree)   (Disagree)

1. In wartime, women between the ages of
21 and 35 without children should be
drafted.   1   2   3   4   5

2. In general, men should leave the
housework to women.   1   2   3   4   5

3. I feel that politicians do not understand
the needs of the average military person.   1   2   3   4   5

4. Societal goods and services should be
distributed to individuals primarily on
the basis of their talent.   1   2   3   4   5

5. Married women, particularly if they have
children, should not expect to have any
kind of a career.   1   2   3   4   5

6. I oppose the death penalty for persons
convicted of murder.   1   2   3   4   5

7. Parents should guide their children into
traditional roles and goals appropriate for
their sex.   1   2   3   4   5

8. Women should take a supportive
position in society, marriage, and the
world of work.   1   2   3   4   5

9. Our society, not nature, teaches women
to prefer homemaking to work outside
the home.   1   2   3   4   5

10. Women have just as much chance to get
big and important jobs; they just aren't
interested.   1   2   3   4   5

11. Raising a child provides many rewards, but as a full-time job it cannot keep most women satisfied.   1   2   3   4   5

12. Women are as intelligent as men.   1   2   3   4   5

13. Women should have as much sexual freedom as men.   1   2   3   4   5

14. Women "libbers" are women with nothing better to do than to cause trouble.   1   2   3   4   5

15. It's about time women did something to protest the real injustices they've faced for years.   1   2   3   4   5

16. I am very happy at the present time.   1   2   3   4   5

17. Military or police aggression is justified to maintain law and order.   1   2   3   4   5

18. All persons should willingly serve for a period of time in their country's army or navy if they are able.   1   2   3   4   5

19. My country should strive for power in the world.   1   2   3   4   5

20. Our country should not give up any of its military power to a world government.   1   2   3   4   5

PART IV. (for all respondents)

We are interested in your reaction to the following statements about women's roles. As in the other sections, there are no right or wrong answers. Please indicate your agreement or disagreement with each of the following statements by circling the number that comes closest to your feelings.

+3: Strong Agreement; +2: Moderate Agreement; +1 Slight Agreement, 0: Neutral; −1: Slight Disagreement; −2: Moderate Disagreement; −3: Strong Disagreement

Strongly Agree _____ Strongly Disagree
+3   +2   +1   0   −1   −2   −3

1. Except in emergencies, the physical care of children should be very largely the mother's rather than the father's job.

+3   +2   +1   0   −1   −2   −3

2. Except in special cases or situations, the wife should do all the cooking and housecleaning and the husband should provide the financial income.

+3   +2   +1   0   −1   −2   −3

3. Except in cases of great financial need, mothers with preschool or young school-age children should not work outside the home.

+3   +2   +1   0   −1   −2   −3

4. It is not necessary for women, as for men, to go to college and/or graduate school.

+3   +2   +1   0   −1   −2   −3

5. If a wife goes to school or works for reasons other than actual financial necessity, she should not expect her husband to share in the household tasks.

+3   +2   +1   0   −1   −2   −3

6. When it gets right down to it, the woman has the final responsibility for birth control.

+3   +2   +1   0   −1   −2   −3

PART V. IF YOU ARE IN THE MILITARY, please answer the questions in this section. If not, skip to the final section, Part VI.

How much of a problem is each of the following for you as a military person? (Please check only one per question.)

FACTOR	NOT APPLICABLE (N/A)	CAUSED ME TO CONSIDER LEAVING THE MILITARY	SOURCE OF MAJOR CONCERN	SOURCE OF MINOR CONCERN	NO PROBLEM
1. Child-care help or arrangements	___	___	___	___	___
2. Low financial rewards	___	___	___	___	___
3. Inadequate educational opportunity	___	___	___	___	___
4. Assignment out of MOS area	___	___	___	___	___
5. Sexism in work group	___	___	___	___	___
6. Opportunity for satisfying intimate relationships	___	___	___	___	___

FACTOR	NOT APPLICABLE (N/A)	CAUSED ME TO CONSIDER LEAVING THE MILITARY	SOURCE OF MAJOR CONCERN	SOURCE OF MINOR CONCERN	NO PROBLEM
7. Military medical care					
8. Overseas assignment					
9. Equal opportunity for advancement					
10. Sexist attitudes					
11. Male atmosphere of work setting					
12. Military justice					
13. Inadequate living arrangements					
14. Underutilization of talent at work					

15. Lack of courtesy, sexist comments, jokes   _____

16. Interference with my off-duty life by military   _____

17. Poor reception to my ideas and suggestions at work   _____

18. Lack of trust and confidence in members of work group   _____

19. Training for combat and field duty   _____

20. Job pressure   _____

21. Little credit for good work   _____

FACTOR	NOT APPLICABLE (N/A)	CAUSED ME TO CONSIDER LEAVING THE MILITARY	SOURCE OF MAJOR CONCERN	SOURCE OF MINOR CONCERN	NO PROBLEM
22. Supervisor's sexist attitudes					

23-25. What are some other problems faced by military personnel?

_____

_____

_____

26. If you could change three things in your life as a military person, which three things would you change and how would you change them?

1. _____

2. _____

3. _____

27.   Check category(ies) that applies to you:

For Enlisted Personnel: _____1. First term, plan to get out.
                           _____2. First termer, plan to reenlist.
                           _____3. Have reenlisted but don't plan a
                                     military career.
                           _____4. Have reenlisted, plan a military
                                     career until retirement.
                           _____5. Other: _____
                                     _____

For Officer Personnel: _____1. I plan to resign in _____ years.
                           _____2. I plan a military career until
                                     retirement.
                           _____3. Other: _____
                                     _____

PART VI. FINAL SECTION FOR ALL RESPONDENTS

1. What are the most significant social problems faced by military
women?

2. Comments on problems of women in your unit:

3. Other comments:

Thank you for your cooperation.

INDEX

279

ABOUT THE AUTHOR

Michael Rustad received his Ph.D. from Boston College. He was a lecturer in the European Division of the University of Maryland from 1975 to 1978. He worked as a research assistant from 1979 to 1981 at the Wellesley College Center for Research on Women.

Dr. Rustad is presently an adjunct assistant professor of sociology at Boston College and a student at Suffolk University Law School.